Enterprise JMS™
Programming

Enterprise JMS™ Programming

Shaun Terry

MICHAEL A. MARÇAL
2 MAY 2005

M&T Books

An imprint of Hungry Minds, Inc.

New York, NY • Cleveland, OH • Indianapolis, IN

Enterprise JMS™ Programming

Published by
M&T Books
An imprint of Hungry Minds, Inc.
909 Third Avenue
New York, NY 10022
www.hungryminds.com

Library of Congress Control Number: 2001098044

ISBN: 0-7645-4897-2

Printed in the United States of America

10 9 8 7 6 5 4 3 2 1

1O/RR/QS/QS/IN

Distributed in the United States by Hungry Minds, Inc.

Distributed by CDG Books Canada Inc. for Canada; by Transworld Publishers Limited in the United Kingdom; by IDG Norge Books for Norway; by IDG Sweden Books for Sweden; by IDG Books Australia Publishing Corporation Pty. Ltd. for Australia and New Zealand; by TransQuest Publishers Pte Ltd. for Singapore, Malaysia, Thailand, Indonesia, and Hong Kong; by Gotop Information Inc. for Taiwan; by ICG Muse, Inc. for Japan; by Intersoft for South Africa; by Eyrolles for France; by International Thomson Publishing for Germany, Austria, and Switzerland; by Distribuidora Cuspide for Argentina; by LR International for Brazil; by Galileo Libros for Chile; by Ediciones ZETA S.C.R. Ltda. for Peru; by WS Computer Publishing Corporation, Inc., for the Philippines; by Contemporanea de Ediciones for Venezuela; by Express Computer Distributors for the Caribbean and West Indies; by Micronesia Media Distributor, Inc. for Micronesia; by Chips Computadoras S.A. de C.V. for Mexico; by Editorial Norma de Panama S.A. for Panama; by American Bookshops for Finland.

For general information on Hungry Minds' products and services, please contact our Customer Care department within the U.S. at 800-762-2974, outside the U.S. at 317-572-3993 or fax 317-572-4002.

For sales inquiries and reseller information, including discounts, premium and bulk quantity sales, and foreign-language translations, please contact our Customer Care department at 800-434-3422, fax 317-572-4002 or write to Hungry Minds, Inc., Attn: Customer Care Department, 10475 Crosspoint Boulevard, Indianapolis, IN 46256.

For information on licensing foreign or domestic rights, please contact our Sub-Rights Customer Care department at 212-884-5000.

For information on using Hungry Minds' products and services in the classroom or for ordering examination copies, please contact our Educational Sales department at 800-434-2086 or fax 317-572-4005.

For press review copies, author interviews, or other publicity information, please contact our Public Relations department at 317-572-3168 or fax 317-572-4168.

For authorization to photocopy items for corporate, personal, or educational use, please contact Copyright Clearance Center, 222 Rosewood Drive, Danvers, MA 01923, or fax 978-750-4470.

 is a trademark of Hungry Minds, Inc.

 is a trademark of Hungry Minds, Inc.

Credits

ACQUISITIONS EDITOR
Chris Webb

PROJECT EDITOR
Andy Marinkovich

TECHNICAL EDITOR
Nicholas P. Jacobs

COPY EDITORS
Michael D. Welch
Roxane Marini

EDITORIAL MANAGER
Mary Beth Wakefield

PROJECT COORDINATOR
Dale White

GRAPHICS AND PRODUCTION SPECIALISTS
Sean Decker
LeAndra Johnson
Kristin McMullan
Laurie Petrone

QUALITY CONTROL TECHNICIAN
John Bitter

PROOFREADING AND INDEXING
TECHBOOKS Production Services

COVER IMAGE
© Noma/Images.com

About the Author

Shaun Terry is a Senior Java Architect with the Sun Java Center, the Java application practice of Sun Microsystems' professional services group. In this capacity, Shaun has spent the past five years helping a variety of companies design and develop the next generation of Java- and Internet-enabled enterprise systems. Before joining Sun, Shaun spent ten years working in the financial services industry, primarily at Merrill Lynch, where he led a team responsible for creating a major real-time, multi-tiered, fixed-income trading system. Shaun has extensive experience designing and programming systems that use inter-application messaging. Shaun is currently attempting to avoid traveling for work so he can spend as much time as possible in New York, his favorite city and home.

To my mother

Preface

The demand for easy and reliable methods of exchanging information over a network between two or more applications has existed for some time now. While the prevalence of systems that rely on network-oriented messaging has steadily increased since the 1980s, in recent years the development of systems that depend on messaging in one form or another has increased in pace. Aided in no small part by the Internet popularity explosion, the desire of corporations large and small to enable their applications to converse with other internal and external applications has resulted in the rapid incorporation of messaging technology into many of their new systems.

JMS is an application programming interface (API) that is designed to provide a common way for various applications to communicate with one another using messaging. Most messaging vendors support JMS, which is designed for applications written for the Java platform but enables the exchange of messages between Java and non-Java systems.

This book guides the developer in the effective use of JMS in Java applications. In addition to thoroughly covering the essentials of JMS programming, it also discusses architectural approaches and issues related to using JMS in the real world. Both developers and architects will find it useful.

JMS is a standards-based API supported by numerous vendors. As JMS itself is vendor-neutral, I have attempted to be as vendor-neutral as possible in the writing of this book. Examples that depend on a particular vendor's product, even if only in a small way, are clearly labeled as such. Otherwise, all examples and descriptions of functionality should apply to all vendors' products equally. I also address situations where it is important to understand how a vendor's particular product is implemented in areas that aren't specifically governed by the JMS specification.

You can find the companion Web site for this book at http://www.hungryminds.com/extras. It has all the code examples from the book as well as any important updates or corrections to the information the book contains.

Who Should Read This Book

I've geared this book toward Java developers who wish to learn how to write applications that incorporate inter-application messaging based on JMS products. It is also designed for the person who, having learned JMS programming (either from this book or elsewhere), wants to learn more about some of the best ways to design systems that rely heavily on JMS.

Readers with at least an intermediate-level knowledge of programming for the Java platform will be able to understand the concepts presented herein. In particular, some experience with the server-side Java technologies such as Enterprise

JavaBeans will be useful. Knowledge of client-side technologies and graphical user interfaces (such as AWT or Swing) is not necessary.

Some basic familiarity with the following specific Java technologies and concepts will be helpful, though not essential:

- ◆ Network-oriented programming (such as sockets)
- ◆ Transactions
- ◆ Enterprise JavaBeans (EJB)

Because there is currently little use for JMS outside the corporate computing environment, I've geared the examples in this book toward the enterprise developer and architect.

This book addresses JMS specification version 1.0.2b.

How This Book Is Organized

I've divided *Enterprise JMS Programming* into three parts. It is not necessary to read this book in its entirety before being able to effectively use a JMS product. Each part covers a different area of JMS — programming, administration, and architecture — and the reader can tackle each part when he or she is ready. It is best, however, to read the parts in order.

- ◆ **Part I, "JMS Programming,"** thoroughly covers the JMS API and related programming concepts and models. After reading this section, you will understand what a JMS message is and be able to write applications that send and receive the various types of JMS messages (MapMessage, TextMessage, ObjectMessage, and so on) using both the JMS publish/ subscribe and queue-based delivery modes. This section also covers more advanced JMS programming topics such as message-driven beans, transactions, security, and performance.

- ◆ **Part II, "JMS Administration,"** talks about what processes and procedures are handled administratively in a typical JMS installation and how the roles of the JMS developer and administrator can be both overlapping and distinct. I present detailed real-world examples of how to administer two JMS products, WebLogic Server and iPlanet Message Queue.

- ◆ **Part III, "JMS Architecture,"** is designed for more advanced readers who wish to design enterprise systems based on JMS messaging technology. Using four fictional systems for illustration, I guide the reader through the process of requirements gathering to final architecture. I also discuss the pros and cons of various design alternatives.

Conventions

This book uses the following conventions that make the material easier to follow and understand:

- *Italics* indicate the use of a new term.

- **Boldface** indicates the name of a standard JMS message property or text the reader is to enter in a window or dialog box.

- `Code font` is used for source code, file names, file extensions, and URLs.

 A Note icon contains a noteworthy piece of information aside from the text.

 A Tip icon provides useful techniques and helpful hints.

Acknowledgments

No book like this sees the light of day based on the efforts of the author alone. It's a collaboration of many people. I'd like to make a special point of thanking Chris Webb at Hungry Minds and my project editor, Andy Marinkovich, for making my first book project go so smoothly. A special thanks also goes to Nick Jacobs for doing such a great job as technical editor.

I'd like to thank my managers at Sun, Ari Shamash and Sunil Mathew, for the support and encouragement they gave me while I was writing this book. And finally, I'd like to acknowledge the contributions of my friends and colleagues who helped me with their advice and also dedicated their time to reviewing various parts of the book for me: Douglas Hill, Joseph Mattina, Peter Nowell, John Prentice, Chris Roberts, Heidi Schuster, and Bernard Van Haecke.

Contents at a Glance

Contents

Part I

JMS Programming

CHAPTER 1
Introducing JMS

CHAPTER 2
The JMS Message

CHAPTER 3
Sending Messages

CHAPTER 4
Receiving Messages

CHAPTER 5
Publish/Subscribe Messaging

CHAPTER 6
Point-to-Point Messaging

CHAPTER 7
Building Message-Driven Beans with EJB 2.0

CHAPTER 8
JMS Transactions

CHAPTER 9
Securing JMS

CHAPTER 10
Maximizing JMS Performance

Chapter 1

Introducing JMS

IN THIS CHAPTER

- ◆ A brief history of JMS
- ◆ JMS and J2EE
- ◆ JMS as industry standard
- ◆ A quick tour of JMS features

THE DAYS OF THE STANDALONE COMPUTER ARE LONG GONE. The true power of a computer is best realized when it's connected to other computers, either via a local area network or the Internet. Effectively networking systems has long been a goal inside large corporations where development teams have been challenged to integrate any number of disparate systems and platforms, including Unix machines, mainframes, PCs, and Macs. In the eighties, prior to the widespread adoption of standardized network technologies, the primary challenge was just getting computers talking to each other at all. Most operating system vendors employed their own proprietary communications protocol that was quite useful for connecting their brand of machines while generally excluding everybody else's. But the protocol wars are finally over, and we've settled on TCP/IP, the native language of that ever-growing beast, the Internet.

Now, rather than figuring out how to integrate machines, users worry about how to integrate applications. Just as computer systems are implemented in a variety of different ways — operating systems, architectures, and so on — so, too, are applications. Some are written in Java, some in C++, some in COBOL, etc. Since no program can be an island in this day and age, how can applications be integrated effectively? Application integration is the domain of *messaging*.

This book covers everything you need to know to begin effectively using a specific messaging technology, called Java Message Service (JMS). This chapter provides a quick overview and history of JMS. In subsequent chapters, we move on to the nuts and bolts of developing and architecting JMS applications.

An Overview of JMS

Java Message Service (JMS) is a specification, not a product. It is an effort by Sun Microsystems and its partners to develop an industry standard application programming interface (API) that covers several common types of inter-application messaging. As such, you can freely download the JMS specification from Sun's Web site at `http://java.sun.com/products/jms`, but unlike the Java programming environment itself, there is no production-ready JMS implementation you can download along with it (the J2EE 1.3 reference edition does come with a JMS implementation; see `http://java.sun.com/j2ee`). Sun defines the JMS API; third party vendors supply the actual implementation.

In this culture of free software and open source software, corporations still pay top dollar for messaging systems, which serve as a key part of many enterprise computing infrastructures where high performance and reliability are paramount concerns.

Messaging systems permeate Wall Street institutions – they are involved in virtually every financial transaction that takes place in the global markets – and they are vital to the manufacturing, transportation, and telecommunications industries. Any top-level software architect must have a strong command of messaging concepts and capabilities in order to do his or her job effectively.

As Java has steadily become the dominant Internet and enterprise development platform, the need to cleanly integrate messaging into Java-based applications has increased in importance as well. Achieving this integration is where JMS comes into play.

The History of JMS

Part of the appeal of the original Java platform was that it came "out of the box" with a lot of technology that developers had previously relied on third party libraries for. Graphical toolkits, threading and synchronization, socket programming, and I/O were all neatly integrated into the base Java development kit (JDK), thus providing an easy-to-use and, more importantly, *standard* way of incorporating many common programming tasks into your application.

While sockets are an effective programming device for delivering information from one application to another, they tend to be unsuitable for transferring data between large numbers of applications because they are connection-oriented (that is, they don't scale well). Connection-oriented approaches require that applications must have a fair amount of *a priori* knowledge about the other applications they will be communicating with.

For years prior to the advent of Java, companies such as Tibco and IBM sold messaging software that provided enterprise-wide messaging services with a greater degree of performance and reliability than a typical in-house development team would be able to achieve writing the same services itself.

The availability of such products is important because high-speed, reliable messaging is vital in many computing environments – possibly none more so than on Wall Street, but the medical, manufacturing, and telecommunications fields rely heavily on messaging technology as well.

As Java rose rapidly in prominence, most messaging vendors quickly Java-enabled their wares by providing a Java library that made it possible for Java-based applications to make use of their messaging services. This was essential because the JDK only dealt with lower-level socket programming, not the more sophisticated messaging.

Because one of the key selling points of the Java platform is its ability to hide the particulars of the underlying technology from the developer, it was not in the Java spirit to have so many different APIs available in the marketplace all doing roughly the same thing. After all, a graphics system is basically a graphics system whether it's on a Mac, a Solaris box, or Windows. And a messaging system is basically a messaging system no matter which platform it's on and no matter which vendor provides it.

Sun set about to resolve the incompatibility issue by creating a standard messaging API that could be used with any (cooperating) vendor's software. The first draft of the JMS specification, made available in August of 1998, was the result of that effort.

Unlike many Java technologies created by Sun which, though influenced by previous technologies, were created completely from scratch, JMS was designed from the beginning with some restrictions. The restrictions existed because, unlike some Java-based technologies, say for instance, Remote Method Invocation (RMI), JMS had to conform to product features already found in the marketplace rather than define those features. Although this restricted the range of capabilities that could be built into JMS, it did make it easier to define a sensible and efficient API because messaging technology was already well understood and fairly mature.

At the same time, if the JMS API was to gain acceptance in the marketplace, it was equally important that it be backwards-compatible with the large number of current messaging installations in the world. Lack of backwards-compatibility would have drastically limited its usefulness to the ordinary developer.

The J2EE Specification

About the time JMS first saw the light of day, Sun was also proposing to the industry a new model for server-based Java applications called Enterprise Java Beans (EJBs). Simply put, each bean is a semi-independent module that provides some service or services to client applications and is accessible via some well-known interface.

If this sounds like something you might see in an object request broker (ORB) such as CORBA, it is. But while at a high level these two technologies are very similar, the difference is that EJBs are designed to run in an *application server*, which is a specialized application (also called a *container*) that is responsible for providing a variety of run-time services to the bean, including security, session management, and transaction management.

By offloading these functions to the container, the EJB programmer's job is simplified. An additional advantage is that the way in which the bean uses these services can be configured declaratively (for example, in a configuration file) rather than programmatically (in the code), thus resulting in better manageability.

Soon after application servers were introduced, Sun announced a technology and branding initiative called Java 2 Enterprise Edition (J2EE), a suite of Java technologies deemed to be essential to any enterprise technology environment. Included in these technologies are (among others) JavaMail, Java Naming and Directory Interface (JNDI), Java Server Pages (JSP), EJB, and, of course, JMS.

EJBs must run in an application server, but JMS does not require a server to operate correctly. Indeed, JMS does not need any of the other J2EE technologies except for some JNDI (this will be explained in Chapter 3).

Except for the capability to include JMS activity inside a J2EE transaction, JMS traditionally has not been very well integrated with the other J2EE components. The latest EJB specification (2.0) has sought to remedy this through the *message driven bean*, a new type of EJB that can be invoked asynchronously upon receipt of a JMS message. I discuss message driven beans in more detail in Chapter 8.

Role of Vendors

As mentioned earlier, JMS is merely a specification; it is the role of the messaging vendor to supply the implementation behind the specified API. At the time JMS was developed, the major messaging vendors already had implementations so of course it was a fairly straightforward matter to support JMS, especially because many of them had partnered with Sun to define the specification. Naturally, they still had to support customers using an older Java API. In most cases, a vendor's original API and the JMS API are both still supported today, although newer entrants to the messaging market tend to support only the JMS API for Java applications.

The provider model

The *provider* is an important concept in JMS and it will be referred to frequently in this book. Remember, JMS is an API only and many vendors supply implementations that conform to the JMS API. The implementation modules a vendor makes available that do the actual heavy lifting in JMS are collectively known as the provider.

The thing that makes a system based on a provider model different than one based on a library model is that applications that use libraries must be recompiled whenever you want to replace one library with another, even if the new library supports the exact same interfaces as the old library. Applications that use providers, on the other hand, do not need to be recompiled whenever you want to use a different vendor's product because the provider's code gets loaded and instantiated by an application dynamically at runtime.

Use of a provider model allows an application to freely use any vendor's JMS implementation without alteration to the original application. Providers can even be changed during the execution of a program and multiple providers can be used at the same time.

Figure 1-1 illustrates how the various layers of code fit together.

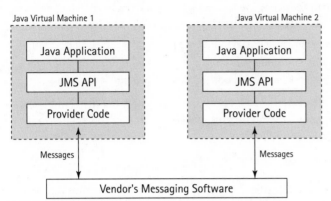

Figure 1-1: Interaction of two Java applications and vendor's messaging software

Some important restrictions

Figure 1-1 highlights two important restrictions of JMS you need to know about. The first is that the JMS API is completely Java-centric, meaning that there are no provisions for using it in anything but a Java program. As a Java developer, do you care? Probably not. Just don't expect that having learned JMS you'll immediately be able to incorporate messaging into your C++ application.

Most vendors provide compile time libraries for accessing their software from languages other than Java. And while they certainly will look different than JMS, they may even behave differently. The good news is that there's no reason you can't have an application written in C++ send messages to one written in Java and *vice versa*.

The second restriction you should consider is that JMS defines only a Java program's interaction with the messaging software and some basic underlying required functionality. It says nothing about how the bytes that make up a message are actually delivered from point A to point B.

In fact, this is an industry standards issue beyond the scope of what JMS currently addresses. A long time ago (in software terms anyhow), this same issue existed in the distributed object world where one vendor's object request broker (ORB) could not talk to another vendor's because each used a proprietary data transmission protocol. This was solved by the creation of the standards-based Internet Inter-ORB Protocol (IIOP), which defined the exact protocol to be used when invoking a remote object. Efforts to allow JMS systems to interoperate with other messaging technologies such as CORBA, and even with other vendor's implementations of JMS, are just now getting off the ground.

Be careful not to confuse message *protocols* and message *formats*. XML, for instance, is often touted as the technology that will finally link all sorts of disparate entities together by providing a common messaging platform. However, XML merely defines the format of a message. It says nothing about how it should be transmitted from one application to another. HTTP, an example of a network protocol, is one means of delivering XML messages.

JMS is neither a protocol nor a message format. It is simply a client-oriented API that hides lower-level messaging details such as protocols and formats from your application.

What this means to the system architect using JMS is that you should have no expectation that a message sent through one vendor's messaging product will be able to be received by another vendor's messaging product, even though both products advertise themselves as JMS-compliant.

When to Use JMS

As a system architect, the first thing to keep in mind when deciding whether to use JMS in your system or not is that JMS is an inter-application technology, not an intra-application technology, like Sun's InfoBus. So, while there is nothing in JMS that prevents an application from receiving messages sent to itself (and this may be just what you want in some cases), you would typically not use JMS if there were no other applications involved.

As illustrated in Figure 1-1, you can use JMS to deliver messages from one Java-based application to another Java-based application. These applications do not, of course, need to be running on the same machine or even be of the same architecture. One can be running on a Windows PC in New York and the other on a mainframe in San Francisco.

Remember, however, that many messaging products are language neutral. They are designed to work with programs written in a variety of languages, running on a variety of different machine architectures and operating systems. This is one of their greatest strengths and reasons for using them.

A valid variation of Figure 1-1 is shown in Figure 1-2.

In the scenario shown in Figure 1-2, the messaging software is responsible for translating the contents of the message from its Java-language representation to the receiver's native format. For example, a Java Unicode string would be automatically converted to EBCDIC before being delivered to a mainframe application.

This capability to easily link together disparate computing worlds is one of the best reasons for using messaging software and why, as an architect, you need to remember that JMS is useful not only in all-Java environments but those based on other technologies as well.

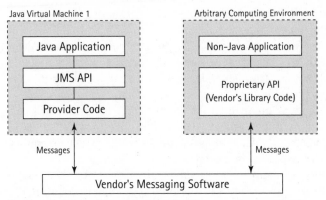

Figure 1-2: Interaction of Java application, non-Java application, and vendor's messaging software

Type of Messaging and Messages Supported

JMS is designed to handle the delivery of messages between applications that know little or nothing about each other. In practice, this typically means that applications passing data back and forth never communicate with each other via a direct network connection; typically they ask a separate running program (sometimes called a *bus* or *queue*) to handle the delivery of the message on their behalf.

This is different from remote procedure call (RPC) models such as the object request broker (ORB), Simple Object Access Protocol (SOAP), and Java's own Remote Method Invocation (RMI). Those technologies are *interface-centric*, whereas JMS is *data-centric*. In an interface-centric system, a message sender has the expectation that there is (in general) only one logical receiver of the data. This implies that the receiver is currently available, that the receiver will perform a well-known operation on the data, and (in general) return some data to the caller (at a minimum, a status code).

In a data-centric environment, the sender of a message does not need to be concerned with who will receive the messages. The sender merely sends (or *publishes*) the message and then goes about its business. After a message is sent, it is then delivered to all receivers (or *subscribers*) who are interested in it. There may be zero or more subscribers currently waiting to receive the sent message and the message may or may not end up being delivered to anyone at all.

As you'll see in Chapter 8, the J2EE message driven bean attempts to blur the distinction between interface-centric and data-centric environments but the basic concept still holds.

You can think of the software responsible for receiving and delivering the messages as a specialized router that looks at a message's *address* and delivers it to the appropriate parties (more on this in Chapter 2). This router is usually an independent process running on some machine accessible to both the sender and receiver applications.

In most cases, the router is a messaging-specific piece of software provided by the vendor. However, it can also be a generic database system that has had some messaging features added on to it. Tibco's *Rendezvous* is an example of the former; Oracle's *Advanced Queuing* the latter.

Interestingly enough, there is no requirement in the JMS specification for a separate, independent message router process. Given the right provider, a JMS-based messaging infrastructure would work just fine between two cooperating applications, such as in a peer-to-peer environment.

In practice, however, most enterprise messaging systems rely on a message router application. Doing so helps ensure the stability and response time of the overall system by allowing each application to physically deliver all its messages to one destination rather than many and by relieving them of the burden of having to store persistent messages. A centralized router application can also be tuned at runtime (say, to remove unwanted messages from the persistent queue) much more easily than a distributed system can.

When discussing enterprise messaging, regardless of product, the following concepts are critical to understand. They come into play with respect to JMS messaging in all aspects, from coding to architecture.

Asynchronous messaging

Because the receiver of a message does not operate in lock-step with its sender, the two applications can be said to be operating in an *asynchronous* manner. Systems built around asynchronous messaging can achieve overall better throughput than synchronous systems because they allow each participant to operate as independently as possible, thereby wasting fewer CPU cycles waiting for messages to be processed. All JMS messaging is presumed to be asynchronous.

Reliable and unreliable messaging

Some messages are too important to be lost in transit. When a large corporate customer places an order for 10,000 widgets through your brand-spanking-new Internet site, you can't afford to lose that message due to a system failure or network outage before it makes it to your back-end fulfillment system.

On the other hand, many messages are transitory and it doesn't matter if they never make it to their destination. Stock quotes, for instance, would likely have been superceded by a more recent quote by the time a system recovered from an outage.

This notion of reliable or unreliable message delivery is supported in the JMS API through what it calls *permanent* and *non-permanent* messaging. Why wouldn't you just declare that every message be delivered reliably? The answer is performance. The overhead associated with ensuring that each message is safely written to disk before delivery can be significant and can greatly impact overall throughput.

The publish/subscribe model

Publish/subscribe (commonly shortened to pub/sub) messaging systems existed long before JMS arrived on the scene. Pub/sub can refer to any system in which two or more applications arrange to exchange data by using a common, logical name as a system-wide delivery identifier. It's not an implementation-dependent notion but because of real-world considerations, the designers of JMS went to great pains to distinguish between two domains that tend to be implemented in different ways: one is publish/subscribe and the other is point-to-point.

Historically, vendors supplied either what were known as pub/sub systems or they supplied queuing systems. Pub/sub systems tended to support the delivery of large numbers of transient messages between many applications very quickly. Queuing systems tended to be more concerned with the safe, reliable delivery of messages from one application to another application.

Naturally, because of advances in technology, the software packages supplied by the pub/sub vendors now support many of the features traditionally associated with those of the queue-based vendors and *vice versa*.

Still, the classifications persist and in order to accommodate the few differences in the way existing products on the market operate, JMS must distinguish between products based on the point-to-point (queue) model and those based on the pub/sub (mass distribution) model.

When Not to Use JMS

Because JMS is only meant to be used with pub/sub or point-to-point messaging, you should not consider using it in situations for which it is not suited.

While e-mail, for instance, certainly is a form of messaging – and an asynchronous one, no less – it is already well supported by an industry standard infrastructure (SMTP, IMAP, and so on) and by a specialized Java API (JavaMail).

Streaming audio/video, because it's connection-oriented, isn't supported by JMS either. Refer to the Java media APIs instead for real-time protocol information.

One general class of applications JMS is not well-suited to is that involving a large audience receiving data over the Internet. This incompatibility is not due to a problem of any sort with the JMS API; rather, the current limitations of the Internet prevent this from being a viable option. So if you're planning on pumping out real-time quotes to the 500,000 subscribers of your *Market News Today* Web site, you best think twice since the technology just isn't there yet. I discuss this issue in greater detail in the architectural example chapters in Part III of this book.

Summary

By now you should have a good idea of what JMS technology is, why it exists and how the vendors (providers) fit into the overall picture. As a developer using any software library, you are always confronted with dual problems of figuring out whether the function you are using actually behaves the way the documentation says it does and, even more challenging, figuring out what the *un*documented behavior is.

Because JMS is not a product available from a single vendor, the usual state of affairs is magnified due to each provider's imperfect implementation of an imperfect specification. In short, don't always take what the JMS specification says as gospel; the details can vary subtly from provider to provider. Verify everything with thorough testing.

In the next chapter, you'll learn about writing programs using the JMS API, beginning with a description of what a JMS message looks like to your program.

Chapter 2

The JMS Message

IN THIS CHAPTER

◆ Types of JMS messages

◆ Addressing JMS messages

◆ Message headers and properties

◆ XML and JMS

GIVEN THAT JMS IS A MESSAGING SYSTEM, it's important to understand the specifics of what a message is. In this chapter I discuss what a JMS message looks like from a developer's point of view, and explore what constitutes a message and how to interact with it. At the end of the chapter, I explain a little about XML and show how a JMS system can easily be used to transport XML messages.

Types of Messages

In the previous chapter, I used the word *message* liberally without attempting to provide a formal definition for it. For the most part, no definition is necessary because when we refer to a JMS message, we are basically relying on the common meaning of the word *message* – that is, an arbitrary collection of information communicated between two or more parties.

JMS messages can contain any kind of byte data, including plain text, HTML, XML, images, documents, and so on. Although the JMS specification mandates no size limitations on messages, in the real world there are always practical limitations to contend with. Just as the Internet's Standard Mail Transfer Protocol (SMTP) does not restrict message size, while your Internet service provider (ISP) probably does, so too with JMS.

The particular JMS provider you use will likely have some sort of total size restriction on messages. This limit will probably be higher for a queue provider because it's likely that it uses permanent storage to transfer the message (as opposed to a pure network transmission), but you should be sure to check your provider's documentation if you're planning on transmitting very large messages. In many transaction-oriented systems, messages tend to be smaller so message size probably won't be an issue. Designers of some workflow systems, on the other hand, may wish to include such things as word processing documents and design schematics in their messages. JMS does not preclude this — just be sure to check on the feasibility of it when selecting a messaging model and provider.

JMS has some predefined message structures that can be used for various types of messages. The following sections include descriptions of the five message types that JMS supports. As far as your code is concerned, each message is defined by a Java interface in the `javax.jms` package, all of which implement the `javax.jms.Message` interface. For example, `javax.jms.TextMessage` defines the text message API.

The TextMessage

The `TextMessage` is just about the simplest JMS message there is. And, depending on how you design your application, it is something you will use a lot (if your messages are all based on simple text) — or perhaps never (if your messages only carry binary data).

`TextMessage` is designed to carry a single string only. As such, it would only seem to be useful for delivering simple, human-readable messages to be used possibly for alerts *("System going down in 5 minutes")* or perhaps some sort of home-grown instant messaging system *("Wanna grab a coffee while the system's being rebooted?")*.

However, because the computer industry seems to be on a relentless drive to define a text representation for every possible data type (e.g. HTML, XML, WML, VRML, OFX, RTF) — you name the domain, there's probably a text mapping for it — it turns out `TextMessage` can be quite useful indeed. Whether this is anywhere near the most efficient way to transmit information is irrelevant; text-based messaging is a fact of life today.

Befitting its simple functionality, `TextMessage` adds only the methods found in Table 2-1 to the `Message` interface.

TABLE 2-1 TEXTMESSAGE METHODS

Return Value	Method
java.lang.String	getText()
void	setText(java.lang.String text)

The BytesMessage

BytesMessage is appropriate when you have "raw" information to send. In most cases, messaging software performs automatic data-representation conversion between host architectures for you (see the section "Inter-platform message delivery" later in this chapter). For instance, integers may need to be converted from a big-endian representation on one computer to a little-endian one on another.

The use of BytesMessage means the provider should ignore the content of the message and deliver it to its destination as is. If the receiver cannot understand the content of the message, that's not the provider's problem. The most common reason you might want to send a message composed only of raw bytes is if you're delivering a message that is already in some well-known format or is not destined to be directly interpreted by the receiving application: for instance, a Microsoft Word document or a JPEG image.

For the most part, however, for messages that are in an application-specific format — one that you have created explicity for use in your system — you would not use BytesMessage. In fact, most of the time, even if you are sending raw data, you can easily use the byte[] facility of StreamMessage to do so. Because you'll probably be using StreamMessage fairly frequently, you may not want to bother learning about BytesMessage, which only really comes in handy if you want to put raw data into your message on a field by field basis. BytesMessage has a number of methods similar to those found in java.io.DataOutput for this purpose, as shown in Table 2-2.

TABLE 2-2 BYTESMESSAGE METHODS

Return Value	Method
void	writeBoolean(boolean value)
void	writeByte(byte value)
void	writeBytes(byte[] value)

Continued

TABLE 2-2 BYTESMESSAGE METHODS *(Continued)*

Return Value	Method
void	writeBytes(byte[] value, int offset, int length)
void	writeChar(char value)
void	writeDouble(double value)
void	writeFloat(float value)
void	writeInt(int value)
void	writeLong(long value)
void	writeObject(java.lang.Object value)
void	writeShort(short value)
void	writeUTF(String value)
boolean	readBoolean()
byte	readByte()
int	readBytes(byte[] value)
int	readBytes(byte[] value, int length)
char	readChar()
double	readDouble()
float	readFloat()
int	readInt()
long	readLong()
short	readShort()
int	readUnsignedByte()
int	readUnsignedShort()
java.lang.String	readUTF()

The ObjectMessage

An ObjectMessage is used to send a single Java object between Java applications. Naturally, the object must be serializable (that is to say, must implement the java.io.Serializable interface) so that it can be transmitted over the wire. Of course, a single Java object can be a standalone object or an object that encapsulates other objects or a collection of objects. As long as the entire object's structure is recursively serializable, the message is deliverable. Table 2-3 lists the methods `ObjectMessage` provides for setting and retrieving its content.

TABLE **2-3** OBJECTMESSAGE METHODS

Return Value	Method
java.io.Serializable	getObject()
void	setObject(java.io.Serializable object)

When you call `setObject()`, the object you pass is immediately serialized and stored internally so that you can continue to manipulate the supplied object (for example, sending a slightly modified copy of it to another recipient). Any modifications made to the original object subsequent to the call to `setObject()` will not be reflected in the message when it is finally sent. Because of this, you don't have to worry about any changes that take place to the object between the time you place it in the `ObjectMessage` and the time you call the method that sends the message somewhere. Of course, as always you are still responsible for ensuring that access to the object is appropriately synchronized and that the object is in a stable state while it is being serialized.

As I mentioned, objects passed between virtual machines in an `ObjectMessage` must conform to the standard Java serialization rules. The messaging bus will provide no explicit support for Java objects. In fact, a vendor's messaging software will only see the object as an opaque array of bytes while it is being delivered.

Deserialization of objects occurs in the destination client's virtual machine. This is analogous to the situation that exists when using RMI and if you plan on using `ObjectMessage`, you should be intimately familiar with the logic RMI uses to locate and load the required *.class* files it needs when reconstructing a serialized object, as well as how you can implement custom serialization procedures.

The MapMessage

A `MapMessage` is very similar in concept to the `java.util.HashMap` or `java.util.Hashtable` classes with the exception that the keys to the map can only be strings and the values can only be one of a small set of predefined types. All the values must be one of the following basic Java types:

◆ boolean

◆ byte

- ◆ byte[] (a byte array)
- ◆ char
- ◆ double
- ◆ float
- ◆ int
- ◆ long
- ◆ short
- ◆ String

`MapMessage` provides a setter and getter method for each of these data types to enable you to set the fields of the message in a type-safe manner: `setInt(String key, int value)`, `getFloat(String key)`, and so on (see Table 2-4).

TABLE 2-4 MAPMESSAGE METHODS

Return Value	Method
boolean	getBoolean(String)
byte	getByte(String name)
byte[]	getBytes(String name)
char	getChar(String name)
double	getDouble(String name)
float	getFloat(String name)
int	getInt(String name)
long	getLong(String name)
java.util.Enumeration	getMapNames()
Object	getObject(String name)
short	getShort(String name)
String	getString(String name)
boolean	itemExists(String name)
void	setBoolean(String name, boolean value)
void	setByte(String name, byte value)

Return Value	Method
void	setBytes(String name, byte[] value)
void	setBytes(String name, byte[] value, int offset, int length)
void	setChar(String name, char value)
void	setDouble(String name, double value)
void	setFloat(String name, float value)
void	setInt(String name, int value)
void	setLong(String name, long value)
void	setObject(String name, Object value)
void	setShort(String name, short value)
void	setString(String name, String value)

Do not be fooled by the setObject() method in MapMessage. This method will not allow you to place an arbitrary Java object in a MapMessage and send it. This method only exists to make it easier for you to set values in a MapMessage in cases where you prefer to do so using a java.lang object wrapper class that represents one of the supported types – for instance, an Integer object rather than a native Java int. If you attempt to supply an unsupported object to MapMessage using setObject(), a javax.jms.MessageFormatException will be thrown.

If you want to send a Java object, you should use an ObjectMessage, if at all possible. If you really, really have to send a Java object in a MapMessage, then serialize the object to a byte array, place it in the message using setBytes(), and then explicitly deserialize the object after the message is received.

The MapMessage class is extremely handy. It has all the features programmers like in HashMap – ease of use, random access to fields, and so on – and it's great for sending messages back and forth between Java and non-Java applications as many vendors supply a MapMessage equivalent for any non-Java clients they support with their product. (See the section "Inter-platform message delivery" later in this chapter for more details.)

Figure 2-1 illustrates a simple MapMessage you could use for a stock quote.

Key (String)	Value	Value Type
"Ticker"	XYZ	String
"Bid"	50.2	float
"Ask"	50.5	float
"Last Trade"	50.3	float

Figure 2-1: A simple MapMessage

Another extremely valuable feature of MapMessages is that they can help shield the internal logic of your application from the specifics of the message content. For example, let's say you have a simple system architecture in which you have a ticker plant application that pumps out the stock quote message from Figure 2-1. The message is then received by many instances of client applications where each client application falls into one of two categories: trading system or analytics system (see Figure 2-2).

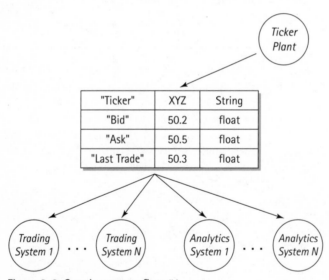

Figure 2-2: Sample message flow #1

Suppose now that the users of the analytics system request a change to the application that requires the addition of a field to the message sent from the ticker plant. If you had an architecture by which you sent out only fixed-format messages such as an ObjectMessage, you would need to recompile, retest, and redeploy all three types of applications because each application would need to be modified to handle the new message format.

However, by using a MapMessage, you do not need to make any changes to the trading system. Because the trading application extracts fields only by logical name (the map key), it will remain blissfully unaware of any information present in the message it receives that it is not interested in, as shown in Figure 2-3.

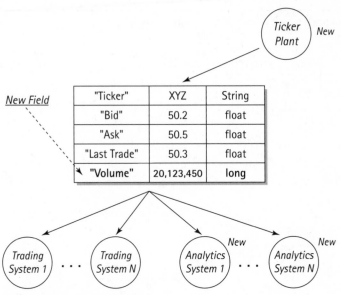

Figure 2-3: Sample message flow #2

Of course, there are limits to how much you can change in a message without impacting all applications. For instance, if you were to change the data type of one of the message fields, in all likelihood, you would have to modify and redeploy all applications.

The StreamMessage

A StreamMessage supports all the same data types as MapMessage, and *only* those data types. The difference is that the fields of the message do not have keys associated with them; there is an explicit ordering to the fields determined by the sequence in which they are written into the message object. This means that the fields must be read out of a StreamMessage in the same sequence in which they were written in order for the data to make any sense. Note that the writeObject() method in StreamMessage conforms to the same rules as the setObject() method in MapMessage. Table 2-5 shows a complete listing of StreamMessage methods.

TABLE 2-5 STREAMMESSAGE METHODS

Return Value	Method
boolean	readBoolean()
byte	readByte()

Continued

TABLE 2-5 STREAMMESSAGE METHODS *(Continued)*

int	readBytes(byte[] value)
char	readChar()
double	readDouble()
float	readFloat()
int	readInt()
long	readLong()
Object	readObject()
short	readShort()
String	readString()
void	reset()
void	writeBoolean(boolean value)
void	writeByte(byte value)
void	writeBytes(byte[] value)
void	writeBytes(byte[] value, int offset, int length)
void	writeChar(char value)
void	writeDouble(double value)
void	writeFloat(float value)
void	writeInt(int value)
void	writeLong(long value)
void	writeObject(Object value)
void	writeShort(short value)
void	writeString(String value)

Why might you prefer to use a StreamMessage over a MapMessage? The answer is efficiency. Because the fields on a StreamMessage are not "indexed" by strings, the amount of data that needs to be transmitted is greatly reduced and the CPU cycles required to convert the indexes back and forth from one platform's representation to another's are eliminated. This can be a boon to performance for systems with high volumes of messages, at the loss, of course, of the data-extraction flexibility you get from `MapMessage`. If you're mainly concerned with maximizing performance and throughput, you should probably use `StreamMessages`.

The empty message

Note that it's also possible to have a completely empty message, too. This message's type is, simply, `Message`. While this might not seem to be useful, you'll see shortly that there's a lot more information associated with a JMS message than the "content." In some rare cases, this additional information may be all you really need.

Note that each message type is defined as a Java interface and that providers' implementations must conform to these interfaces. These interfaces are all defined in the `javax.jms` package. `Message` not only defines the interface for the empty message, it is also the parent interface for all the other message types. The UML diagram shown in Figure 2-4 illustrates the relationship of the standard Java interfaces to each other, and to the provider's implementation.

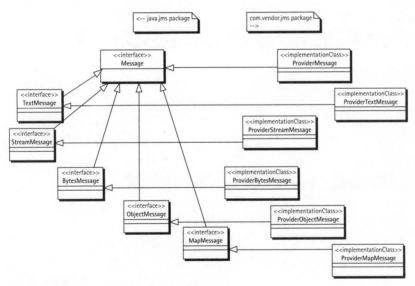

Figure 2-4: Relationship of message classes

As a developer, you of course only care about the JMS interface's API. In Chapter 3, I will demonstrate the appropriate way to create each of the preceding message types and how to populate them.

Inter-platform message delivery

Why doesn't JMS define just one basic type of message holder and allow you to just give it some arbitrary object or array of bytes? There are two reasons.

First, having several message types can simplify the interface for the programmer, thereby cutting down on programming errors and aiding in ease of use and debugging.

The more significant reason, however, has to do with the way information is shuttled back and forth in the provider's messaging software. Remember from Chapter 1 that a primary function of most messaging software is not only to transmit data from one location to another, it is also to provide automatic conversion of the data from one platform's internal representation to another's.

Thus, if a messaging bus is to be required to transmit messages handed to it by a Java application running on a Solaris server to a C++ application on a Windows PC, it must be able to perform a conversion from Java's internal data representation to, say, an Intel 32-bit architecture representation.

For example, imagine a simple market volume message being sent under the just described conditions. Figure 2-5 shows the data translation the messaging bus would perform before handing off the message to the C++ application.

Java-based sender

Field Name	Value	Native Representation
Ticker	"XYZ"	Java String
Time	992846170670	Java long (big-endian)
Volume	65000000	Java int (big-endian)

Messaging software translates

PC-based C++ receiver

Field Name	Value	Native Representation
Ticker	"XYZ"	null-terminated char array
Time	992846170670	C++ 32 bit long (little-endian)
Volume	65000000	C++ 32 bit long (little-endian)

Figure 2-5: Data translation from Java to Intel Pentium/C++

Only the StreamMessage, MapMessage, and TextMessage can have their contents translated from one platform to another. For this reason, these classes accept only a small number of fixed data types. Messaging providers cannot prefer Java applications over those written in other languages; they can only really translate the basic data types that exist on all computing platforms.

Addressing Messages

So far, I've talked quite a bit about the various types of JMS messages and how to manage their contents. A message isn't any good, however, unless the message router knows where to deliver it. Like mail in the physical world, JMS messages need to be addressed. It is your application's responsibility to do this prior to sending any message. You do this by specifying a message *destination*.

 JMS addresses are logically similar to Internet Protocol (IP) addresses but don't confuse the two. An IP address is just a unique number used to distinguish your computer from others on the same network. A JMS address is a string of no particular format. It is unique and meaningful only within one particular vendor's messaging environment. An address is the identifier that links senders with interested receivers. One of the advantages of using messaging software is that applications do not need to be concerned with the actual location of the other applications. Thus, as a JMS programmer you won't need to be concerned with such location-dependent details as IP addresses.

JMS destinations come in two flavors, each of which is specific to a messaging domain. Pub/sub destinations are called *topics* and are defined by the `javax.jms.Topic` interface. Point-to-point destinations are called *queues* and are defined by the `javax.jms.Queue` interface. Both are subinterfaces of `javax.jms.Destination`. Despite the distinction, as far as addressing is concerned there's really no difference between the two; they're both just simple strings of whatever length you like.

Like message objects, topic and queue destinations are created by provider factories, so don't expect to be able to just write something like `Topic topic = new Topic("ABC")` to create a topic. Creating destinations programmatically will be discussed in Chapter 3.

Although it is not a technology issue *per se*, an effective message addressing scheme is important to any large scale JMS installation. A good architect will recognize that the manner in which messages are addressed can have a pronounced effect on how efficient a system is and can also affect other system properties such as maintainability. The architectural chapters in Part III of this book cover this issue in more detail.

A popular convention in the pub/sub world is the dot-delimited topic. Using this technique, a topic string contains two or more pieces of information, each separated by a period (or dashes, or commas, or whatever symbol you like) – for instance, "A.B.C". The values between the dots typically are also contained inside the message itself. The reason for duplicating the information in the topic is that it's usually easier and more efficient to examine just the header of a message – using it to filter out unwanted messages – than it is to parse the whole incoming message just so the contents can be examined and a determination can be made as to whether to process it or not. In JMS, this message filtering is accomplished with *message selectors,* which I discuss in Chapter 4.

In addition to separating the data elements with dots, the convention is also to order the elements in order of increasing specificity – that is, to make it hierarchical. The meaning of this hierarchy is completely artificial and must be implicitly agreed upon by the sending and receiving applications. As far as JMS is concerned, it is an application convention that has no real significance to the provider's messaging software, although historically some messaging systems do provide specific capabilities that allow dot-delimited topics to be routed more efficiently than non-delimited topics.

In an all-JMS environment, the use of the delimited topic is obviated by the ability to attach arbitrary properties to a message. Properties offer a much richer way to filter messages than stuffing a lot of information into the topic name. However, because in many enterprise systems all participants will not be JMS-aware – and, hence, some will lack support for properties – the delimited topic technique can still be useful.

See the "Order Taking" sample architecture in Chapter 15 for an example of filtering based on message properties.

Properties of Messages

It is common in messaging systems to divide the structure of a message into two main parts: the header and the content (also known as the body). Internet e-mail is the most recognizable example of this. Typically, the header is a hodge-podge of information that describes such things as the content of the message, delivery instructions, timestamps, and a variety of other things. The body, of course, is just the information you want to send.

JMS jargon makes a distinction between header values and what it calls *message properties*. Properties are simple name/value pairs of information that are associated with a message. There are some standard properties that client applications can utilize. Clients also have the option of adding any number of arbitrary properties to a message.

Message headers are essentially required properties that are present in all messages, though some can be null or disabled. Both headers and properties are set through methods found in the `javax.jms.Message` interface which, as I mentioned earlier in this chapter, all message types implement. The main difference is that headers have special named methods that can be used to access them and properties just have a single generic method.

Following is a discussion of each of the JMS-defined message headers. To simplify matters, I will refer to headers generically as *properties*.

JMSDestination

The **JMSDestination** property is accessed with the `setJMSDestination()` and `getJMSDestination()` methods. Its value type is `Destination`.

While it's tempting to assume that you specify the address of a message by setting the **JMSDestination** property on it, this is not the case. Although you can call `setJMSDestination()` again and again, it will never have any effect on the message. **JMSDestination** is a set-on-call property, which means it is basically read-only. It is set by the provider's code when it delivers a message. The **JMSDestination** property is meant to be used by the receiver application, not so much the sender.

You may wonder why this property even has a setter method. It's for the benefit of the developer who writes the provider's JMS implementation because they'll need to set the destination property inside their JMS library. However, it's not terribly useful for the end-user developer. You will see in the next chapter how to correctly specify the address of a message.

JMSDeliveryMode

JMS defines two message delivery options: reliable and unreliable. As discussed in Chapter 1, the term *reliable* implies that messages are stored on disk so that they can be recovered in the event of a system failure, whereas unreliable messages are delivered in a best-effort fashion. The delivery mode property should be one of the following two integer constants: `javax.jms.DeliveryMode.PERSISTENT` or `javax.jms.DeliveryMode.NONPERSISTENT`, both of whose names naturally refer to the expected reliability of the messaging.

The `setJMSDeliveryMode()` and `getJMSDeliveryMode()` methods are used to access this property. Like **JMSDestination**, however, the setter method is irrelevant; the desired delivery mode is not specified via the property.

 The JMS specification calls reliable message delivery "once and only once" and unreliable "at most once." A correctly implemented JMS provider will ensure that each receiving application will never be delivered the same message twice under normal conditions.

JMSExpiration

This property indicates the time after which a message is no longer valid. It is a standard Unix-style timestamp – a long integer indicating the current GMT-based time. A zero value means the message never expires.

Because of the difficulties associated with managing timestamps between systems, JMS says this property is only advisory. It's entirely possible your application may receive a message that has expired.

If your provider supports message expiration, be sure to investigate its capabilities thoroughly before depending on it for anything more than very course-grained time control. It exists more for queue maintenance purposes (to allow a disk-based queue to be periodically purged) than it does to support applications that want messages to live for, say, no more than a few seconds.

If you do want to support precise expiration behavior, there's nothing to stop you from doing so at the application level. All you have to do is drop any incoming messages whose expiration time is greater than the current time. Of course, if you're doing this across systems, you have to be sure the times on each machine are properly synchronized in order to be able to get the correct behavior. This is a challenge in itself if you require sub-second granularity.

The `setJMSExpiration ()` and `getJMSExpiration()` methods are used to access the **JMSExpiration** property. It is also a set-on-call property.

JMSPriority

The priority property is an integer in the range 0 to 9 where by convention 0–4 indicates degrees of "normal" delivery and 5–9 indicates degrees of "expedited" delivery. It is not required that a provider honor the **JMSPriority** property in any particular way or even at all.

Thus, even if your provider supports priority delivery, it's hard to see as an architect how you could make good use of it in your design. Because there are no well-defined semantics associated with it, you won't be able to count on getting any particular behavior out of your system. And, of course, if you were to change providers, the behavior of your system might change as well. For these reasons, it's probably best to avoid using the priority property entirely.

The `setJMSPriority()` and `getJMSPriority()` methods are used to access this property. It is also a set-on-call property.

JMSMessageID

JMS defines a message ID to be a string that uniquely identifies the message across some arbitrary, provider-specific domain. It will always start with the token "ID:". Of course, this value will be generated and set by the provider.

When would you use a message ID? Because JMS provides no facility for retrieving previously delivered messages, let alone retrieving a message by its ID, it's not used to retrieve old or expired messages. Its only real use is in conjunction with the **JMSCorrelationID** property.

If, for instance, you have one application sending out messages that are somehow related to another message that had previously been sent, you would set the correlation ID of the subsequent message(s) to the message ID of the original message. Of course, in order for this to work, the sending application must have access to the message ID that the provider generates for the original message so that it can cache it for later use. For this reason, JMS specifies that the provider must set the message ID property on the message immediately when the message is submitted for delivery. Thus, the order of operations for the sender would be as follows:

1. Submit a message for delivery.

2. Retrieve the message ID from the message object with the `getJMSMessageID()` method.

3. Store the message ID somewhere (memory, disk).

4. Set the correlation ID of any related messages to the saved message ID *prior* to sending the related messages.

The message ID is also commonly used in request/reply circumstances. An application that is responding to another application's request will set the correlation ID of the response message to the message ID of the original message so that the receiving application can correctly pair up the response with the original request.

For efficiency reasons, JMS provides a way to turn off the message ID functionality. See Chapter 3 for more on this.

Architecturally speaking, the message and correlation ID properties are of little practical use. In a business setting, your goal generally is to tie one *transaction* to another *transaction* and you almost always use some data element in the record to do so — say, order number. Keeping message IDs around for a long time as a means of referring to a previous business event is not practical or efficient. Message IDs are really only useful for messages that live a short period of time, as in a request/reply situation.

JMSTimestamp

JMSTimestamp is a GMT-based timestamp like **JMSExpiration**. This represents the time a client application submitted a message to the provider for delivery. If a message is being transmitted between two different machines, this time may not be in sync with the time on the destination machine, so in some situations a JMS timestamp on a received message may indicate a message was sent in the future.

The `setJMSTimestamp()` and `getJMSTimestamp()` methods are used to access this property. It is also a set-on-call property.

JMSCorrelationID

As discussed in the **JMSMessageID** section, the **JMSCorrelationID** property is generally the provider-generated ID string from a previous message's ID. However, because providers are not allowed to perform any referential integrity checking on this value, it actually can be any string you like. Thus, the correlation ID can be used in such a way that it only has meaning to the applications sharing the message.

JMS actually allows the correlation ID to be one of two data types: string or byte array. The byte array option provides a catch-all way for applications to correlate messages in any way they like. Whether a string or a byte array, the correlation ID has no meaning to the JMS provider.

JMSCorrelationID is a read/write property. Unlike with many of the other header properties, it is the responsibility of the sending application to set this property appropriately prior to sending the message.

The `setJMSCorrelationID()`, `getJMSCorrelationID()`, `setJMSCorrelation IDAsBytes()`, and `getJMSCorrelationIDAsBytes()` methods are used to access this property.

JMSReplyTo

This property is of type `javax.jms.Destination` and — if you want to set it at all — it should be set by an application prior to sending the message. Keep in mind that the use of this property is completely application-driven. JMS providers do not have any automated response or acknowledgment mechanisms that you can use to determine if a message was received or not. Any sender that sets this property is probably expecting that the receiving application will respond back to it with some message, but JMS makes no assurances this will actually ever happen. See Chapter 10 for more information on using the reply-to field.

The `setJMSReplyTo()` and `getJMSReplyTo()` methods are used to access this property.

JMSType

JMSType is a simple string that can be anything your application desires. It exists because some providers (albeit very few) maintain meta-data about various message types and they can use the **JMSType** to tie a message to its meta-data. In most cases, you won't need to worry about doing this, but because the JMS documentation strongly recommends setting **JMSType** to *something* even if it's not used, you can just make a habit of setting it to something short and innocuous.

The `setJMSType()` and `getJMSType()` methods are used to access this property.

JMSRedelivered

JMSRedelivered is a boolean property that is set to true by the provider if the provider is making a second attempt to deliver a message to an application. Although I said earlier that JMS requires that no message be delivered more than once to the same client, strictly speaking this is not true. The rule is more precisely stated as: no *properly acknowledged* message will be delivered to the same client more than once.

So even though an application has already received a message, if the application it was delivered to never acknowledges it — either due to application or provider failure of some sort — the provider *may* attempt to redeliver it. I discuss message acknowledgment further in Chapter 4.

The `setJMSRedelivered()` and `getJMSRedelivered()` methods are used to access this property. It is also a set-on-call property.

Additional properties

In addition to the header properties, JMS defines some additional standard properties. You can add any number of your own properties as well. These differ from the headers in that they don't have specific named methods for accessing them. You set and retrieve them using their string name.

Not including the header properties mentioned previously, all message property values must be one of the following Java types: `boolean`, `byte`, `short`, `int`, `long`, `float`, `double`, or `String`. They are set on a message using the property name string and the method that corresponds to their type. Here are a couple of examples:

```
Example #1: setIntProperty("JMSXGroupSeqID", 3)
Example #2: setFloatProperty("Price", 32.69);
```

You can use the general method `setObjectProperty()` to set properties, but the supplied object must be the Java object equivalent of one of the supported native types (for example, `java.lang.Integer` for `int`) or a `javax.jms.MessageFormatException` will be thrown. There are, of course, corresponding `getXXXProperty()` methods as well.

Table 2-6 lists the standard properties defined by JMS and includes a brief description of each. They may or may not be useful to you and they may or may not even be supported by your provider (with the exception of **JMSXGroupID** and **JMSXGroupSeq**, which must be supported by all providers). Be sure to consult your provider's documentation before relying on the behavior associated with any of these properties.

TABLE **2-6 STANDARD PROPERTIES AND THEIR DEFINITIONS**

Property	Definition
JMSXUserID	The system user ID (as a string) that the sending application is running under. If supported, this value is automatically set by the provider.
JMSXAppID	The application ID (as a string) of the sending application. If supported, this value is automatically set by the provider. The meaning of an application ID is completely provider-specific.
JMSXDeliveryCount	The number of times the current message has been delivered: 1 for the first delivery attempt, 2 for the first redelivery attempt, and so on. If supported, this value is set by the provider.
JMSXGroupID	A string set by the sending application prior to submitting a message for delivery. The meaning of this string is completely application-dependent. It can be used in a similar fashion as JMSCorrelationID.

Continued

TABLE 2-6 STANDARD PROPERTIES AND THEIR DEFINITIONS *(Continued)*

Property	Definition
JMSXGroupSeq	An integer representing an ordering of messages in a group of messages. It is set by the application prior to sending a message and is generally used in conjunction with JMSXGroupID.
JMSXProducerTXID	
JMSXConsumerTXID	A string identifying the transaction in which a message was sent or received. These are not of much use to your application.
JMSXRcvTimestamp	The time a message was delivered to the client.
JMSXState	For internal provider use.

Remember, however, that applications are entirely free to attach any number of their own application-specific properties to a message. So, even if your provider does not automatically create a "JMSXUserID" property for you, there's no reason your application can't define its own user ID property. Just don't call it "JMSXUserID" because all property names that start with "JMSX" are reserved.

The value of creating your own message properties will become clearer when we cover message filtering in Chapter 4.

Automatic type-conversion

One final note on properties. JMS provides for the automatic conversion of properties set as one type to another type. Thus, the receiving application can read a property as a different type than the one the sending application supplied as long as the types are compatible.

For instance, a sender might set a property like so:

```
msg.setObjectProperty("Total", new Integer(1000));
```

And the receiver might extract the property like this:

```
float total = msg.getFloatProperty("Total");
```

This automatic conversion of value types is meant as a small aid to reduce the amount of test and conversion code a receiver must write when processing a message's properties.

Figure 2-6 shows which types are automatically converted for the receiver. If a receiver attempts to extract a property as an incompatible type, a `javax.jms.MessageFormatException` will be thrown. For instance, using the previous example, the following code would result in an exception:

```
boolean b = msg.getBooleanProperty("Total");
```

	boolean	byte	short	int	long	float	double	String
boolean	✓							✓
byte		✓	✓	✓	✓			✓
short			✓	✓	✓			✓
int				✓	✓			✓
long					✓			✓
float						✓	✓	✓
double							✓	✓
String	✓	✓	✓	✓	✓	✓	✓	✓

Figure 2-6: Valid type conversions from the row type to the column type

XML and JMS Messages

Everyone is jumping on the XML bandwagon these days and, of course, the designers of JMS are no different. `TextMessage` has been positioned as a great message holder for XML and, truth be told, it is. But this is only because an XML message of any complexity can be expressed as a single Java string.

The fact of the matter is, however, that currently there is no explicit support for XML in JMS. As is the case with any standards-based effort, individual vendors are racing ahead, adding proprietary XML features to their JMS implementations. In some cases, they're adding features to aid in creating JMS messages from XML document structures. In others, JMS's defined message selection capabilities (see Chapter 4 for a description of message selectors) have been extended to allow for filtering based on the content of an XML message.

Most likely, similar capabilities will be incorporated into future revisions of the JMS specification. For now, as with any proprietary addition to an industry standard, you should avoid using any of them unless you have a very good reason to do so. Using a vendor's proprietary extensions removes the option of easily swapping in another JMS vendor, one of the primary reasons for programming to a standard API in the first place.

By all means, however, use XML in your applications if you want to. Just stuff your XML message in a JMS `TextMessage` when sending it and parse it at the receiver's end using any of the myriad XML tools available. Be prepared, however, to pay a significant performance penalty for this kind of messaging. Chapter 10 contains further discussion of the performance issues regarding JMS and XML messaging.

Summary

In this chapter, we thoroughly covered the five types of JMS messages: how they differ in the way they manage their content, and how they're the same in the way they support message headers and properties.

When architecting a distributed system, it's important to remember that many vendors allow JMS messages to be exchanged between Java and non-Java environments. Your provider's messaging software will provide automatic data conversions between the native data representation of the various computing platforms it supports.

Now that you understand JMS messages, in the next chapter I delve into the steps you need to know in order to open a connection to your provider's software and get it to send a message.

Chapter 3

Sending Messages

IN THIS CHAPTER

- ◆ Using JNDI to instantiate your provider
- ◆ Working with JMS factories, connections, and sessions
- ◆ Creating and populating messages
- ◆ Sending messages

IN CHAPTER 2, I described the various elements of a JMS message and how you might use them. In this chapter, I discuss how to use the JMS API to create a message and actually send it somewhere.

As I've explained, JMS is primarily an API layer that rides on top of an actual messaging implementation, known as a provider. As a developer, you code to the JMS API as defined by the JMS specification (currently, version 1.0.2). From an end-user developer's point of view, this API is entirely defined by the classes in the `javax.jms` package, most of which are Java interface definitions. Not counting some very simple functionality, when you invoke one of the published JMS methods, you're more likely than not invoking one of the corresponding methods in the library supplied by your vendor of choice.

In this chapter, I demonstrate how to prepare and send a message. I also examine what's going on inside the provider's code that might not be readily apparent to a JMS developer.

Specifying a Provider via JNDI

Providers are largely interchangeable because they must support the same API. In fact, because JMS allows you to specify a provider dynamically, you can change providers at runtime; your application can even interact with more than one provider at the same time.

You might have an application talking to two providers at once because your application is serving as a software bridge linking the JMS messaging systems from two different vendors. As I mentioned in Chapter 1, JMS systems from two different vendors will not be interoperable. If you want to receive a message from provider A and then want to turn around and publish it using provider B, you have to write the code to extract the data from A's message and then resend a new message using B.

Each provider's implementation you access — and in most cases it will be only one — must be loaded at runtime. Typically, you would do this during the initialization portion of your program.

The base object you must create first is either the `TopicConnectionFactory` (for pub/sub messaging) or the `QueueConnectionFactory` (for point-to-point messaging). These objects are the single points of access for creating all the other messaging objects you will need.

Remember that in JMS API terminology *topic* is always used to refer to the pub/sub messaging domain and *queue* is always used to refer to the point-to-point messaging domain. Rather than separate the domain at the package level, JMS has chosen to segregate the two messaging domains at the class name level. Thus, we have a `TopicConnectionFactory` class for pub/sub messaging and its analogue for point-to-point messaging, `QueueConnectionFactory`. In this and subsequent chapters you will see many cases of classes that follow this naming convention.

You create an initial connection factory with the Java Naming and Directory Interface (JNDI) API. JNDI is a standard part of J2SE 1.2 and above; if you are using an earlier JDK, you will have to download the JNDI library from Sun's Web site (`http://java.sun.com/products/jndi`).

Because JNDI uses a provider model just like JMS, you will have to first specify the JNDI provider you are interested in using. Then, you can look up the appropriate connection factory from that provider. A JNDI provider could be one that interacts with a standard directory service — for example, LDAP — or it may be a custom one that only knows how to interact with your JMS provider's proprietary directory service. In either case, you will have to consult your JMS provider's documentation to figure out how to use JNDI to get access to the appropriate directory service. Fortunately, this will be the only vendor-specific portion of your code and, as I'll show at the end of this chapter, even this vendor-specific portion can be avoided.

TIP No matter which JNDI provider you are using, be sure the appropriate directory service is running before attempting to access it. Otherwise your
lookups will fail. For example, in the case of *WebLogic* you will need to start
the application server first. Of course, your directory service also needs to
have the right JMS provider registered with it. How you do this will vary
greatly from vendor to vendor, so if you're responsible for configuring JMS
on a machine, be sure to read your vendor's administration documentation
thoroughly before attempting any JMS programming.

For example, to create JMS connection factories using WebLogic 6.1, you would
write the following code in Listing 3-1:

Listing 3-1: Creating JMS ConnectionFactories

```java
import javax.jms.*;
import javax.naming.*;
import java.util.*;

public class JMSLookup
{
    public static void main(String[] args)
    {
        try
        {
            Hashtable hash = new Hashtable();
            hash.put(Context.INITIAL_CONTEXT_FACTORY,
                "weblogic.jndi.WLInitialContextFactory");
            hash.put(Context.PROVIDER_URL,
                "t3://localhost:7001");

            Context context = new InitialContext(hash);

            // "XXXX" and "YYYY" are the symbolic names for
            // WebLogic connection factories. You create them
            // through WebLogic's
            // administration facilities.

            TopicConnectionFactory tcFactory =
                (TopicConnectionFactory) context.lookup("XXXX");

            QueueConnectionFactory qcFactory =
```

Continued

Listing 3-1 *(Continued)*

```
                (QueueConnectionFactory) context.lookup("YYYY");
        }
        catch (NamingException ex)
        {
            ex.printStackTrace();
        }

    }
}
```

Note that you must first decide which type of messaging you will be using: topic or queue. There is nothing to stop you from using both kinds in your application of course; it's just that the APIs for pub/sub messaging are not entirely the same as the APIs for point-to-point messaging (though they are very similar). To use both kinds of messaging, you would have to create both a `TopicConnectionFactory` and a `QueueConnectionFactory`. Be aware, though, that providers are not required to support both types — only one or the other.

Creating Connections and Sessions

The connection factory represents the vendor's provider that you have chosen to use but getting the initial connection factory object is only step one of the JMS setup process. Once you have the connection factory object, you need to use it to create a connection object.

The connection object represents a live connection to your provider's messaging software — in this respect it's very similar to a connection to a database — and like the connection factory, it comes in topic and queue flavors. Typically, your application will need to have only one connection open at a time. Once you have a connection, you then use it to create a session.

For example, let's extend the example from Listing 3-1 to create a connection and session each for pub/sub and point-to-point messaging, as shown in Listing 3-2.

Listing 3-2: Creating JMS Connections and Sessions

```
import javax.jms.*;
import javax.naming.*;
import java.util.*;

public class JMSInitialize
{
    public static void main(String[] args)
    {
        try
        {
```

```
                    Hashtable hash = new Hashtable();
                    hash.put(Context.INITIAL_CONTEXT_FACTORY,
                            "weblogic.jndi.WLInitialContextFactory");
                    hash.put(Context.PROVIDER_URL,
                            "t3://localhost:7001");

                    Context context = new InitialContext(hash);

                    // Pub/sub set up

                    TopicConnectionFactory tcFactory =
                            (TopicConnectionFactory) context.lookup("XXXX");

                    TopicConnection topicConn =
                            tcFactory.createTopicConnection();

                    TopicSession tcSession =
                            topicConn.createTopicSession(false
                                        Session.AUTO_ACKNOWLEDGE);


                    // Point-to-point set up

                    QueueConnectionFactory qcFactory =
                            (QueueConnectionFactory) context.lookup("YYYY");

                    QueueConnection queueConn =
                            qcFactory.createQueueConnection();

                    QueueSession qcSession =
                            queueConn.createQueueSession(false,
                                        Session.AUTO_ACKNOWLEDGE);
                }
                catch (NamingException ex)
                {
                    ex.printStackTrace();
                }
                catch (JMSException ex)
                {
                    ex.printStackTrace();
                }
        }
}
```

If you look at the methods of a JMS `Connection` object you'll see there are only a couple of them — connection objects just don't do very much. Their primary function is to let you create a session, which you then use to send and receive messages. Why does JMS define both connection objects *and* session objects? JMS expects that while most applications will have just one connection per provider open at any given time, some applications will have more than one simultaneous active session. To see why this might be the case, we need to examine the parameters accepted by the `createTopicSession()` and `createQueueSession()` methods.

The first parameter of both methods is a `boolean`, which indicates whether all activity in the session takes place within a transaction (see Chapter 7 for more on transactionalized messaging). The second parameter is an `int`, which must be one of three constants: `Session.AUTO_ACKNOWLEDGE`, `Session.CLIENT_ACKNOWLEDGE`, or `Session.DUPS_OK_ACKNOWLEDGE` (the meaning of these values will be explained in Chapter 4). Although you might assume there can be up to six (2 times 3) different variations on a JMS session, it's really only four because transacted sessions perform acknowledgment automatically; thus, the second parameter is irrelevant when the value of the first is true.

As a practical matter, most applications will be designed to use just one session (that is to say, one *type* of session) but there are legitimate reasons for using two or more different session types in one application. The reasons for this will be more clear after you read about message acknowledgment strategies in the next chapter.

To summarize, in order to initialize your JMS provider in preparation for sending or receiving messages, you need to perform the following operations:

For pub/sub messaging:

1. Point JNDI at the appropriate directory service by using `javax.naming.InitialContext`. (Note that you may need to pass in vendor- and/or environment-specific properties.)

2. Obtain your provider's `TopicConnectionFactory` object by doing a JNDI context lookup.

3. Use the `TopicConnectionFactory` to create one or more `TopicSession` objects.

For point-to-point messaging:

1. Point JNDI at the appropriate directory service by using `javax.naming.InitialContext`.

2. Obtain your provider's `QueueConnectionFactory` object by doing a JNDI context lookup.

3. Use the `QueueConnectionFactory` to create one or more `QueueSession` objects.

Finally, notice how all the code is enclosed in a `JMSException` try/catch block. All exceptions thrown by JMS methods — except, of course, for runtime exceptions — are either directly a `JMSException` or a subclass of it. Additionally, because it's not really known ahead of time exactly what operations a provider's code might perform in any particular method, practically all JMS method invocations are defined to throw a `JMSException`. The bottom line is that you should just get in the habit of expecting all method invocations — even trivial setters and getters — to potentially throw a `JMSException`. Be sure to structure your code accordingly.

Constructing the Message

Although the APIs for the pub/sub and point-to-point messaging domains adhere to different naming conventions, one portion that is identical in both is the creation of JMS message objects. This is accomplished through the `javax.jms.Session` interface, which both `TopicSession` and `QueueSession` inherit from.

It is important to note, however, that even though, for instance, the method call to create a pub/sub `MapMessage` is identical to the method call to create a point-to-point `MapMessage`, the internal implementation is still tied to a particular session and, hence, to a particular messaging domain and provider. This means, for example, that if you have an application that receives messages via pub/sub, does some processing, and then places the same message on an outbound queue, you will have to extract all the necessary values (content *and* properties) from the pub/sub message and populate a newly created queue message with them prior to retransmitting the message.

As I described in Chapter 2, there are six different types of JMS messages: Text, Map, Bytes, Object, Stream, and the empty message. A JMS session object has the following factory methods, which should be used to create each type of message.

- ◆ `TextMessage createTextMessage()`

- ◆ `MapMessage createMapMessage()`

- ◆ `BytesMessage createBytesMessage()`

- ◆ `ObjectMessage createObjectMessage()`

- ◆ `StreamMessage createStreamMessage()`

- ◆ `Message createMessage()`

A couple of additional convenience methods are also available:

- ◆ `TextMessage createTextMessage(String text)`

- ◆ `ObjectMessage createObjectMessage(Serializable object)`

You must use the factory methods to create messages because the actual implementation class of each message is hidden from you in the provider's library.

Now that you know how to create the various types of message objects, let's walk through each to see how to populate it with data.

TextMessage

Because it's so simple, the TextMessage has only one method for setting its content. A basic example is as follows:

```
Session session = (a previously created session);

TextMessage msg = session.createTextMessage();

msg.setText("Hello World!");
```

Want to send an XML message instead? XML is string-based so it's a piece of cake:

```
String xml = "<?xml version=\"1.0\" ?>" +
             "<message>" +
             "   <text>Hello World!</text>" +
             "</message>";

Session session = (a previously created session);

TextMessage msg = session.createTextMessage();

msg.setText(xml);
```

Of course, in the real world, you'd probably be using an object-to-XML package, such as Sun's JAXB (Java Architecture for XML Binding) to generate XML rather than hard coding it in your program — but you get the picture.

Remember from Chapter 2 that messages can also have properties associated with them and that there are essentially two kinds: standard JMS properties and application-defined properties. Most of the standard properties are set by the provider's software. You're free, however, to attach any number of additional properties to a message. The example that follows shows how to add some additional information to a text message without affecting the original content of the message.

```
Session session = (a previously created TopicSession or
QueueSession);

TextMessage msg = session.createTextMessage();

msg.setText("Hello World!");

msg.setBooleanProperty("IsMyFirstMessage?", true);
msg.setStringProperty("SourceState", "California");
msg.setObjectProperty("SourceCity", "San Francisco");
```

MapMessage

As you recall from Chapter 2, the content of a MapMessage is a set of name/value pairs. The name is always a simple string and the value must be one of an allowed set of types. Each value type has a corresponding named method that you must use to set it. For example, to create a simple order message you might do something like this:

```
Session session = (a previously created TopicSession or
QueueSession);

MapMessage msg = session.createMapMessage();

msg.setLong("OrderNumber", 12345);

msg.setInt("Quantity", 5);

msg.setFloat("Price", 65.88f);

msg.setString("ProductID", "JM0425");

msg.setObject("CustomerNumber", new Long(4563345));

msg.setBytes("SourceIP",
        InetAddress.getLocalHost().getAddress());
```

BytesMessage

A BytesMessage is used exclusively when you want to deliver raw data. Say, perhaps, you want to send a JPEG image using point-to-point messaging. The following code fragment illustrates how you could populate a BytesMessage with the image data:

```
File file = new File("image.jpg");

int len = (int) file.length();

byte[] data = new byte[len];

DataInputStream dis = new DataInputStream(new
FileInputStream(file));

dis.readFully(data);

dis.close();
```

```
BytesMessage msg = new BytesMessage();

msg.writeBytes(data);
```

ObjectMessage

Like TextMessage, ObjectMessage accepts only one type of data, so there is only one setter method: setObject(Serializable object).

Using the order example from the MapMessage section previously in this chapter, you might write code as follows:

```
public class Order implements java.io.Serializable
{
    long orderNumber;
    int quantity;
    float price;
    String productID;
    long customerNumber;
    byte[] sourceIP;

    public Order() {}

    void setOrderNumber(long orderNumber)
    {
        this.orderNumber = orderNumber;
    }

    void setQuantity(int quantity)
    {
        this.quantity = quantity;
    }

    void setPrice(float price)
    {
        this.price = price;
    }

    void setProductID(String productID)
    {
        this.productID = productID;
    }

    void setCustomerNumber(long customerNumber)
    {
        this.customerNumber = customerNumber;
```

```
    }

    void setSourceIP(byte[] sourceIP)
    {
        this.sourceIP = sourceIP;
    }
}
Session session = (a previously created TopicSession or
QueueSession);

ObjectMessage msg = session.createObjectMessage();


Order order = new Order();

order.setOrderNumber(12345);

order.setQuantity(5);

order.setPrice(65.88f);

order.setProductID("JM0425");

order.setCustomerNumber(4563345);

order.setSourceIP(InetAddress.getLocalHost().getAddress());


msg.setObject(order);
```

Remember that using an `ObjectMessage` makes sense only when both the sender and receiver are Java applications *and* when the receiving application's class loader can successfully resolve the class definition of the sent object.

StreamMessage

`StreamMessage` takes its name from the fact that you supply values to it by sequentially writing them into the message one at a time. It's very similar to how you would interact with a `java.io.DataOutputStream`.

Adapting the Order example from the `MapMessage` description section earlier in this chapter to the `StreamMessage` type gives code that looks like the following:

```
Session session = (a previously created TopicSession or
QueueSession);
```

```
StreamMessage msg = session.createStreamMessage();

// OrderNumber
msg.writeLong(12345);

// Quantity
msg.writeInt(5);

// Price
msg.writeFloat(65.88f);

// ProductID
msg.writeString("JM0425");

// CutomerNumber
msg.writeObject(new Long(4563345));

// SourceIP
msg.writeBytes(InetAddress.getLocalHost().getAddress());
```

The empty message

Of course, the empty message has no methods for setting its content because by
definition it has no content. The only thing you can do with an empty message is
set properties on it.

You can use an empty message, for example, to implement a simple heartbeat
facility. Heartbeats are often used to monitor applications. Generally, when
implementing heartbeats, an application periodically sends out small messages
letting some monitoring application know it is alive and functioning properly. If
the monitor does not receive a heartbeat message within some predetermined
amount of time, it can alert a human being to look into the problem.

You might construct a simple heartbeat message as follows:

```
Session session = (a previously created TopicSession or
QueueSession);

Message msg = session.createMessage();

msg.setStringProperty("ApplicationName", "OrderSystem");

msg.setBooleanProperty("IsHeartbeat", true);
```

Sending the Message

Now that you know how to create and populate a message, you are ready to send it somewhere. For sending messages, we must return to our domain-based thinking because the process is slightly different for pub/sub messaging than it is for point-to-point.

Creating message producers

To send a message in the pub/sub domain, JMS defines an object (interface) called a `TopicPublisher`. In the point-to-point domain, the object used to send messages is the `QueueSender`. JMS refers to both generically as *message producers* and, thus, both classes inherit from the `MessageProducer` interface.

Publishers and senders are created on a per `Destination` (address) basis, which means that if your application sends messages to more than one address, you will need to create multiple publishers and/or senders.

The following code fragment demonstrates how to create a `TopicPublisher` and `QueueSender`:

```
TopicSession tsession = (a previously created session);

Topic topic = tsession.createTopic("PUBSUBADDRESS");

TopicPublisher publisher = tsession.createPublisher(topic);
QueueSession qsession = (a previously created session);

Queue queue = qsession.createQueue("QUEUEADDRESS");

QueueSender sender = qsession.createSender(queue);
```

Note that for performance reasons you'll want to reuse the `TopicPublisher` and `QueueSender` instances you create; there's no need to create a new one every time you send a message. Unless your application is extremely memory-conscious, you should cache these instances and reuse them for as long as the session that created them is still valid.

Creating destinations

In the code fragment in the previous section, I used the session to create a `Topic` object and a `Queue` object. You must have an instance of a valid `Topic` or `Queue` before creating a `TopicPublisher` or `QueueSender`, respectively. One way to get a valid instance is to use the appropriate session factory method: `createQueue()` or `createTopic()`. The JMS documentation strongly discourages you from doing this, however.

The JMS vision is that the definition of valid Topics and Queues is a messaging administration function not to be left up to the programmer. JMS was designed with the expectation that the corporate messaging software administrator will be responsible for defining what destinations are valid and for configuring various delivery options related to a destination.

Administratively, defining a destination is a vendor-specific task that is beyond the scope of the JMS specification. However, JMS does say that a client program will get a handle to the desired destination via a JNDI lookup. For instance:

```
import javax.jms.*;
import javax.naming.*;
import java.util.*;

public class DestinationLookup
{
    public static void main(String[] args)
    {
        try
        {
            Hashtable hash = new Hashtable();
            hash.put(Context.INITIAL_CONTEXT_FACTORY,
                "weblogic.jndi.WLInitialContextFactory");
            hash.put(Context.PROVIDER_URL,
                "t3://localhost:7001");

            Context context = new InitialContext(hash);

            Topic topic = (Topic) context.lookup("PUBSUBNAME");

            Queue queue = (Queue) context.lookup("QUEUENAME");
        }
        catch (NamingException ex)
        {
            ex.printStackTrace();
        }
    }
}
```

In this example, "PUBSUBNAME" and "QUEUENAME" are directory reference names; they are not necessarily the actual destination names. You will need to refer to an individual vendor's documentation to see how it maps JNDI's logical lookup name to an actual JMS destination.

TEMPORARY DESTINATIONS

Two types of Destinations that can *only* be created in code are TemporaryTopic and TemporaryQueue. These Destinations are only good for the life of the current open connection. The primary reason for using temporary destinations is in request-reply situations where you need to uniquely identify yourself to some other application so it can respond to you – and only you.

Generally, you would use the **JMSReplyTo** property for this purpose, as follows:

```
TopicSession tsession = (a previously created session);

Topic me = tsession.createTemporaryTopic();

TextMessage msg = session.createTextMessage();

msg.setText("Hello World!");

msg.setJMSReplyTo(me);
```

For the most part, a temporary destination is only useful when your application is expecting a response within a relatively short period of time. Because your application will never receive its response should it happen to be restarted between the time it sends the request portion of the exchange and the time it receives the response, temporary destinations should only be used when the receipt of the response message is not vital to the correct functioning of the overall system.

Configuring delivery properties

In the "Properties of Messages" section of Chapter 2, I outlined the various standard properties (headers) that are associated with a JMS message. Although some properties can be set directly by client code using the message's setXXXProperty() method, several of them cannot; they must be specified in another manner. You accomplish this through methods in the MessageProducer interface.

Because both pub/sub publishers and point-to-point senders support this same interface, the process is the same in both messaging domains. Also, because these properties are configured on a per producer basis, they apply to all messages delivered using that producer – that is, all messages sent to a given Topic or Queue.

JMSDELIVERYMODE

The delivery mode is used to indicate whether messaging is persistent or non-persistent (the default is persistent) – that is, whether a message will be delivered successfully even in the event of a system failure.

For example, to specify that all messages sent via a particular queue-based message sender are to be recoverable, you would write code similar to the following fragment:

```
QueueSession qsession = (a previously created session);

Queue queue = (a previously acquired queue);
```

```
QueueSender sender = qsession.createSender(queue);

// Cast to producer just for clarity
MessageProducer producer = (MessageProducer) sender;

producer.setDeliveryMode(DeliveryMode.PERSISTENT);
```

JMSEXPIRATION

If you examine the expiration property of a received message, you will see that its value represents an absolute time. However, you never set an explicit expiration time on any message. It is always a calculated value, which is a time-to-live value – that is, a duration – added to the timestamp of the message. The value is specified in milliseconds.

For example, to set a 30 second lifetime on a message producer you would do the following:

```
MessageProducer producer = (a previously created producer);

long duration = 30 * 1000;    // 30 seconds, in milliseconds

producer.setTimeToLive(duration);
```

Setting the time-to-live to the constant `Message.DEFAULT_TIME_TO_LIVE` (or zero) will cause it to never be expired.

JMSPRIORITY

A priority value must be in the range 0 to 9, inclusive, where 0 is the lowest and 9 is the highest. Given the vague definition JMS has of exactly how a vendor's messaging software should react to the various priority levels, it's probably best to use the default priority (`Message.DEFAULT_PRIORITY`) for all your messages – that is, do not set the priority at all.

If you decide to do so anyway, however, you would use the `setPriority()` method as follows:

```
MessageProducer producer = (a previously created producer);

producer.setPriority(9);     // Highest priority
```

JMSMESSAGEID

Message IDs are simply arbitrary (but unique) strings set by the messaging software. They cannot be set explicitly in your application code. If you're concerned about maximizing performance and you don't need message IDs, JMS does allow you to tell the vendor's software that you are not interested in using them. In this way, the vendor's software can optimize its behavior by avoiding the overhead associated with creating a unique ID for every message.

Disabling ID generation is only a hint to the provider, though. A particular provider may choose to always tag each message with an ID if the vendor has determined that the performance gain would be negligible – or if the provider just hasn't gotten around to implementing this feature yet. Keep this in mind if you attempt to disable message IDs but still see them in your received messages, or if you aren't getting the performance boost you expected.

The following code fragment shows how to disable use of IDs:

```
MessageProducer producer = (a previously created producer);

producer.setDisableMessageID(true);
```

Note that you can only disable message IDs on a per producer basis. There is no global way to disable this feature for all producer objects even though this is frequently what you'll want to do.

JMSTIMESTAMP

The timestamping of messages can also be disabled. Disabling timestamps is only a hint to the provider, just like disabling message IDs is – and all the same rules apply.

```
MessageProducer producer = (a previously created producer);

producer.setDisableMessageTimestamp(true);
```

Depending on your vendor's software's capabilities, you may have the option for an administrator to specify values for these properties outside of the applications. The advantage of this is that it centralizes the configuration of message delivery and relieves the developer of the burden of performing this task programmatically. However, it's important to remember that any property values specified administratively will silently override programmatically specified ones. See Chapter 11 for more information on configuring JMS installations.

Sending the message

Once you've got your message producer and you've populated a message object, sending the message is a simple matter:

For pub/sub:

```
TopicSession tsession = (a previously created session);

TopicPublisher publisher = (a previously created publisher);

TextMessage msg = tsession.createTextMessage();
```

```
msg.setText("Hello World!");

publisher.publish(msg);
```

For point-to-point:

```
QueueSession qsession = (a previously created session);

QueueSender sender = (a previously created sender);

TextMessage msg = tsession.createTextMessage();

msg.setText("Hello World!");

sender.send(msg);
```

You should be aware of a couple of variations on publish() and send() methods as well. One variation has an additional three parameters. Each parameter corresponds to one of three delivery properties that you can specify on the message producer. These properties are: delivery mode, priority, and time-to-live.

The overloaded methods signatures are as follows:

```
TopicPublisher.publish(Message msg, int deliveryMode, int priority,
long timeToLive)

QueueSender.send(Message msg, int deliveryMode, int priority, long
timeToLive)
```

If you specify delivery properties in the publish() or send() method, the values will apply only to the current message being sent and will not change the current configuration of the message producer used to deliver the message.

One other set of overloaded send methods allows you to specify the Topic or Queue name at send time. They are as follows:

```
TopicPublisher.publish(Topic topic, Message msg)

QueueSender.send(Queue queue, Message)

TopicPublisher.publish(Topic topic, Message msg, int deliveryMode,
int priority, long timeToLive)

QueueSender.send(Queue queue, Message msg, int deliveryMode, int
priority, long timeToLive)
```

When you create a producer object, as we did in the section "Creating message producers," I said you must specify a Topic or Queue and that every message sent using that producer will be delivered to the same topic or queue destination. You are allowed, however, to create a producer with a null destination. You then have what JMS calls an *unidentified producer*. With an unidentified producer, you must use one of the variations of the send() or publish() method that allows you to specify the message destination as the first parameter.

The JMS specification is not clear on whether it's permissible to specify a destination name when sending a message via a non-unidentified producer. Therefore, some providers may allow it and some may not. As in all situations where certain behavior is not guaranteed to be the same across vendor's products, it's best to use only that functionality which is clearly defined.

Putting It All Together

So far, I've covered everything you need to set up a JMS connection, create a message, and hand it off to a JMS provider for delivery. Now let's pull it all together in one complete program. First, I show a pub/sub example (Listing 3-3) and then a point-to-point example (Listing 3-4):

Listing 3-3: A complete pub/sub sending example

```
import javax.jms.*;
import javax.naming.*;
import java.util.*;
import java.net.*;

public class JMSPubSubSend
{
    public static void main(String[] args)
    {
        try
        {
            // Context is loaded from the jndi.properties file
            Context context = new InitialContext();

            TopicConnectionFactory tcFactory =
                    (TopicConnectionFactory)
context.lookup("TOPICFACTORY");

            TopicConnection topicConn =
                    tcFactory.createTopicConnection();

            TopicSession tcSession =
topicConn.createTopicSession(false,
```

Continued

Listing 3-3 *(Continued)*

```
Session.AUTO_ACKNOWLEDGE);

        Topic topic = (Topic) context.lookup("PUBSUBNAME");

        TopicPublisher publisher =
tcSession.createPublisher(topic);

        publisher.setDeliveryMode(DeliveryMode.NON_PERSISTENT);

        // End of setup code

        // Now we can create as many different message types
        // as we like and send them as often as we like

        MapMessage msg = tcSession.createMapMessage();

        msg.setLong("OrderNumber", 12345);

        msg.setInt("Quantity", 50);

        msg.setFloat("Price", 65.88f);

        msg.setString("ProductID", "JM0425");

        msg.setObject("CustomerNumber", new Long(4563345));

        msg.setBytes("SourceIP",
            InetAddress.getLocalHost().getAddress());

        // Put some of the message's values in header properties
so the
        // message can be filtered by the receiver using a
message selector
        // (see Chapter 4, "Receiving Messages")
        msg.setObjectProperty("ProductID",
msg.getObject("ProductID"));

        msg.setObjectProperty("Quantity",
msg.getObject("Quantity"));


        publisher.publish(msg);

        System.out.println("Sent pub/sub message OK");
```

```
                        tcSession.close();
                        topicConn.close();
                }
                catch (NamingException ex)
                {
                        ex.printStackTrace();
                }
                catch (JMSException ex)
                {
                        ex.printStackTrace();
                }
                catch (UnknownHostException ex)
                {
                        ex.printStackTrace();
                }
        }
}
```

Listing 3-4: A complete point-to-point sending example

```
import javax.jms.*;
import javax.naming.*;
import java.util.*;
import java.net.*;

public class JMSPointToPointSend
{
    public static void main(String[] args)
    {
        try
        {
            // Context is loaded from the jndi.properties file
            Context context = new InitialContext();

            QueueConnectionFactory qcFactory =
                    (QueueConnectionFactory)
context.lookup("QUEUEFACTORY");

            QueueConnection queueConn =
                    qcFactory.createQueueConnection();

            QueueSession qcSession =
queueConn.createQueueSession(false,
```

Continued

Listing 3-4 *(Continued)*

```
Session.AUTO_ACKNOWLEDGE);

        Queue queue = (Queue) context.lookup("QUEUENAME");

        QueueSender sender = qcSession.createSender(queue);

        sender.setDeliveryMode(DeliveryMode.PERSISTENT);

        // End of setup code

        // Now we can create as many different message types
        // as we like and send them as often as we like

        MapMessage msg = qcSession.createMapMessage();

        msg.setLong("OrderNumber", 12345);

        msg.setInt("Quantity", 50);

        msg.setFloat("Price", 65.88f);

        msg.setString("ProductID", "JM0425");

        msg.setObject("CustomerNumber", new Long(4563345));

        msg.setBytes("SourceIP",
            InetAddress.getLocalHost().getAddress());

        // Put some of the message's values in header properties
so the
        // message can be filtered by the receiver using a
message selector
        // (see Chapter 4, "Receiving Messages")
        msg.setObjectProperty("ProductID",
msg.getObject("ProductID"));

        msg.setObjectProperty("Quantity",
msg.getObject("Quantity"));


        sender.send(msg);

        System.out.println("Sent point-to-point message OK");
```

```
            qcSession.close();
            queueConn.close();
        }
        catch (NamingException ex)
        {
            ex.printStackTrace();
        }
        catch (JMSException ex)
        {
            ex.printStackTrace();
        }
        catch (UnknownHostException ex)
        {
            ex.printStackTrace();
        }
    }
}
```

You may be wondering, after reviewing these code samples, how the programs know how to communicate with the WebLogic server (or whatever JMS provider you're using, for that matter). The answer lies in the behavior of the `InitialContext` class. When an `InitialContext` is created, it must be configured through the use of Java properties so that it knows where to find the naming service it needs to talk to. One way to configure it is in the source code itself (as I did in Listings 3-1 and 3-2) by explicitly placing the required values in a Java `Hashtable` and passing the hashtable into the `InitialContext` constructor.

Another way — which is the one I'm using for the examples — is to place the required values in a Java properties file called `jndi.properties` (Listing 3-5). As long as this properties file is named correctly and located anywhere in the application's classpath, then the values will be loaded automatically when the `InitialContext` is created. Using an external file to specify the context values has the advantage of allowing them to be changed without having to recompile the code. This can make life a lot easier for you when the machine your JMS server is running on changes, or when swapping in a new JMS provider.

See the `javax.naming.InitialContext` Javadoc for full details on the various ways in which an `InitialContext` can be created and configured.

Listing 3-5: The jndi.properties file used by the code examples

```
java.naming.factory.initial=weblogic.jndi.WLInitialContextFactory
java.naming.provider.url=t3://localhost:7001
```

Listing 3-6 shows a `build.xml` file that can be used to compile and run the sample programs from Listings 3-3 and 3-4 using the *ant* build tool. The "compile" target is executed by default and is used to compile the source files. The "runpubsubsend" and "runptpsend" targets are defined for running the programs pub/sub and point-to-point programs. Thus, you would use *ant* as follows:

To compile: `ant`

To run the pub/sub program: `ant runpubsubsend`

To run the point-to-point program: `ant runptpsend`

 Ant is a command line source code build tool that is gaining in popularity. It is similar to the more traditional *make* but it is extensible and designed to operate more consistently across a variety of platforms. *Ant* files are written in XML and the default configuration file is called `build.xml`. *Ant* itself is written in Java. To find out more about *ant,* refer to `http://jakarta.apache.org/ant`.

Listing 3–6: An ant build.xml file for building and running the example programs

```xml
<project name="JMSTest" default="compile" basedir=".">

  <property name="WL_HOME" value="c:/wlserver6.1"/>
  <property name="jmslib" value="${WL_HOME}/lib/weblogic.jar"/>

  <path id="runclasspath">
    <pathelement location="."/>
    <pathelement location="./classes"/>
    <pathelement location="${WL_HOME}/lib/weblogic.jar"/>
  </path>

  <target name="prepare">
    <mkdir dir="./classes"/>
  </target>

  <target name="compile" depends="prepare">

    <javac srcdir="." destdir="./classes" classpath=".;${jmslib}">
    </javac>

  </target>

  <target name="runpubsubsend" depends="compile">
    <java classname="JMSPubSubSend" fork="yes">
      <classpath refid="runclasspath"/>
```

```
    </java>

  </target>

  <target name="runptpsend" depends="compile">
    <java classname="JMSPointToPointSend" fork="yes">
      <classpath refid="runclasspath"/>
    </java>

  </target>

  <target name="clean">
    <delete dir="./classes"/>
  </target>

</project>
```

Summary

In this chapter, you saw that there's a fair amount of setup and initialization work that needs to be done in your application before you're in a position to send a message anywhere. Always remember that your JMS application is merely a client of another application – the provider – that is doing all the actual messaging on your application's behalf. Because of this, you need to be sure that the provider is running and properly configured before attempting to access it, just as you would with a vendor's database software, for instance.

Fortunately, once you've gotten all the configuration issues out of the way (or found someone to do it for you!) sending messages using JMS is simple and straightforward.

In the next chapter, you learn how to receive messages in your application. All the setup code required for receiving is the same as for sending, but that's been covered already in this chapter so we'll be able to focus exclusively on receipt-specific functionality.

Chapter 4

Receiving Messages

IN THIS CHAPTER, I show you how to receive and process messages in your JMS application. You'll find detailed information about the various types of message acknowledgment modes and how to best employ them. Finally, I discuss a powerful feature of JMS known as *message selection*, which allows you to pre-screen incoming messages before they reach your application without having to write a lot of special code whose job it is to examine and discard unwanted messages.

Creating Message Consumers

Just as JMS applications that send messages are referred to as *message producers* and are supported by the `MessageProducer` interface, applications that receive messages are called *message consumers* in JMS parlance, and are supported by the `MessageConsumer` interface. As with `MessageProducer`, `MessageConsumer` has two subinterfaces that correspond to the two messaging domains: `TopicSubscriber` for pub/sub and `QueueReceiver` for point-to-point.

In order to create the required consumer objects, you must execute all the same setup steps that you did to create producer objects. In particular, you must use JNDI to locate the correct provider's implementation and then create session and destination objects. See Chapter 3 for detailed examples of how to do this.

You use the consumer object to tell the provider which messages you are interested in receiving. Messages are delivered to your application based on two pieces of information: a `Topic` or `Queue` name and a message selector. For now, we won't worry about message selectors; I cover their use later in this chapter.

Listing 4-1 provides a complete source example that shows how to initialize your JMS application and create the consumer objects required to receive pub/sub and point-to-point messages. As in Chapter 3, the examples are based on

WebLogic 6.1. The JNDI portion of the code will vary somewhat depending on the requirements of your particular provider.

Listing 4-1: Creating TopicSubscribers and QueueReceivers using *WebLogic* 6.1

```
import javax.jms.*;
import javax.naming.*;
import java.util.*;

public class JMSInitialize
{
    public static void main(String[] args)
    {
        try
        {
            Hashtable hash = new Hashtable();
            hash.put(Context.INITIAL_CONTEXT_FACTORY,
                "weblogic.jndi.WLInitialContextFactory");
            hash.put(Context.PROVIDER_URL,
                "t3://localhost:7001");

            Context context = new InitialContext(hash);

            // Pub/sub set up

            TopicConnectionFactory tcFactory =
                (TopicConnectionFactory) context.lookup("XXXX");

            TopicConnection topicConn =
                tcFactory.createTopicConnection();

            TopicSession tcSession =
topicConn.createTopicSession(false,

Session.AUTO_ACKNOWLEDGE);


            // Point-to-point set up

            QueueConnectionFactory qcFactory =
                (QueueConnectionFactory) context.lookup("YYYY");

            QueueConnection queueConn =
                qcFactory.createQueueConnection();
```

```
        QueueSession qcSession =
queueConn.createQueueSession(false,

Session.AUTO_ACKNOWLEDGE);


            // Create a pub/sub consumer

            Topic topic = tcSession.createTopic("PUBSUBADDRESS");

            TopicSubscriber tsubscriber =
tcSession.createSubscriber(topic);


            // Create a queue consumer

            Queue queue = qcSession.createQueue("QUEUEADDRESS");

            QueueReceiver qreceiver =
qcSession.createReceiver(queue);

            // Allow messages to be delivered

            topicConn.start();
            queueConn.start();
        }
        catch (NamingException ex)
        {
            ex.printStackTrace();
        }
        catch (JMSException ex)
        {
            ex.printStackTrace();
        }
    }
}
```

In Listing 4-1, you should notice, in particular, how the start() method was invoked on the connection objects. I did not mention the use of start() in Chapter 3 because it is not required when sending messages. However, it must be invoked when receiving messages because it tells the provider that it should start delivering messages to your application.

Because it's a highly distributed system, any number of serious errors can occur in a JMS application — from your provider's messaging program dying to a network outage. Errors such as these would normally first be detected inside your provider's code. If you want your application to find out about them when they happen, you have to register an exception handler with your `TopicConnection` or `QueueConnection` object, as follows:

```
conn.setExceptionListener(new ExceptionListener()
{
    void onException(JMSException ex)
    {
        ex.printStackTrace();
    }
}
```

Registering a Callback Method

Something important is missing in Listing 4-1. I've told the provider what messages I want to receive and I've told it to start delivering them, but I have not written any code to process the messages once they arrive. As it stands now, messages will be delivered to my application and then immediately discarded.

Remember from Chapter 1 that JMS handles only asynchronous message delivery between applications. However, *inside* an application, JMS gives you the option of processing messages either synchronously or asynchronously.

Before I discuss how to code your application to receive messages one way or the other, let's take a peek under the hood to see what a provider's implementation of a delivery mechanism typically looks like. Figure 4-1 is a logical representation of how a provider delivers pub/sub messages to your application.

Although Figure 4-1 uses pub/sub naming as an example, depending on your provider, point-to-point messaging might operate in exactly the same way — or it might not. Unfortunately, JMS does not completely define the semantics of queue-based delivery. In particular, it's left up to the provider to determine what happens if there are multiple receivers defined for a single `Queue`.

Some providers might deliver the same message to each registered `QueueReceiver` just as in pub/sub. Other providers will deliver one copy of the message only on a first-come first-served, or random, basis. Unfortunately, this can result in wildly different application behaviors from one provider to the next. Be sure you investigate fully the operational parameters of your provider when using point-to-point receivers.

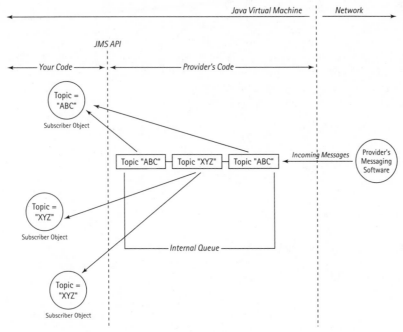

Figure 4-1: A provider's message delivery mechanism

It's important to keep in mind that a provider keeps track of deliveries to individual consumers – not to individual applications – and that each consumer is represented by a separate instance of a `TopicSubscriber` object. It is entirely possible for two or more objects within the same virtual machine to receive the same message, either because they have subscribed to it in exactly the same way or because they have subscribed to it in different ways (that is, using differing message selectors) but the message matches both subscriber's criteria.

Processing messages synchronously

Consuming messages in a synchronous fashion means that your application will be required to make a blocking JMS call, which will wait until an appropriate message is available on the internal queue. As soon as one arrives, it will be delivered to your application as a return value from the call.

For example:

```
TopicSubscriber tsubscriber = (a previously created subscriber);

while (true)
{
    // Wait forever until a message is available

    Message msg = tsubscriber.receive();
```

```
    // ... process the message here
}
```

Of course, unless you have an extremely simple application, you want to be sure the preceding code is run in a separate Java thread in order to avoid blocking your whole application while it waits for messaging input.

You can avoid blocking by using the `receiveNoWait()` method to poll for messages:

```
TopicSubscriber tsubscriber = (a previously created subscriber);

while (true)
{
    // Check to see if a message is available

    Message msg = tsubscriber.receiveNoWait();

    if (msg != null)
    {
        // ... process the message here
    }
    else
    {
        // ... no message is available, do some other stuff
    }
}
```

Generally, you won't use `receiveNoWait()` because the most efficient use of resources is to block on any I/O and perform any simultaneous processing in a separate thread. Non-blocking I/O operations are usually employed when there are many hundreds or thousands of input channels – not likely in a JMS application – and you don't want to dedicate a separate thread to manage each.

Non-blocking message receipt using `receiveNoWait()` could be useful when your application is running in resource restricted environments – such as a PDA or smartcard – where memory and threads are at a premium because it allows you to code your application in a way that makes the best use of the resources available while at the same time minimizing the need to create extra threads.

Processing messages asynchronously

Although it is possible to receive messages synchronously, you're almost never going to want to choose to do so because it requires too much thread management on the part of the developer and does not allow for the most efficient use of system resources. It also is not in line with the general Java model used by most APIs that rely on callbacks, or *listeners,* to provide for just-in-time invocation. The JFC (Swing) API, for example, makes heavy use of listeners.

The preferred method of receiving messages is asynchronous. In order to receive messages asynchronously, you must register the object that will receive the incoming messages with the consumer object. Your listener object must implement JMS's `MessageListener` interface — a very simple interface that has only one method: `void onMessage(Message msg)`. For example:

```
public class MessageHandler implements MessageListener
{
    public void onMessage(Message msg)
    {
        System.out.println("Got a message!");
    }
}


TopicSubscriber tsubscriber = (a previously created subscriber);

tsubscriber.setMessageListener(new MessageHandler());
```

Unlike many Java libraries that support listeners and allow you to register multiple listener objects for a particular event — each of which will be called when a certain event occurs — a JMS consumer can have only one listener at a time attached to it. If you want a message to be delivered to more than one place in your application, you must write the code to do so yourself — or subscribe to the message more than once by creating multiple subscriber objects.

Keep in mind that the synchronous/asynchronous determination is made on a per consumer object basis. Thus, it is possible to write your application in a way so that some messages are processed synchronously and some asynchronously.

Also, although both the synchronous and asynchronous message receipt examples in this chapter reference pub/sub messaging, the message receipt and listener registration calls are actually part of the `MessageConsumer` interface that is the parent interface of both `TopicSubscriber` and `QueueReceiver`. Thus, the method calls and behaviors are identical for point-to-point messaging.

Threading concerns

In general, it's a good idea to ensure you have a separate instance of a listener object to handle each message destination you are processing — that is, one listener object per consumer.

If you choose to share listener instances between consumers, however — perhaps to conserve memory — then you are free to use the same object instance to handle messages without regard to threading and synchronization issues, provided that the consumers you are listening with were created from the same source session. That is because JMS sessions are, by specification, single-threaded, so no call to `onMessage()` in any object will be made prior to the completion of a previous call. In effect, all calls to `onMessage()` for the same session are automatically synchronized for you.

Reusing listener instances between sessions is a big no-no, however, because each session potentially operates under a separate thread of control. Thus, there is no implied ordering to the calls.

For example, the following code is okay:

```
QueueConnection qConn = (a previously created connection);

QueueSession qcSession = queueConn.createQueueSession(false,
                            Session.AUTO_ACKNOWLEDGE);
Queue queue1 = qsession.createQueue("QUEUEADDRESS1");

Queue queue2 = qsession.createQueue("QUEUEADDRESS2");

QueueReceiver qreceiver1 = qcSession.createReceiver(queue1);

QueueReceiver qreceiver2 = qcSession.createReceiver(queue2);

MessageListener listener = new MessageHandler();

qreceiver1.setMessageListener(listener);

qreceiver2.setMessageListener(listener);
```

while the following code is *not* thread-safe:

```
QueueConnection qConn = (a previously created connection);

QueueSession qcSession1 = queueConn.createQueueSession(false,
Session.AUTO_ACKNOWLEDGE);

QueueSession qcSession2 = queueConn.createQueueSession(false,
                            Session.AUTO_ACKNOWLEDGE);
Queue queue1 = qsession1.createQueue("QUEUEADDRESS1");

Queue queue2 = qsession2.createQueue("QUEUEADDRESS2");

QueueReceiver qreceiver1 = qcSession1.createReceiver(queue1);

QueueReceiver qreceiver2 = qcSession2.createReceiver(queue2);

MessageListener listener = new MessageHandler();

qreceiver1.setMessageListener(listener);

qreceiver2.setMessageListener(listener);
```

Processing the Message

Whether a message is received by an active call to `receive()` or by a passive message listener callback, it is always delivered to your code as the type `Message`, which all JMS message classes implement. Unless you know, based on your application design, that you will always receive the same type of message for a given destination, the first thing you must do after receiving a message is to determine its actual type. Because JMS does not require that all messages delivered to a particular destination be of the same type, it's possible, for instance, to receive a `TextMessage` followed by a `MapMessage`.

Message types are readily determined with the `instanceof` operator, as shown in Listing 4-2.

Listing 4-2: A basic message handler class

```
import javax.jms.*;

public class MessageHandler implements MessageListener
{
    public void onMessage(Message msg)
    {
        if (msg instanceof TextMessage)
            System.out.println("Got a text message.");

        else if (msg instanceof MapMessage)
            System.out.println("Got a map message.");

        else if (msg instanceof ObjectMessage)
            System.out.println("Got an object message.");

        else if (msg instanceof StreamMessage)
            System.out.println("Got a stream message.");

        else if (msg instanceof BytesMessage)
            System.out.println("Got a bytes message.");

        else
            System.out.println("Got an empty message.");
    }
}
```

Once the message type has been determined, it's a simple matter of extracting the information you need. This is very much the reverse of the process described in Chapter 3 for populating a message. What you do with the extracted data is, of course, completely up to you as the application designer.

Unless you are using the JMS `ObjectMessage` to receive real Java objects in your application, you are likely to want to use the extracted information to populate a local object, which can then be used elsewhere in your program.

The code in Listing 4-3 uses the `MapMessage` in this manner to create a stock quote object.

Listing 4-3: Creating a stock quote message using MapMessage

```java
import java.util.Date;

public class StockQuote
{
  String symbol;
  float bid, ask;
  Date time;

  public StockQuote() {}

  public void setSymbol(String symbol) { this. symbol = symbol; }

  public String getSymbol() { return symbol; }

  public void setBid(float bid) { this.bid = bid; }

  public float getBid() { return bid; }

  public void setAsk(float ask) { this.ask = bid; }

  public float getAsk() { return ask; }

  public void setQuoteTime(Date time) { this.time = time; }

  public Date getQuoteTime() { return time; }
}

import javax.jms.*;
import java.util.Date;

public class MessageHandler implements MessageListener
{
  public void onMessage(Message msg)
  {
      if (msg instanceof MapMessage)
      {
          MapMessage mm = (MapMessage) msg;
```

```
        StockQuote quote = new StockQuote();

        try
        {
            quote.setSymbol( mm.getString("TickerSymbol") );

            quote.setBid( mm.getFloat("Bid") );

            quote.setAsk( mm.getFloat("Ask") );

            quote.setQuoteTime( new Date(mm.getLong("Time")) );
        }
        catch (JMSException ex)
        {
            // Unexpected error encountered
            ex.printStackTrace();
            return;
        }

        someBusinessObject.setQuote(quote);
    }

    // else message type is unexpected, do nothing
  }
}
```

Let's now create the same stock quote object but with the contents from a StreamMessage, as shown in Listing 4-4:

Listing 4-4: Creating a stock quote message using StreamMessage

```
public class MessageHandler implements MessageListener
{
  public void onMessage(Message msg)
  {
      if (msg instanceof StreamMessage)
      {
          StreamMessage sm = (StreamMessage) msg;

          StockQuote quote = new StockQuote();

          try
          {
              quote.setSymbol( sm.readString() );
```

Continued

Listing 4-4 *(Continued)*

```
        quote.setBid( sm.readFloat() );

        quote.setAsk( sm.readFloat() );

        quote.setQuoteTime( new Date(sm.readLong()) );
    }
    catch (JMSException ex)
    {
        // Unexpected error encountered
        ex.printStackTrace();
        return;
    }

    someBusinessObject.setQuote(quote);
    }

    // else message type is unexpected, do nothing
    }
}
```

Notice how in the `MapMessage` example (Listing 4-3), the order of calls to the quote object's setter methods can be rearranged arbitrarily. This is not the case in the `StreamMessage` example (Listing 4-4), however, because the values in the message are not named.

One final note: whenever a JMS message object is received by your client code, the message is always in read-only mode. This means that any attempt to set any value on the message or its properties – not counting the headers, though – will result in a `MessageNotWriteableException` being thrown. Requiring the message to be read-only allows the provider to potentially optimize its internal implementation.

In any case, this should rarely, if ever, prove to be an inconvenience because it's always a good idea to create a brand new message object whenever you need one. Always use the appropriate session factory method to get a new message object rather than attempting to reuse an existing one. If you're creating a new message that is supposed to contain some or all of the information from an existing message, you'll of course have to do a field-by-field copy of the required information from the old message object to the new.

Acknowledging Messages

Acknowledgment is an important part of the message delivery process because it tells the JMS provider that your consumer has satisfactorily processed the message and that it can officially mark it "delivered." Once a message has been delivered to all interested consumers, the provider can free up the resources used to store it, whether they be disk or memory.

Remember that sessions are created with two parameters: the transaction indicator and the acknowledgment mode. The following code creates a non-transacted session with an acknowledgement mode of "client acknowledge":

```
TopicSession session = topicConnection.createSession(false,
Session.CLIENT_ACKNOWLEDGE);
```

This code creates a transacted session. Notice the use of 0 instead of an explicit acknowledgement constant.

```
QueueSession session = queueConnection.createSession(true, 0);
```

Messages that are received in the context of a transacted session are always acknowledged automatically when the outstanding session transaction is committed; hence, the second parameter is not important when the first is true. See Chapter 8 for the specifics on how to work with transacted sessions.

Messages that are received in a normal, or non-transacted, session fall into one of three acknowledgment categories. Each is described in the sections that follow.

AUTO_ACKNOWLEDGE

Messages received in this type of session require no explicit acknowledgment on the part of the receiver. The JMS provider presumes the client has successfully processed the message as long as the onMessage() method returns normally.

Because the MessageListener interface defines onMessage() as returning void and throwing no exceptions, the only possibility of a non-normal return is if some activity inside onMessage() — or something called by it — results in a RuntimeException being thrown. A prime example of a RuntimeException is NullPointerException, which, as we know, can happen all too frequently.

One thing to keep in mind when using automatic acknowledgement is that it is possible, given some sort of failure in the system, for a message to be delivered to a client twice. Your application may have finished processing a received message, for example, but a failure outside your code may prevent the provider from properly acknowledging it. In this case, the provider would redeliver the last message (and only the last message) to your application.

CLIENT_ACKNOWLEDGE

This mode requires a specific acknowledgment on the part of the receiver. Failure to acknowledge a given message will not result in that message being redelivered, though, unless there is a system failure of some sort. In fact, the main reason for using the client-acknowledge mode is to increase performance by allowing for a whole series of records to be processed and then acknowledged as a whole.

Acknowledging any message effectively acknowledges all preceding unacknowledged messages as well.

Deferring acknowledgment in this way can be dangerous, however. If a JMS system failure occurs, the consumer will potentially end up processing duplicate records. This may be harmless or very harmful, depending on the design of your application. Additionally, failure to acknowledge messages for too long may lead to excessive use of resources inside the provider, potentially resulting in lost messages due to buffer overruns or exhaustion of other resources.

DUPS_OK_ACKNOWLEDGE

This mode has the least overhead associated with it because it reduces the internal bookkeeping a provider must perform by allowing it to deliver a message more than once. Redelivery of any message will only occur, however, if there is a JMS system failure of some sort.

This mode is definitely the way to go in a high-volume system, provided that your application can effectively deal with the delivery of a few duplicate messages. Applications are duplicate-tolerant if the repeat processing of a duplicate record does not cause any state change in the application or if the application has a mechanism in place for detecting and discarding duplicates.

An example of the latter would be an application that looked at all incoming messages that had their **JMSRedelivery** property set to true and compared some unique identifier in the message content to a list of previously processed identifiers—for example, an invoice number that had already been stored in the database. Already processed messages would need to be discarded.

No matter what the current acknowledgment mode for a session is, the way to acknowledge a message is fortunately always the same line of code:

```
msg.acknowledge();
```

Unfortunately, it's not always clear where to place that one line of code. Certainly, a message should not be acknowledged prior to extracting all the values you need from it. This way, in the rare case there's a transient error in the provider code, you give the provider the opportunity to recover from it and redeliver the message.

The more complicated issue arises when determining whether to acknowledge a message before the execution of your business logic or after it. In Listing 4-4, I created a quote object from the message and passed it to some other business object that performed some operation on it (updated the screen, wrote a record to a database, and so on). What would you do if an error occurred in this code? It depends on what the source of the error was. If you encountered an exception that you can recover from, you should execute whatever recovery steps are necessary and retry the operation.

If the encountered exception is *not* recoverable (perhaps there's a bug in the code that prevents it from properly handling the received message), then you're either going to want to drop the message and report the error *or*, if the error is big enough – perhaps there's a database failure – you want to stop processing messages altogether. In either case, the implication is that messages should always be acknowledged before any business logic is invoked because if our application just can't handle the message, there's no point in having the provider hang on to it.

Remember that the preceding discussion is for *non-transacted* sessions only. Transacted sessions should always be used if it's imperative the received message be successfully delivered.

Even though it is not required to make a call to `acknowledge()` for `AUTO_ACKNOWLEDGE` sessions or for transacted sessions, it is good practice to do so anyway. By always explicitly acknowledging messages any time the characteristics of the session are changed elsewhere in the code, you won't have to track down every message handler in your code to be sure it acknowledges messages properly.

If I extend the example from Listing 4-4 to explicitly acknowledge messages, the code would now look like the following:

```
public class MessageHandler implements MessageListener
{
  public void onMessage(Message msg)
  {
      if (msg instanceof StreamMessage)
      {
          StreamMessage sm = (StreamMessage) msg;

          StockQuote quote = new StockQuote();

          try
          {
              quote.setSymbol( sm.readString() );

              quote.setBid( sm.readFloat() );

              quote.setAsk( sm.readFloat() );

              quote.setQuoteTime( new Date(sm.readLong()) );

              // Acknowledge as soon as is appropriate

              sm.acknowledge();
          }
          catch (JMSException ex)
          {
              // Unexpected error encountered
              ex.printStackTrace();
              return;
          }
```

```
        someBusinessObject.setQuote(quote);
    }

    // else message type is unexpected, just ACK it
    else sm.acknowledge();
  }
}
```

Filtering with Message Selectors

All delivered messages are automatically filtered by destination by the provider's software prior to delivery to your application. Traditionally, this is the only piece of information messaging software has used to determine which consumers received which messages.

JMS extends this capability by allowing a client to express an interest in messages based on almost any property attached to the message (refer back to Chapter 2 for a discussion of message properties).

In all cases, you must indicate which Topic or Queue you're interested in when creating a MessageConsumer. You also have the option of specifying a *message selector,* which will be applied to each message to determine if it should be delivered to a consumer.

A message selector is a string that is essentially identical to the "where" clause of a simple SQL statement. (Technically speaking, JMS defines it as "a subset of the SQL92 conditional expression syntax.") In JMS SQL, however, the table column names generally used in an SQL statement for a database query are replaced by JMS message property names.

For example, suppose an application publishes a MapMessage as shown in Figure 4-2.

Header Values	
JMSDestination	"TRADENOTIFICATION"
JMSType	"Trade"
JMSPriority	4
JMSReplyTo	null
Message Properties	
"MarketType"	"Equity"
"TradeSize"	12500
MapMessage Content	
"TickerSymbol"	"XYZ"
"TradePrice"	45.128
"TradeSize"	12500
"CustomerAccount"	"1234-567-89"

Figure 4-2: A sample MapMessage with properties

Let's say we have two applications. The first application is interested in receiving all trade notifications, while the second is only interested in receiving notifications for trades of 10,000 or more shares. Both applications will need to create the appropriate pub/sub consumer object for receiving messages sent to the "TRADENOTIFICATION" destination. The second application, however, can further qualify the messages it receives by specifying a message selector.

For example, the first application would create a consumer as I've discussed earlier in this chapter:

```
TopicSession tcSession = (a previously created session);

Topic topic = tcSession.createTopic("TRADENOTIFICATION");

TopicSubscriber tsubscriber = tcSession.createSubscriber(topic);
```

The second application would create a consumer as follows, however:

```
TopicSession tcSession = (a previously created session);

String msgSelector = "TradeSize >= 10000";

Topic topic = tcSession.createTopic("TRADENOTIFICATION");

TopicSubscriber tsubscriber =
    tcSession.createSubscriber(topic, msgSelector, true);

    // the last parameter means we're not interested
    // in messages published through the same connection
    // in which we're receiving them, if any
```

It's important to note that the "TradeSize" I'm using in this example is the message property, not the field in the MapMessage content. It is not possible to use a message selector that references the content of a message. Specifying a selector such as "TradeSize >= 10000 AND TradePrice >= 50" in this case would not prevent this message from being delivered to us because "TradePrice" is not a property of this message. No exception is thrown when a non-existent property is used in a selector because, as far as JMS is concerned, it is perfectly okay to reference a non-existent – it just treats it as a null value.

Of course, we can assume that when the publishing application was created, its designers knew that some receiving applications would be interested in looking only at large trades. That's why "TradeSize" is inside the message and is a property as well. If the designers had not anticipated the use of trade size in this manner, the receiving application would have no choice but to examine all incoming messages and discard the ones it didn't want after extracting and testing the trade size field from the content of each message.

Figure 4-3 lists all the possible operators you can use in a message selector and provides an example of each.

Operator	Description	Examples
>	Greater than	"Total>32", "JMSTimestamp > 878382928134"
>=	Greater than or equal	"Quantity >= 100"
<	Less than	"Price < 55.75"
<=	Less than or equal to	"Days <= 0"
=	Equal	"Year = 1977" "Name = 'Joey'", "First = TRUE"
<>	Not equal	"X <> 100" "City <> 'Washington, D.C.'"
NOT	Boolean NOT	"NOT Present" (where 'Present' is a boolean value)
AND	Boolean AND	"x > 50 AND y > 25"
OR	Boolean OR	"LastName = 'McDonald' OR LastName = 'MacDonald'"
+	Addition	"Cost + Commission > 100"
-	Subtraction	"Range - 10 < 50"
/	Division	"ShippingCost / TotalCost > .5"
*	Multiplication	"A * B > 1000"
()	Precedence ordering	"HireYear < 2000 AND (Salary > 100000 OR Bonus > 15000)"
IS [NOT] NULL	Null comparator	"MiddleInitial IS NOT NULL", "EventCode IS NULL"
[NOT] BETWEEN	Range comparator	"Salary BETWEEN 80000 AND 100000", "Age NOT BETWEEN 18 AND 70"
[NOT] IN	Set comparator	"Borough IN ('Manhattan', 'Queens', 'Brooklyn')"
[NOT] LIKE	Wildcard comparator	"SSN LIKE '540-%'" "Exchange LIKE 'A_'" Note: The wildcard characters are '_' and '%'. '_' represents 1 and only 1 character, '%' represents 0 or more characters.

Figure 4-3: Allowed message selector operations

Property names are case sensitive, so if you have a property named "Price" in your message and it has a value of 10, the selector "Price > 5" will match the message but "price > 5" will not because the token "price" will evaluate to NULL.

Also, there is no direct support for date/time processing because the properties themselves do not support the Java Date type directly. Dates in properties must be passed around as Java longs, which means that any selector operators involving date/time values must use long numbers as well (refer to the first example in Figure 4-3). This is inconvenient to be sure, but doable.

Finally, note that all message properties are fully selectable with the exception of the header properties. Only the following header properties are selectable: **JMSDeliveryMode, JMSPriority, JMSTimestamp, JMSMessageID, JMSCorrelationID,** and **JMSType.**

Because it is possible for a sender to attach any number of arbitrary properties to a message, the use of selectors can be a quite powerful way of screening out unwanted messages. And the earlier you can filter out unwanted data, the better your performance will be. See Chapter 10 for a discussion of performance issues related to message selectors.

As you will see in Part III of this book, selectors are also valuable traffic distribution tools.

Putting It All Together

I've explained all the elements related to receiving messages. Now, let's combine them all together into one complete program as shown in Listings 4-5 (pub/sub) and 4-6 (point-to-point). (Note that the jndi.properties file used by the programs is the same as the one in Listing 3-5 from Chapter 3.)

Listing 4-5: A complete pub/sub receiving example

```
import javax.jms.*;
import javax.naming.*;
import java.util.*;

public class JMSPubSubReceive
{
    public static class MessageHandler implements MessageListener
    {
        String id;

        public MessageHandler(String id)
        {
            this.id = id;
        }

        public void onMessage(Message msg)
        {
            // If message type is unexpected, just ACK it
            if (!(msg instanceof MapMessage))
            {
                try { msg.acknowledge(); }
                catch (JMSException e) {}
            }

            MapMessage mm = (MapMessage) msg;

            try
            {
```

Continued

Listing 4-5 *(Continued)*

```
            System.out.println("Handler = " + id +
                    ";  ProductID = " +
mm.getString("ProductID") +
                    ";  Quantity = " +
mm.getInt("Quantity"));
        }
        catch (JMSException ex)
        {
            // Unexpected error encountered
            ex.printStackTrace();
            return;
        }
        finally
        {
            try { mm.acknowledge(); }
            catch (JMSException e) {}
        }
    }
}

public static void main(String[] args) throws Exception
{
    try
    {
        // Context is loaded from the jndi.properties file
        Context context = new InitialContext();

        TopicConnectionFactory topicFactory =
                (TopicConnectionFactory)
context.lookup("TOPICFACTORY");

        TopicConnection topicConn =
                topicFactory.createTopicConnection();

        TopicSession topicSession =
topicConn.createTopicSession(false,

Session.AUTO_ACKNOWLEDGE);

        Topic topic = (Topic) context.lookup("PUBSUBNAME");

        TopicSubscriber subscribeAll =
topicSession.createSubscriber(topic);
```

```
            String selector =
               "ProductID LIKE 'JM%' AND Quantity > 20";

            TopicSubscriber subscribeSome =
topicSession.createSubscriber(topic,
                                    selector, true);

            subscribeAll.setMessageListener(
                  new MessageHandler("ALL MESSAGES"));

            subscribeSome.setMessageListener(
                  new MessageHandler("SELECTED MESSAGES"));

            // Indicate we're ready to start receiving messages.
            topicConn.start();

            // Block so we don't exit while waiting for messages
            Thread.sleep(60 * 60 * 1000);
        }
        catch (NamingException ex)
        {
            ex.printStackTrace();
        }
        catch (JMSException ex)
        {
            ex.printStackTrace();
        }
    }
}
```

Listing 4-6: A complete point-to-point receiving example

```
import javax.jms.*;
import javax.naming.*;
import java.util.*;

public class JMSPointToPointReceive
{
    public static class MessageHandler implements MessageListener
    {
        String id;

        public MessageHandler(String id)
        {
```

Continued

Listing 4-6 *(Continued)*

```java
            this.id = id;
        }

        public void onMessage(Message msg)
        {
            // If message type is unexpected, just ACK it
            if (!(msg instanceof MapMessage))
            {
                try { msg.acknowledge(); }
                catch (JMSException e) {}
            }

            MapMessage mm = (MapMessage) msg;

            try
            {
                System.out.println("Handler = " + id +
                        ":  ProductID = " +
mm.getString("ProductID") +
                        ":  Quantity = " +
mm.getInt("Quantity"));
            }
            catch (JMSException ex)
            {
                // Unexpected error encountered
                ex.printStackTrace();
                return;
            }
            finally
            {
                try { mm.acknowledge(); }
                catch (JMSException e) {}
            }
        }
    }

    public static void main(String[] args) throws Exception
    {
        try
        {
            // Context is loaded from the jndi.properties file
            Context context = new InitialContext();

            QueueConnectionFactory queueFactory =
```

```
                    (QueueConnectionFactory)
context.lookup("QUEUEFACTORY");

         QueueConnection queueConn =
               queueFactory.createQueueConnection();

         QueueSession queueSession =
queueConn.createQueueSession(false,

Session.AUTO_ACKNOWLEDGE);

         Queue queue = (Queue) context.lookup("QUEUENAME");

         QueueReceiver receiveAll =
queueSession.createReceiver(queue);

         receiveAll.setMessageListener(
               new MessageHandler("ALL MESSAGES"));

/*
// Only one receiver at a time can be active for any queue. We can
read
// from the QUEUENAME queue using _either_ the "receiveAll" receiver
or
// the "receiveSome" receiver, but not both.

         String selector =
            "ProductID LIKE 'JM%' AND Quantity > 20";

         QueueReceiver receiveSome =
queueSession.createReceiver(queue, selector);

         receiveSome.setMessageListener(
               new MessageHandler("SELECTED MESSAGES"));
*/

         // Indicate we're ready to start receiving messages.
         queueConn.start();

         // Block so we don't exit while waiting for messages
         Thread.sleep(60 * 60 * 1000);
      }
      catch (NamingException ex)
      {
         ex.printStackTrace();
```

Continued

Listing 4–6 *(Continued)*

```
        }
        catch (JMSException ex)
        {
            ex.printStackTrace();
        }
    }
}
```

Listing 4-7 shows a `build.xml` file that can be used to compile and run the sample programs from Listings 4-5 and 4-6. In addition to the "compile" target, the "runpubsubreceive" and "runptpreceive" targets are defined for running the programs pub/sub and point-to-point programs.

Listing 4-7: An ant build.xml file for building and running the example programs

```xml
<project name="JMSTest" default="compile" basedir=".">

  <property name="WL_HOME" value="c:/wlserver6.1"/>
  <property name="jmslib" value="${WL_HOME}/lib/weblogic.jar"/>

  <path id="runclasspath">
    <pathelement location="."/>
    <pathelement location="./classes"/>
    <pathelement location="${WL_HOME}/lib/weblogic.jar"/>
  </path>

  <target name="prepare">
    <mkdir dir="./classes"/>
  </target>

  <target name="compile" depends="prepare">

    <javac srcdir="." destdir="./classes" classpath=".;${jmslib}">
    </javac>

  </target>

  <target name="runpubsubreceive" depends="compile">
    <java classname="JMSPubSubReceive" fork="yes">
      <classpath refid="runclasspath"/>
    </java>

  </target>

  <target name="runptpreceive" depends="compile">
```

```
    <java classname="JMSPointToPointReceive" fork="yes">
       <classpath refid="runclasspath"/>
    </java>

  </target>

  <target name="clean">
    <delete dir="./classes"/>
  </target>

</project>
```

Summary

At this point in the book, I've covered all the JMS steps required to connect your application to a JMS provider, define individual sessions, create and populate the various types of messages, and send, receive, and acknowledge messages – in short, everything you need to send a message from one application and receive it in another.

So far, I've dealt with pub/sub and point-to-point messaging side-by-side because, except for some naming differences, the APIs used to interact with both are virtually the same. In the next couple of chapters, however, I deal with each messaging domain separately so that I can talk in greater detail about the things that pertain only to that domain, both from an API and an implementation standpoint.

Chapter 5

Publish/Subscribe Messaging

IN THIS CHAPTER

◆ Using the TopicRequestor class

◆ Durable topic subscriptions

◆ Typical publish/subscribe implementations and issues

JMS DOES A VERY GOOD JOB of keeping the APIs for pub/sub and point-to-point messaging looking and behaving similarly. For almost every `TopicXXX()` method, there's a corresponding `QueueXXX()` method that accepts the same parameters and performs the same role – this despite the fact the underlying provider's implementations might be radically different. Thus, if you are accomplished at using the JMS pub/sub methods and classes, you are able to use the point-to-point methods and classes.

So far, I've limited the discussion to areas where the pub/sub and point-to-point domains have similar or identical functionality and APIs. In this chapter, I discuss those few areas where there are pub/sub-specific features.

In the latter part of the chapter, you'll see how a typical provider might actually implement a pub/sub system, and I talk about the pros and cons of some of the different approaches a provider might use. Though programmers simply interested in learning the API might not find this immediately useful, architects and designers of systems that require pub/sub JMS need to know what's going on at the network level in order to design robust and scalable systems.

Using the TopicRequestor

In Chapter 3, I discussed how a JMS temporary topic could be used with the **JMSReplyTo** message property to effect an application-level request/reply. Remember that request/reply is used when a client asks another application to perform an operation for it and wants that application to respond to it exclusively rather than broadcasting the response to the whole world.

The application providing the service can be anywhere; the messaging provider routes the request message to it. After the message is received and processed, a reply message containing the desired results is sent back to the requestor. The reply message is sent to the destination identified by the temporary topic in the **JMSReplyTo** property of the request message.

Because this is a common scenario, JMS provides a utility class that allows a developer to implement a request/reply in the application without a lot of setup coding. This class is `javax.jms.TopicRequestor`.

With the `TopicRequestor` class, a developer can send a message and wait for its reply all in one blocking method call. To code all this manually, a developer would have to take the following steps (after any initial JMS session creation):

1. Create (or reuse) a temporary topic

2. Set the **JMSReplyTo** property of the request message to the temporary topic

3. Create a topic subscriber that listens only for messages with a destination of the temporary topic

4. Send the request message

5. Receive the response message using `TopicSubscriber.receive()`

6. Destroy the subscriber object properly using `TopicSubscriber.close()`

With the `TopicRequestor` class, you simply:

1. Create (or reuse) a TopicRequester object

2. Use `TopicRequestor.receive(msg)` to both send the request and receive the response

3. Destroy the `TopicRequestor` object properly using `TopicRequestor.close()` (only if not intending to reuse it)

Not only does the `TopicRequestor` class provide a huge savings in coding time to be sure, it also reduces the amount of housekeeping necessary and makes your code more readable. Listing 5-1 shows an example using the `TopicRequestor` class.

Listing 5-1: Using the TopicRequestor class

```
TopicSession session = (a previously created TopicSession);

Topic requestTopic = = (a previously created topic);

TextMessage msg = session.createTextMessage();

msg.setText("Hello World!");

TopicRequestor requestor = new TopicRequestor(session,
```

```
requestTopic);

// Warning: This is a blocking call that can take a
// relatively long time to process. It should always be
// executed in a separate thread so as not to block
// the entire application.
// Be sure you've called start() on your topic connection object
// before executing this call. Otherwise you will not be able
// to receive the reply message.
Message reply = requestor.receive(msg);

requestor.close();
```

Although request/reply scenarios are pretty basic, there are, architecturally speaking, several things that can go wrong. An application designer must always consider the following possibilities when implementing request/reply messaging:

♦ There is no service application running. Naturally, no response message would be sent in this circumstance and the `TopicRequestor` would block forever waiting for one. Unless your provider gives you a way to administratively configure one, you should always implement some sort of timeout behavior on the requestor side to cover this eventuality. Fiorano Software, for example, provides proprietary requestor classes with its *FioranoMQ* product that allow you to specify a timeout when sending a request message. Always keep in mind that using proprietary APIs results in non-standard, non-portable code, however.

♦ The server application is not coded properly to respond to requests, or it encounters a runtime error that prevents it from responding. In this case, the client would also never get a response. Timeouts should be implemented as in the previous point.

♦ There's more than one service application running and responding to the same request topic. With JMS, there's no way to ensure only one application is subscribed to a pub/sub topic at any given time. If more than one instance of a server is receiving and processing request messages, the result would be that the request message would be delivered to multiple server applications, thus causing the client to receive multiple replies.

Note that you don't have to worry about more than one client application subscribing to the same temporary topic at the same time — and, thus, potentially receiving the same response message. JMS guarantees that all created temporary topics are unique for the runtime life of the messaging provider.

Using Durable Topic Subscribers

A special kind of message delivery mechanism that pertains only to pub/sub messaging is the *durable subscription*. A durable subscription is one where the messaging provider is required to hold a message in nonvolatile storage for any subscribers that are not running at the time the message is delivered. If this sounds remarkably like the queue-based delivery mechanism used in point-to-point messaging, it is. The difference, however, is that while point-to-point messages are usually delivered to a single client, durable subscription messages maintain pub/sub semantics and can be delivered to multiple clients, some of which may be running when the provider receives the message and some of which may not be.

 According to the JMS specification, a provider must store a message for a durable subscriber until all interested subscribers have read the message or the message expires. Unfortunately, it says nothing about what happens to messages that are never delivered and never expire. Most providers enable you to specify a maximum time to live for a durable subscription message in order to prevent the internal queue from growing forever as a result of a subscriber that never reads all its messages.

Even with the ability to administratively override message expiration values, however, you won't want to use durable subscriptions to distribute very high volume messages because a single inactive client — or even one that's active but very slow — can cause the internal message queue to grow rapidly and possibly drag down the performance of the overall messaging infrastructure.

If a client subscribes to a topic, receives some messages, exits, and then wishes to pick up where it left off the next time it's started, how does the provider know it's the same application when it comes up the second time? The client must identify itself to the provider via a string that is unique across client applications known to the provider. This string is known as the *client identifier*. It exists on a per connection basis and can be manipulated through the setClientID() and getClientID() methods in the javax.jms.Connection interface that the TopicConnection class implements.

How you create a unique client identifier is completely up to you; JMS provides no facility to help you do this. You are not required to set a client ID at all unless you are creating durable subscriptions. If you do need to set a client ID, you can do so programmatically through setClientID() or you can pre-populate the desired value administratively when you define a TopicConnectionFactory using your provider's JMS administration tool (see Chapters 11 and 12 for more information on administrative procedures).

Like point-to-point messages, durable subscription messages are guaranteed to be delivered and the provider will ensure that all unacknowledged messages are redelivered in the event of a system failure (see Chapter 3 for more information).

The `TopicSubscriber` object associated with durable subscriptions has all the same functions as a normal `TopicSubscriber` object; however, it must be initially created by a call to `TopicSession.createDurableSubscriber()` rather than the more typical `TopicSession.createSubscriber()`. Notice that calls to `createDurableSubscriber()` require an extra `name` parameter to be supplied. This name is a secondary *subscription identifier* that uniquely identifies the particular durable subscription within the domain already determined by the client identifier. That is to say, the subscription identifier refers to a particular {topic, message selector} pair within an application instance, and the application instance itself is uniquely identified by the client identifier.

Listing 5-2 is based on Listing 4-5 from Chapter 4 but it has been adapted to explicitly set the client identifier for the application and to create durable subscriptions instead of regular subscriptions.

Listing 5-2: Setting up a durable subscriptionimport javax.jms.*;

```
import javax.naming.*;
import java.util.*;

public class JMSDurablePubSubReceive
{
    public static class MessageHandler implements MessageListener
    {
        String id;

        public MessageHandler(String id)
        {
            this.id = id;
        }

        public void onMessage(Message msg)
        {
            // If message type is unexpected, just ACK it
            if (!(msg instanceof MapMessage))
            {
                try { msg.acknowledge(); }
                catch (JMSException e) {}
            }

            MapMessage mm = (MapMessage) msg;

            try
```

Continued

Listing 5-2 *(Continued)*

```
            {
                System.out.println("Handler = " + id +
                        ":  ProductID = " +
mm.getString("ProductID") +
                        ":  Quantity = " +
mm.getInt("Quantity"));
            }
            catch (JMSException ex)
            {
                // Unexpected error encountered
                ex.printStackTrace();
                return;
            }
            finally
            {
                try { mm.acknowledge(); }
                catch (JMSException e) {}
            }
        }
    }

    public static void main(String[] args) throws Exception
    {
        try
        {
            // Context is loaded from the jndi.properties file
            Context context = new InitialContext();

            TopicConnectionFactory topicFactory =
                    (TopicConnectionFactory)
context.lookup("TOPICFACTORY");

            TopicConnection topicConn =
                    topicFactory.createTopicConnection();

            // Here is where the client ID is specified. Each
durable
            // subscription client must have a unique ID. This ID
can
            // typically also be set administratively.
            topicConn.setClientID(args[0]);

            TopicSession topicSession =
topicConn.createTopicSession(false,

Session.AUTO_ACKNOWLEDGE);
```

```
            boolean doUnsubscribe = false;

            if (doUnsubscribe)
            {
                // Durable subscriptions are removed for a
particular
                // client ID by calling the unsubscribe() method.
                topicSession.unsubscribe("UNIQUENAME");

                System.out.println("Unsubscribed for client: "
                                    +
topicConn.getClientID());

                topicSession.close();
                return;
            }

            Topic topic = (Topic) context.lookup("PUBSUBNAME");

            // Here is where the durable subscription is created.
Notice
            // the difference from creating a normal subscription.
            TopicSubscriber durableSub =
                    topicSession.createDurableSubscriber(topic,
"UNIQUENAME");

            durableSub.setMessageListener(
                new MessageHandler("MSGHANDLER"));

            // Indicate we're ready to start receiving messages.
            topicConn.start();

            // Block so we don't exit while waiting for messages
            Thread.sleep(60 * 60 * 1000);
        }
        catch (NamingException ex)
        {
            ex.printStackTrace();
        }
        catch (JMSException ex)
        {
            ex.printStackTrace();
        }
    }
}
```

Listing 5-3 shows a sample ant `build.xml` file that can be used to compile and run the example program in Listing 5-2. Notice that there are two run targets, each of which hands different client ID parameters to the application. This ID string is used in the `setClientID()` method to uniquely identify particular instances of the application.

To test durable subscription behavior, you can run the following two commands, each in a separate window:

```
ant rundurpubsubreceive1
```

and

```
ant rundurpubsubreceive2
```

The former command will create an instance of the pub/sub receiver identified as "CLIENT_ID1" and the latter as "CLIENT_ID2". Both application instances will subscribe to the "PUBSUBNAME" topic. If you were to then run the sample program from Listing 3-3 in Chapter 3, you would see that both instances receive the sent message.

If you kill one of the instances and then send more messages, you'll then see that one instance will continue to receive the messages in real-time. However, unlike with non-durable delivery, when the killed instance is run for a second time, it will immediately receive all messages that had been sent to the "PUBSUBNAME" topic while it was inactive. This behavior will continue until such time as the durable subscription is terminated by executing the code in the `if (doUnsubscribe) {}` block in Listing 5-2.

Notice also that the sample sending program from Listing 3-3 did not need to be modified in any way in order to send messages to the Listing 5-2 durable subscription program. This is good news because it means that JMS allows us to design our pub/sub senders without regard to whether a receiver is durable or non-durable; it is completely up to the provider to determine if a message needs to be queued up for a particular pub/sub client or not.

Keep in mind, though, that unless the provider is aware that a subscriber is interested in having its pub/sub messages queued — that is, only if the subscriber has previously defined a durable subscription using the `createDurableSubscription()` method — then any messages delivered to a particular topic prior to the client defining a durable subscription will never make it to the durable subscriber. Contrast this behavior to point-to-point queues which store any messages sent, using them regardless of whether any client application has told the provider whether it is interested in receiving such messages at the time the message is sent.

Listing 5-3: An ant build.xml file for building and running the example program

```xml
<project name="JMSTest" default="compile" basedir=".">

    <property name="WL_HOME" value="c:/wlserver6.1" />
```

```
<property name="jmslib" value="${WL_HOME}/lib/weblogic.jar"/>

<path id="runclasspath">
  <pathelement location="."/>
  <pathelement location="./classes"/>
  <pathelement location="${WL_HOME}/lib/weblogic.jar"/>
</path>

<target name="prepare">
  <mkdir dir="./classes"/>
</target>

<target name="compile" depends="prepare">

  <javac srcdir="." destdir="./classes" classpath=".;${jmslib}">
  </javac>

</target>

<target name="rundurpubsubreceive1" depends="compile">
  <java classname="JMSDurablePubSubReceive" fork="yes">
      <arg value="CLIENT_ID1"/>
      <classpath refid="runclasspath"/>
  </java>
</target>

<target name="rundurpubsubreceive2" depends="compile">
  <java classname="JMSDurablePubSubReceive" fork="yes">
      <arg value="CLIENT_ID2"/>
      <classpath refid="runclasspath"/>
  </java>
</target>

<target name="clean">
  <delete dir="./classes" />
</target>

</project>
```

Note that within an application, only one session at a time can have a durable subscription active for any particular named subscription – that is, for any particular client ID/subscription ID combination. So, while for a normal subscription you are allowed to subscribe to the same topic via separate sessions within the same virtual machine, you are effectively prohibited from doing this with durable subscriptions (though there's nothing to stop you from subscribing to the same topic non-durably in other sessions). Because it's rare to have two JMS sessions actively subscribed to the same topic in the same application, you probably don't need to be too concerned with this restriction.

You are allowed to re-use a subscription identifier (e.g. the "UNIQUENAME" ID from Listing 5-2) whenever you like. However, should you re-use a subscription identifier by creating a durable subscriber with a different topic name and/or message selector than that currently associated with the identifier, then the effect will be the same as if you unsubscribed from the old subscription associated with the identifier and created a brand new subscription. All pending messages associated with the old identifier will be automatically discarded.

Keep in mind that the overhead associated with durable subscriptions can be substantial because the provider must keep a record of each subscriber in permanent storage and must maintain a separate logical message queue for each topic/subscriber combination. Even worse, the amount of resources used to maintain the subscription list will grow roughly linearly with the number of subscriptions. The bottom line is that you should use durable subscriptions judiciously with a full assessment of the resource impact on your system. And to be on the safe side, always be sure to use `TopicSession.unsubscribe()` to remove a durable subscription when you are finished with it. The resources associated with maintaining the long-term subscription will not be released until you do so.

Figure 5-1 illustrates the path a message must take through the provider's software if any of the subscribers listening for it are durable.

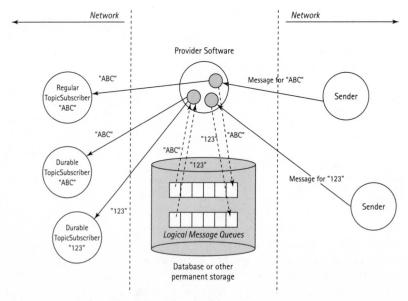

Figure 5-1: Durable subscription message flows

Pub/Sub Implementation

This section covers some of the network protocols and techniques typically used to implement pub/sub messaging. Having some knowledge of how pub/sub systems are implemented will help you better understand the behavior and limitations of any system you architect that relies on pub/sub messaging. It will also aid you in configuring and administering your provider's software. Administration of JMS products will be covered in Chapter 11.

The UDP protocol

If you're reading this book you probably have some familiarity with the TCP/IP network protocol; it is, after all, the networking language of the Internet. Although as developers we generally associate network communications with sockets – connection-oriented, stream-based data delivery constructs – the TCP/IP protocol stack also defines a datagram protocol called *Unreliable Datagram Protocol* (UDP). A *datagram* is roughly equivalent to a JMS message and UDP can be used by an application to send a message simultaneously to a number of listening applications. Java even has built-in support for datagram messaging with its `java.net.DatagramSocket` class. Moreover, if the underlying network supports broadcasts – for example, as Ethernet does – datagram sockets can be used to easily and effectively send a message to a large number of machines with a single method call.

If UDP messaging is free, easy-to-use, and readily available, why use special pub/sub messaging software at all? The answer lies in the details of how UDP behaves. I discuss some key issues in the sections that follow.

PORT NUMBER RESTRICTIONS

When a sender broadcasts a UDP message, the sender specifies the destination by using an integer port number, rather than a string-based destination like JMS uses. The range of possible port numbers is the same as that used when doing stream (that is to say, TCP) socket programming. And, similar to stream socket programming, client applications must specify the particular port number they expect messages to arrive on.

Once an application has begun listening for messages on a particular port number, it has exclusive use of that port. Thus, it is impossible to send a message to more than one client on any given machine without either writing custom message distribution software, which accepts messages sent to a port and redistributes them to all interested applications on the same machine, or by sending the same message to all the ports on a machine that clients are listening on.

Also, the integers that identify port numbers are not particularly descriptive destination names when compared to the string-based destination names that JMS provides. String-based destinations permit a much richer and human-readable way of routing messages.

OS LIMITATIONS

Modern operating systems can very efficiently send and receive network messages. Unix is particularly good because it was created almost from the beginning as a network-aware OS. However, the major concern of all operating systems is delivering an incoming message to the destination application as quickly as possible. While there are internal OS buffers that will hold incoming messages for an application if it is too slow to process them, these buffers are naturally limited in size and when they overflow, any further incoming messages will simply be discarded without any notification to the application. Losing messages due to buffer overflow is not an acceptable state of affairs for most commercial applications.

Also, as they are internal OS constructs, the sizes of these buffers cannot easily be reconfigured on a multi-user system without special permission (and skills!).

NO RESEND MECHANISM

Messages can be lost due to buffer overflow; they can also be lost in transit, although that is relatively rare. Unlike TCP, which employs low-level acknowledgment messages to help guarantee that all data makes it to its destination, UDP has no such capability. This makes it a lighter weight protocol and therefore faster. Speed is gained at the price of reliability, however, which means there is no automated way of resending a message that was dropped due to, say, network congestion. Even worse, if a message is lost, neither the sender nor the recipient will ever know it.

SUBNET SCOPE LIMITATION

Although a lengthy discussion of subnet scope limitation is beyond the range of this book, you should be aware that, for efficiency reasons, large installations of networked computers are typically divided up into *subnets*. Each subnet is the network segment that directly links a group of machines (usually around 100 or less). TCP traffic (for example, sockets) is transparently shuttled back and forth between machines located on different subnets by a router that bridges the two subnets – which is why TCP socket programmers never need be concerned about such details of network topology.

Generally speaking, however, large installations do not automatically route UDP traffic between subnets because the broadcast nature of the protocol would result in a lot of bandwidth being used up on a subnet where perhaps no machines have any interest in the messages sent to it. This means that as an architect, you are now left with the unenviable job of convincing your network administrator to reconfigure their routers to pass through UDP traffic, or of employing a custom software router that picks up your UDP datagrams from one subnet and delivers them to others.

In either case, you must be topology-aware when designing your system. Tailoring your application design to a specific physical network installation is clearly not desirable – especially when the network administrators, who have long since forgotten about your application, decide they want to restructure the network and crash your application in the process.

As a result of subnet scoping, UDP is also not a practical solution for delivering messages over the Internet at large. Bridging many subnets is not feasible because routing all UDP packets to all existing subnets would quickly bring the Internet to its knees.

SECURITY

As with most lower-level protocols, UDP leaves security up to the applications involved in the sending and receiving. So unless all your messages are encrypted, there's nothing to prevent any application with access to your network from receiving all your UDP traffic without detection simply by listening on the right port. Moreover, there's no way to prevent unauthorized applications from sending messages.

The IP multicast protocol

To correct some of the limitations of UDP, a new protocol called *IP multicast* (RFC 1112) was developed. IP multicast is very much like UDP in that it employs datagram messaging and does not guarantee delivery. It also makes use of port-based addressing though, unlike UDP, multiple applications may listen on the same port at the same time.

IP multicast is an improvement over UDP, however, because it is smarter about how it delivers messages to large numbers of machines where perhaps only a few machines are interested in receiving the delivery in the first place. Instead of blindly broadcasting messages, IP multicast can selectively deliver messages to individual machines because it requires that, in addition to specifying a port number, listeners subscribe to a multicast group before receiving messages. Groups are designated by a class D IP address, which are in the range `224.0.0.1` to `239.255.255.255`.

Because groups must be subscribed to — *joined* in IP multicast terminology — network routers can be more efficient about where they deliver messages, thus reducing the amount of wasted bandwidth. For this reason, IP multicast is a much more suitable protocol than UDP for high-volume message delivery (for example, stock quotes, audio/video, and so on) in large network installations or even (theoretically) over the Internet.

Although IP multicast is slowly gaining in popularity — Java supports it via the `java.net.MulticastSocket` class — it's not a message delivery panacea. IP multicast applications still use a lot of bandwidth, partly because of the protocol itself and partly because of the nature of the data most likely to be sent using it. Also, most network administrators are reluctant to configure their routers to allow it even if they have routers that support it, which many still don't.

More importantly from an enterprise messaging perspective, IP multicast solves few of the problems associated with UDP. Although many applications on the same machine can easily receive messages with IP multicast (because multiple clients are allowed to listen on the same port number), the addressing scheme is primitive, messages can still be silently dropped, and there is no improvement in security.

Reliable multicast

To be useful in a corporate environment, a broadcast messaging system must, at a minimum, have the following features:

- Guaranteed delivery

- Guaranteed order of message receipt (on a per sender basis)

- Descriptive destination naming and subscription capabilities

- Message receivable by multiple applications on the same machine

- Fast, efficient delivery

To achieve these goals, many pub/sub products are built using what's generically referred to as *reliable multicast*. Unlike UDP or IP multicast, reliable multicast is not a single industry-wide standard; there are a wide variety of public domain and proprietary protocols in use. A good place to start if you're interested in finding out more about the various reliable multicast protocols out there is `http://www.nard.net/~tmont/rm-links.html`.

Most reliable multicast protocols start with a basic network protocol like UDP or IP multicast and add some additional features (for reliability and so forth) on top of it. This is usually achieved by adding a special software layer between the sender and receiver. Instead of communicating directly with the network as before, an application asks a vendor's software proxy to send and receive messages on its behalf. In this way, the proxy can take on the responsibility of redelivering messages that, for whatever reason, did not make it to their destination. Generally, a lightweight acknowledgment protocol based on sequence numbering of messages is employed to determine which messages were lost in transit.

Additional advantages of utilizing proxy software include the following:

- Because it's a normal application, the proxy can implement message buffering in a much more robust and easily configurable way.

- Multiple applications on a machine can use the same proxy instance.

- Proxies can allow for a much richer and more flexible message subscription scheme.

- Cooperating proxies are in a better position to implement security without involving the endpoint applications. Figures 5-2 and 5-3 depict the high-level architecture of a generic reliable multicast system and the internals of its proxy server, respectively.

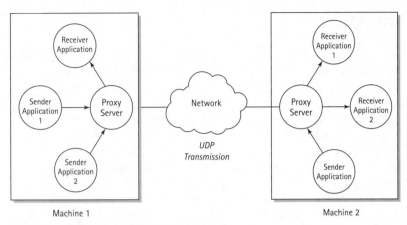

Figure 5-2: A reliable multicast architecture

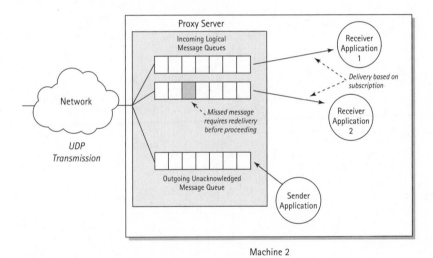

Figure 5-3: The internals of a reliable multicast proxy server

Because of their reliability, it's clear why commercial multicast-based systems have become so popular. You're likely to come across providers that make use of reliable multicast technology when evaluating JMS products. There are, however, some disadvantages aside from the fact that you actually have to pay a lot for the really good ones. First, they are not based on a single standard, so messages cannot automatically be routed between vendor offerings. Also, in most cases, you have to have a special software daemon supplied by the vendor running on every machine participating in the messaging, which makes it hard to add new machines to the messaging bus very quickly.

Summary

In this chapter, I covered some of the JMS features that pertain only to pub/sub messaging. You can use the `TopicRequestor` class to simplify the common task of implementing request/reply messaging. You can use durable subscriptions to combine the guaranteed, long-latency delivery behavior of point-to-point messaging with the multi-client distribution semantics of pub/sub messaging, but durable subscriptions must be used with care and you should be aware of the overhead associated with them.

Finally, you learned some of the ways in which pub/sub messaging is implemented and you read about the network topology considerations associated with it – information that should be helpful to any system architect who is creating a system based on pub/sub messaging.

In the next chapter we'll look at similar issues and concepts related to point-to-point messaging.

Chapter 6

Point-to-Point Messaging

IN THIS CHAPTER

- ◆ Details of point-to-point messaging
- ◆ Using the QueueRequestor class
- ◆ Using the QueueBrowser class
- ◆ Typical point-to-point implementations and issues

IN THIS CHAPTER, I delve into those features of JMS that are particular to point-to-point messaging. While they are relatively few, these queue-specific features and behaviors are important to be aware of for anyone doing JMS point-to-point programming.

In the latter part of this chapter – just as I did with pub/sub messaging in the last chapter – I discuss some of the ways in which message queues are implemented so you can have a better feel for their limitations and performance characteristics.

Details of Point-to-Point Messaging

Before venturing further into the specific point-to-point messaging features provided by JMS, let's clarify a couple of issues that people often find confusing regarding queue-based messaging.

Dealing with multiple queue readers

Although the JMS specification is regrettably vague on the subject, most queue-based providers supply messages to consumers on a first-come, first-served basis. This means that unlike pub/sub messaging where all clients that subscribe to a particular destination receive the same messages, only one client will ever receive a copy of a message delivered via a queue.

Keep in mind that it is still possible to have more than one consumer object – either in the same or different applications – subscribed to any particular destination. This is a good way to implement a simple load balancing scheme, for example, where a pool of like application instances – each perhaps on separate machines – all set themselves up as receivers for the same message destination; each incoming message is then delivered to the first available (not busy) instance. Just be sure that if you have this type of behavior in your system that it's intentional and not accidental!

For example, suppose you defined two queue receiver objects in your application as follows (where the message handler object is the one from Listing 6-2, which appears later in this chapter):

```
QueueReceiver receiver1 = queueSession.createReceiver(queue);

receiver1.setMessageListener(new MessageHandler("HANDLER1"));

QueueReceiver receive2 = queueSession.createReceiver(queue);

receiver2.setMessageListener(new MessageHandler("HANDLER2"));
```

If you send point-to-point messages to a program with two receivers defined in this way, then you will see that one of the receiver's message handler objects will be invoked whenever a message arrives, but never both at the same time like you would see with a pub/sub message. The queue receiver handlers will probably be invoked in alternating fashion but this is not guaranteed.

Persistent vs. non-persistent queues

In discussing point-to-point messaging, I've pointed out that queues are used to hold messages regardless of whether there are any clients actively receiving the messages or not. Since all point-to-point messages are clearly saved somewhere, it may be confusing as to what effect a persistent versus non-persistent delivery mode has when sending such a message (refer to Chapter 3 to review how to specify that a JMS message should be delivered persistently or non-persistently). The answer lies in whether a message is recoverable after a provider failure or intentional restart.

JMS does not prohibit an application from sending point-to-point messages with a delivery mode of PERSISTENT to a queue destination as well as sending messages with a delivery mode of NON_PERSISTENT to the same queue. If you were to send messages with both modes to a queue without reading any of them off the queue, and you then stopped and restarted your JMS provider, you would find that the messages sent as PERSISTENT messages are still present on the queue while the NON_PERSISTENT messages have been lost.

Using the QueueRequestor

The javax.jms.QueueRequestor class is the point-to-point analogue of the TopicRequestor class examined in Chapter 5 (see the section "Using the TopicRequestor"). It is a utility class that encapsulates most of the operations required to implement request/reply messaging over a point-to-point infrastructure.

The operations a `QueueRequestor` performs on behalf of the requesting client are identical to those performed by a `TopicRequestor` – except, of course, they use the equivalent *Queue* API calls rather than the *Topic* API calls. Because I've already thoroughly discussed these operations and the issues associated with them, we can skip a detailed analysis here and go directly to the code. Listing 6-1 shows an example of how to use the `QueueRequestor` class.

Listing 6-1: Using the QueueRequestor class

```
QueueSession session = (a previously created QueueSession);

Queue requestQueue = = (a previously created queue);

TextMessage msg = session.createTextMessage();

msg.setText("Hello World!");

QueueRequestor requestor =
        new QueueRequestor(session, requestQueue);

// Warning: This is a blocking call that will take a
// relatively long time to process. It should always be
// executed in a separate thread so as not to block
// the entire application.
// Be sure you've called start() on your queue connection object
// before executing this call. Otherwise you will not be able
// to receive the reply message.
Message reply = requestor.receive(msg);

requestor.close();
```

Although request/replies transmitted over queues use a very different transport mechanism than topic-based request/replies, the types of things that can go wrong are exactly the same. In particular, these are the problems associated with the lack of a response to the initial request and the implications that has for your application (see Chapter 5 for a complete discussion on this topic).

Not only can the server fail before sending a response, but the client can fail before receiving it. Anything that causes the client's connection to the JMS provider to close prior to the receipt of the reply – including failure of the entire application – falls into this category. Because point-to-point reply messages are, by definition, stored somewhere before delivery, you may be tempted to try to retrieve them after your application restarts. This is not possible when using a `QueueRequestor` because you don't have access to the temporary destination it creates internally. On the other hand, if you're managing the reply process yourself by using an explicitly created `TemporaryQueue` for responses, you will have access to its string name and can store it away somewhere for failure recovery purposes. This is not a good idea, however.

Even if you've stored away the temporary name somewhere, the main problem with trying to recover a reply message after a client application restart is that JMS does not say what is supposed to happen to a message directed to a temporary destination when the currently subscribed receiver goes away. Some providers may leave the message in the queue until it expires, but don't count on that. Because JMS ties a temporary destination to the `QueueConnection` that created it, more likely than not a provider will immediately free up the resources used by such messages destined for connections that have terminated either normally or abnormally.

Using the QueueBrowser

The `javax.jms.QueueBrowser` class is another utility class that is specific to point-to-point messaging. With a `QueueBrowser`, a client can examine the contents of the queue of unread messages without actually removing any of them from the queue. A `QueueBrowser` is created in much the same way as a regular `QueueReceiver`; calling the `QueueSession.createBrowser(Queue)` or `QueueSession.createBrowser (Queue, String msgSelector)` factory method will return a new browser instance.

Unlike `QueueReceivers`, however, `QueueBrowsers` have no `receive()` method and no option for adding a message listener. Instead, an application calls the `QueueBrowser.getEnumeration()` method to get an enumerator object that you then use to review the list of pending messages. The returned `java.util. Enumeration` object allows the caller to scan all the pending (that is to say, unread) messages in the queue that match the given destination name and message selector (if any).

Code Listing 6-2 shows an example program that makes use of a `QueueBrowser`. The program browses the queue five times, once every ten seconds, and prints out the current number of messages in the queue that match the `QueueBrowser`'s queue name and message selector.

You can use the point-to-point sender test program from Chapter 3 (Listing 3-4) to place messages on the queue. Since the sample `QueueBrowser` program only browses — it does not actually read any messages — you will notice that it reports that a larger and larger number of messages are available as time goes by and as you keep sending messages to the queue. The program should report there are as many messages present in the queue as you have sent using the Listing 3-4 program.

I have also included an ant `build.xml` file (Listing 6-3) that can be used to compile and run the browser test program. The ant target to run the program is "runqbrowse".

Listing 6-2: A sample program that uses a QueueBrowser

```
import javax.jms.*;
import javax.naming.*;
```

```
import java.util.*;

public class JMSQueueBrowse
{
    public static void main(String[] args) throws Exception
    {
        try
        {
            // Context is loaded from the jndi.properties file
            Context context = new InitialContext();

            QueueConnectionFactory queueFactory =
                    (QueueConnectionFactory)
context.lookup("QUEUEFACTORY");

            QueueConnection queueConn =
                    queueFactory.createQueueConnection();

            QueueSession queueSession =
queueConn.createQueueSession(false,

Session.AUTO_ACKNOWLEDGE);

            Queue queue = (Queue) context.lookup("QUEUENAME");

            QueueBrowser browser =
                    queueSession.createBrowser(queue, "Quantity >
20");

            // It's not required to call start() if you're just
browsing
            // as we are in this program, but it doesn't hurt.
            queueConn.start();

            for (int i=0; i < 5; ++i)
            {
                int cnt=0;
                for (Enumeration en=browser.getEnumeration();
                                en.hasMoreElements();)
                {
                    ++cnt;

                    Message msg = (Message) en.nextElement();
```

Continued

Listing 6-2 *(Continued)*

```
                    // Calling acknowledge will NOT have the effect of
                    // removing the message from the queue. It will
remain
                    // on the queue until explicitly read from it.
                    //
                    // msg.acknowledge();
                }

                System.out.println("There are " + cnt + " matching
messages" +
                                   " currently in the queue");

                Thread.sleep(10 * 1000);
            }

            // Notice how the same browser object can be used for many
            // browse operations. It does not need to be closed
until you
            // are finished with it entirely.
            browser.close();

            queueSession.close();
            queueConn.close();
        }
        catch (NamingException ex)
        {
            ex.printStackTrace();
        }
        catch (JMSException ex)
        {
            ex.printStackTrace();
        }
    }
}
```

Listing 6-3: An ant build.xml file for building and running the example programs

```
<project name="JMSTest" default="compile" basedir=".">

  <property name="WL_HOME" value="c:/wlserver6.1" />
  <property name="jmslib" value="${WL_HOME}/lib/weblogic.jar"/>

  <path id="runclasspath">
    <pathelement location="."/>
```

```
    <pathelement location="./classes"/>
    <pathelement location="${WL_HOME}/lib/weblogic.jar"/>
</path>

<target name="prepare">
  <mkdir dir="./classes"/>
</target>

<target name="compile" depends="prepare">

  <javac srcdir="." destdir="./classes" classpath=".;${jmslib}">
  </javac>

</target>

<target name="runqbrowse" depends="compile">
  <java classname="JMSQueueBrowse" fork="yes">
    <classpath refid="runclasspath"/>
  </java>
</target>

<target name="clean">
  <delete dir="./classes" />
</target>

</project>
```

Application design issues

Queue browsing is one of those areas where JMS does not really nail down exactly how the provider should be implemented, however. There are two basic options:

- The provider returns a static snapshot of all matching messages in the queue. These messages are then stored in a memory buffer inside your application's JVM and a call to `Enumeration.nextElement()` returns the next message from the buffer.

- The provider designs the enumerator such that each call to `nextElement()` goes back to the physical queue and retrieves the next matching message. This necessitates a context switch to the provider's software for each element retrieved and results in a higher latency for each message retrieved but yields more up-to-date results.

If you have a high-volume system and you're making heavy use of queue browsing, it's important to know which option your provider's implementation has chosen because the second option will have higher negative performance impact than the first, both on the client application and the provider.

The advantage of the second implementation, however, is that the list of messages seen by the client is more likely – but not guaranteed – to reflect the actual contents of the queue. A message retrieved via a browse operation might not be in the physical queue by the time the client sees it because it may have been read by a QueueReceiver somewhere else. This other QueueReceiver may be in another application, or it may even be one that you created in your application running in a different thread.

In fact, the only time you can be absolutely sure that the list of messages returned by the QueueBrowser reflects exactly the list of matching, unread messages in the physical queue is when there are no clients actively reading those messages at all, including the client doing the browsing.

The only pattern that guarantees the option to read every message returned by a browse involves a combination of browsing and synchronous reading (see Chapter 4 for a review of how to read messages synchronously). In order for it to work, you must be able to uniquely identify the browsed messages somehow – the JMSMessageID property is perfect for this – and you must ensure that there's no other client attempting to read the messages you've browsed.

Code Listing 6-4 shows an example of this pattern.

Listing 6-4: Using the reliable QueueBrowser pattern

```
QueueSession session = (a previously created QueueSession);

Queue queue = = (a previously created queue);

QueueBrowser browser = session.createBrowser(queue);

for (Enumeration en=browser.getEnumeration();
            en.hasMoreElements();)
{
    Message msg = (Message) en.nextElement();

    // Determine if you want to actually read the message
    // or not
    boolean doRead = (true/false);

    if (doRead)
    {
        QueueReceiver reader =
            session.createReceiver(queue,
            "JMSMessageID = '" + msg.getJMSMessageID() + "'");

        msg = reader.receive();
```

```
        reader.close();

        // Do something with msg here
    }
}
```

Note that simply calling the `Message.acknowledge()` method on a message object received via a browse will not have the effect of telling the provider that you've consumed that message – though it would be nice if that were the case. In fact, calling `acknowledge()` in this way may have the undesired side effect of acknowledging any other messages that are being received via the same `QueueSession`, or it may cause an exception to be thrown, or it may do nothing at all – it depends on how the provider is implemented.

The current lack of precisely defined behavior opens up the larger question of when you would want to use a `QueueBrowser` at all. The only advantage `QueueBrowser` has over using a message selector is that is allows you to examine the contents of a message before deciding whether to consume it or not; message selectors are limited to examining the JMS properties of a message. But in order for this to work, you would still need to implement the reliable read pattern from Listing 6-3.

If possible, rather than using `QueueBrowser` to pre-screen messages, it's a much better idea to have the sender place whatever information you're trying to filter in a JMS message header property. You can use a standard message selector as a means of receiving only those messages your application is interested in.

Point-to-Point Implementation

In this section, I discuss some of the pertinent implementation details you'll be interested in when architecting a system that uses point-to-point messaging.

Differences from pub/sub

The two primary differences between a point-to-point system and a pub/sub system are that a point-to-point system requires that:

◆ All messages must be stored somewhere prior to delivery; the actual storage location may be either volatile or nonvolatile.

◆ All messages must be cached without regard to who's interested in them.

With the exception of the hybrid durable subscription messages, pub/sub messaging does not require messages to be stored on behalf of the client. Also, whereas pub/sub messaging systems are always aware of which consumers are interested in which messages, point-to-point systems are less intelligent in that they just optimistically assume that some client will be interested in each of the messages flowing through the system. All point-to-point messages are queued even if there currently is not, and never has been, any client subscribed to the particular destination a message is delivered to.

These differences between the pub/sub and point-to-point models are significant considerations when architecting your system and will help decide which is best suited to your needs.

Storing the message

The need to squirrel away all messages in nonvolatile storage explains why databases play such a prominent role in many JMS products. In fact, because they provide transactionalized, nonvolatile storage and efficient searching capabilities, relational databases are particularly well-suited as the underpinning of point-to-point messaging systems. For this reason, most major RDBMS (Relational Database Management System) vendors have their own queuing products – Oracle's *Advanced Queuing* and IBM's *MQSeries* are examples. They are a natural and easy extension to each company's main product line.

Of course, an RDBMS is not an absolute requirement and some JMS vendors use less heavyweight means to store messages on disk – for instance, a transaction manager and the local file system. A lighter weight technology – or at least a light-weight database – is often essential if you want to run your messaging system on a resource-restricted platform such as a PDA or a cell phone.

Delivering the message

As the name implies, point-to-point messages are not broadcast. Each message delivery is a targeted operation in which the message is delivered to a specific client. Because messages are usually delivered to a client over a connection-oriented communications channel such as a stream socket, the specific network topology in use is typically not an architectural concern, as it can be with pub/sub messaging (see Chapter 5 for a review of the influence of network topology on pub/sub transmissions).

Because of the requirement for intermediate storage and the connection-oriented nature of the message delivery, point-to-point messaging typically has higher latency than pub/sub messaging. This does not mean that point-to-point systems cannot be fast, of course, just that they typically cannot deliver messages to a larger audience as efficiently as pub/sub systems operating in an equivalent environment.

Underlying architectures

Of course, a point-to-point provider might choose to implement its system in a variety of ways and it's critical when evaluating any messaging vendor's software to understand, at least at a high level, what its underlying architecture looks like. This will help you satisfy yourself as to whether their claims regarding reliability and scalability are valid.

Following is a brief overview of the three primary point-to-point architectures.

THE CONNECTED ARCHITECTURE

This hub-and-spoke architecture is the most common because it is high performance, highly centralized (and thus easy to manage), and lends itself nicely to internal corporate environments with their access to high-speed networks and high-end database software.

In this architecture, all traffic is funneled through a central machine that manages the message queue. Unlike with many pub/sub implementations, where often a proxy server must be running on each machine (see Chapter 5), queue-clients communicate directly with the central provider software to receive their messages. They either must maintain an open connection to the provider or they must periodically poll the provider in search of new messages.

Often the messaging systems based on this architecture are used for nothing more than to bridge messaging endpoints between two very different computing environments. A common example would be a distributed LAN-based system that needs to exchange messages with a legacy back-end mainframe environment; Figure 6-1 shows a simple example.

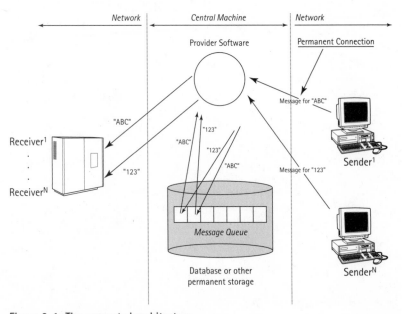

Figure 6-1: The connected architecture

THE SEMI-CONNECTED ARCHITECTURE

The semi-connected architecture is becoming more and more common as the world of wireless communications expands rapidly. This architecture covers environments where many client devices are only intermittently connected to the network – or connected over a high latency (slow) network – and it presents its own set of architectural challenges.

The primary challenge is that multiple physical storage queues are needed to hold the messages. At a minimum, there need to be two queues: one on the client device and one on the server. The client queue is, of course, needed to hold outgoing messages that are generated while the device is disconnected from the network. This enables users to merrily continue along working with their device without regard to whether they are currently connected to the network. The server queue is needed as a place to safely store the incoming messages while waiting for an application to read them.

The outbound queue on the client device will continue to grow until the device is again connected to the network. At that time, the messages will be transferred from the device's queue to the server's. This transfer must, naturally, take place within the context of a transaction so that it is possible to recover from a network failure. For messages outbound from the server, the process is merely reversed. Figure 6-2 provides an illustration of the semi-connected architecture.

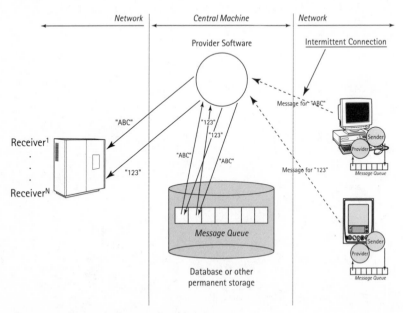

Figure 6-2: The semi-connected architecture

The main disadvantage of this architecture is that a client application can only ever be sure a message it sent was successfully committed to local storage (the device-based queues in Figure 6-2). The application – and thus the user – is never aware of when or how long it takes for the message to actually make it to the server. This is generally not a problem for messages such as e-mail or expense reports but is a big problem for time-sensitive messages such as stock trades.

While it is possible to write the client application in such a way that it always waits for a custom confirmation message – that is, a reply message from the server application – before telling the user the operation has completed, this is a messy and proprietary solution to the problem. It also negates the advantages of using a store-and-forward architecture to begin with. If your application requires reliable, immediate confirmation from the server that a message was received and processes successfully, then it is better to use a synchronous protocol such as HTTP or SOAP to communicate with the server.

THE PEER-TO-PEER ARCHITECTURE

The peer-to-peer (sometimes shortened to P2P) architecture is very similar to the semi-connected architecture, except that instead of having one server machine where all messages are consolidated into a single queue, each node communicates directly with (potentially) every other node. Even though a central server is still typically used to allow a client to locate another client (*a la* Napster), messages themselves are directly exchanged between client devices.

As with the semi-connected architecture, a peer-to-peer architecture is not ideally suited for "real-time" response – that is, when a request/reply operation must complete while a user waits. This architecture works best when operating in the background without time constraints – say, to synchronize a set of files between *Peer A* and *Peer B*. Because of the local queue, a peer architecture is able to wait out any temporary network outage and to store actions and data for later delivery to a temporarily disconnected device such as a roving laptop. Groove Networks' (http://www.groove.com) *Relay Service* works in this manner, for instance. Figure 6-3 provides an illustration of the peer-to-peer architecture.

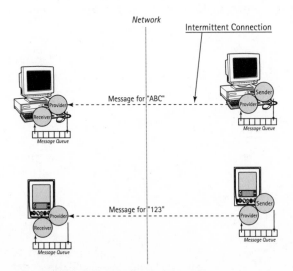

Figure 6-3: The peer-to-peer architecture

So long as messages are exchanged between just two or a few peers, the peer-to-peer architecture can work well. However, the more systems that participate in the messaging, the more connections that are required to deliver information to all interested parties. In the worst case scenario where every peer needs every message, the connections will grow exponentially in relation to the number of peers (order N^2), which can severely impact performance.

Despite all the P2P hype, it's still not clear what role this type of architecture will play in the future of computing. Because of issues such as response-time, service-ability, and traceability, it is a desirable feature of all business-oriented messages that they be funneled through a central point (the corporation), which makes either of the previous two architectures a better choice than this one for most business critical transactions.

On the other hand, perhaps we are about to enter a new era of intelligent agents and direct person-to-person communication free from the institutional intermediary, where peer-to-peer architectures like the one presented here are prevalent (though I wouldn't be betting any money on it).

Summary

The first half of this chapter covered the few APIs and concepts pertaining to point-to-point messaging that had not been dealt with in earlier chapters.

The second half of the chapter dealt with the three basic point-to-point messaging architectures a JMS product (or non-JMS product, for that matter) might use to deliver messages. Understanding how point-to-point systems might be architected from an implementation point of view can be very valuable as it gives you a basis for evaluating various vendor's products beyond the simple issue of JMS API-compliance. Keep in mind, there's no right or wrong point-to-point architecture. The best one is the one that satisfies your application requirements in the most efficient manner.

Chapter 7

Building Message-Driven Beans with EJB 2.0

THIS CHAPTER TALKS ABOUT A NEWER FEATURE of the Enterprise JavaBean (EJB) specification: the *message-driven bean*. Message-driven beans fill a big gap in the EJB model and you'll almost surely be interested in using them in any enterprise scale system you build. First we'll look into the theory behind message-driven beans — what makes them different from ordinary enterprise beans — and then we'll show some usage examples. Lastly, we'll delve into some architectural considerations related to message-driven beans.

This chapter reviews at a high level what an EJB is and how an application server manages it. However, if you do not have a good understanding of what an enterprise bean is and how it is supposed to behave, it may be a good idea to become familiar with that subject before trying to digest the material in this chapter. You can find a good primer on EJBs at `http://java.sun.com/j2ee/tutorial/doc/EJBConcepts.html`.

Working with EJBs

Beans is a generic term for Java components. In this section we'll talk about what types of beans there are because it's definitely an overloaded term in Java. You'll need to have a good grounding in Enterprise JavaBeans before being able to tackle JMS's message-driven bean.

JavaBeans versus Enterprise JavaBeans

Before getting into the details of message-driven beans, let's quickly review what the term "bean" means in the Java world and how beans typically behave. There are two bean-related terms commonly used when talking about the Java platform. The first is *JavaBeans* and the second is *Enterprise JavaBeans*.

New Java developers are often confused by the two terms and rightfully so because, despite the naming, they really don't have a lot in common except that they both mean a type of software component.

THE PLAIN JAVABEAN

A plain JavaBean is simply any Java class that conforms to a certain method naming convention. This convention is meant to facilitate the identification of the properties a component exposes to the outside world, both to humans and to design tools such as Borland's JBuilder or Sun's Forte for Java.

Unlike the more common interface model of development, the beans paradigm does not require that a class implement any particular interface in order to be a bean. It is the application of the convention that determines bean-ness; it is not something built into the language.

One of the notions defined by the JavaBeans specification is the *property*. A property is just a single data element encapsulated in the bean. The convention, or design pattern, a programmer must follow to define a bean property is to write the element's accessor methods in the following way:

Write accessor: `void set`*Name*`(`*DataType*` value)`

Read accessor: *DataType* `get`*Name*`()`

In this example, *Name* would be replaced by the actual property name and *DataType* by its Java type. So, for example, if a bean called "Login" had a property called "user" of type "String" it would be defined as follows:

```
public class Login
{
    void setUser(String user) { ... }
    String getUser() { ... }
}
```

Properties of beans are determined to be readable and/or writeable based on the presence or non-presence of read and write accessor methods in the class. For instance, consider the following Java class:

```
public class QuoteBean
{
    public float getPrice() { ... }

    public void setPrice(float px) { ... }

    public boolean isLatest() { ... }
```

```
    public String getSymbol() { ... }
}
```

The `QuoteBean` class is said to have the following properties:

◆ A read/write property "price" of type `float`.

◆ A read-only property "latest" of type `boolean`.

◆ A read-only property "symbol" of type `String`.

Notice that there is no inheritance from any particular superclass or implementation of any particular interface to identify `QuoteBean` as a JavaBean. It is only the particular coding convention employed that makes the class a bean.

Among the many valuable features of JavaBeans is the ability to programmatically find out what properties a bean supports. This is done through a process called *introspection* (using the `java.beans.Introspector` class). In the example above, introspecting the `Login` class would reveal that it had a property named "user" that was both readable and writeable.

Additionally, the introspector would give us a handle to a `java.lang.Method` object that we could use to set the property and a handle to another `Method` object that we could use to get the value of the property. This is similar to method pointers in other languages, such as C++.

See `http://java.sun.com/products/javabeans` for a complete description of JavaBeans and their associated conventions.

THE ENTERPRISE JAVABEAN

Enterprise JavaBeans are a much more formal concept than the plain Java bean (they do have, after all, a 500+ page specification!). EJBs are the core of J2EE-based component-based architecture that provides, among other things, automated transaction management, automatic persistence, and enhanced scalability through the use of pooling and clustering technologies. EJB components generally contain the bulk of the code that executes in what is often referred to as the business logic tier of an n-tiered application.

EJBs always run in a Java-based program called a *container* – more commonly known as an *application server* – that is responsible for managing the lifecycle of the bean and controlling access to it by client applications. Unlike plain JavaBeans, EJBs must implement specific interfaces and they must behave – and not behave – in certain predefined ways.

An application server sits in between the client and the EJB and mediates requests to the bean. This behavior is essential because the application server is responsible for providing the following basic services on behalf of the client and the EJB:

◆ EJB creation (instantiation)

◆ EJB passivation (allows for reduction of resources used when the bean is not being actively used)

- EJB persistence to and from underlying relational and/or object databases

- EJB destruction (garbage collection)

- Security (rejection of unauthorized access to a particular bean method)

- Transaction management (automatically includes a method call within any existing transaction if configured to do so)

An EJB can certainly be coded to the same conventions as a plain JavaBean — and at times this is desirable. However, with the exception of the entity bean, EJBs tend to be more concerned with exposing *operations* than properties. Thus, the plain JavaBean's conventions are not typically as applicable.

Though from a developer's perspective a call to an EJB method appears to be a local method call — that is, a method call that never leaves the client's JVM — calls to EJBs do, in fact, often travel over the network to another process and are proxied to the actual target EJB by the application server. If this sounds to you a lot like the way CORBA or RMI works, it should. EJBs operate on a similar remote procedure call (RPC) model as traditional object request brokers (ORBs) and, in fact, the latest EJB specification (2.0) requires Internet Inter-ORB Protocol (IIOP) as a supported mechanism for ensuring application server interoperability.

Unlike traditional ORB-based technology, however, some types of EJBs can be defined to be *stateless,* which means that separate calls to the same bean will not necessarily be invoked on the same object instance. Because they do not need to maintain any per-client information between calls to their methods, many instances of a single stateless bean can be pooled by an application server, resulting in greater overall scalability by allowing many calls to a particular bean to be served in parallel. As we'll see later in the chapter, all JMS message-driven beans are stateless EJBs.

For a fuller discussion of Enterprise JavaBeans, refer to `http://java.sun.com/products/ejb`, where you will find the specifications and other documents.

The EJB 1.1 specification

Up through the EJB 1.1 specification there were three types of beans available to a designer:

- **Entity Beans:** A shared, stateful object representing some portion of the application's data model. Represented by the class `javax.ejb.EntityBean`.

- **Stateful Session Beans:** A stateful object providing services to one particular client over the life of the client's session. The container is not required to persist these objects to permanent storage, though some do. Represented by the class `javax.ejb.SessionBean`.

- **Stateless Session Beans:** A stateless object providing service to any client on a first-come, first-served basis. Represented by the class `javax.ejb.SessionBean`.

Stateless session beans, because they are lightweight in nature and promote scalability, are the most commonly used bean.

For our purposes, the key thing to note about all these bean types, however, is that they all operate *synchronously*, meaning that they only become active in response to a method invocation made by a client application (see Figure 7-1).

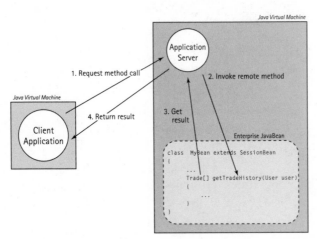

Figure 7-1: Synchronous EJB invocation

Message-driven beans

The EJB 2.0 specification defines an entirely new type of bean called the message driven bean (javax.ejb.MessageDrivenBean). Instead of becoming active in response to a specific client method call, a message-driven bean is invoked by a container in response to an incoming JMS message.

Clearly, any time your application receives a JMS message you're going to want to execute some of your business logic. Since EJBs in application servers are meant to be the place where much of an application's business logic resides, it seems logical that enterprise application designers would be very interested in receiving JMS messages directly in their EJBs. Unfortunately, prior to the advent of JMS's message-driven beans there was no simple way to set up an EJB as a JMS message consumer.

In an effort to get the behavior they desired, designers were forced to include simple proxy programs in their architectures. These proxy programs had the responsibility of listening for JMS messages, interpreting their contents, and then invoking the appropriate EJB methods with the required data. See Figure 7-2 for an illustration.

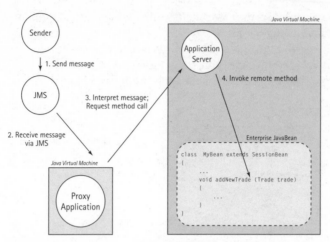

Figure 7-2: Asynchronous EJB invocation via a proxy process

While this model of service invocation certainly worked, it had several key drawbacks:

- The proxy process could not be an EJB because there was no way for an EJB to be "woken up" periodically to look for new messages or to be alerted when a message arrived. The EJB specification also explicitly disallows EJBs from managing their own network connections.

- Because the proxy process could not be an EJB, it had to be run as an independent process outside the application server. It, therefore, could not take advantage of the numerous runtime features offered by application servers, such as security, transaction management, clustering for scalability, and so on.

- There was one extra process that needed to be monitored constantly in case of failure.

To cut out the middleman, in the EJB 2.0 specification it was decided to take the two technologies that were already part of the J2EE platform – JMS and EJB – and link them more closely together. A new interface, `javax.ejb.MessageDrivenBean`, was defined for EJBs that wished to process incoming JMS messages. In addition, EJBs implementing the `MessageDrivenBean` interface must also implement the `javax.jms.MessageListener` interface just as clients operating in non-application server (standalone) environments do. Message-driven bean developers do not have to write any of the usual JMS setup code we saw in previous chapters; this is taken care of for them by the application server. All the developer needs to write is an `onMessage(Message)` method to handle the incoming messages.

In typical application server fashion, the mapping of a JMS destination to an EJB is identified in the deployment descriptor file for the bean (see the "Writing and

Deploying Message-driven Beans" section later in this chapter for an example of how to define an appropriate bean descriptor). The application server is responsible for performing all the housekeeping associated with connecting to the JMS provider, looking up destinations, and registering code callbacks for incoming messages.

Figure 7-3 illustrates how message-driven beans are invoked in response to the receipt of a JMS message.

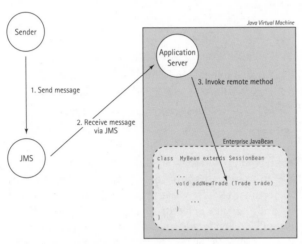

Figure 7-3: Asynchronous EJB invocation via JMS

APPLICATION SERVER BEHAVIORS

In most respects, a message-driven bean is treated the same as a stateless session bean inside an application server. This means that most application servers will allow you to administratively configure the bean so that a pool of bean instances will be created at runtime. Each member of the pool is equivalent and the first free one is assigned to handle the next incoming message. Similarly to stateless session beans, this also means that clients cannot expect message-driven beans to maintain state in between invocations of their `onMessage(Message)` method.

While this pooling capability can greatly increase the scalability of your application, it's important to note how the behavior differs from that of a JMS message consumer running in a standalone application. As we saw in Chapter 4, JMS sessions are single-threaded and all messages received in a JMS session will be distributed to the appropriate consumer object in a serial manner, which means that all incoming messages will be processed in exactly the order they arrived at your application.

In an application server using a pooled set of message-driven beans, however, you have no order-processing guarantee. Though the application server itself receives JMS messages in the correct order, it immediately passes them on to one of the pooled bean instances. Because each bean instance will be running in its own thread, it is possible – depending on how the threads are scheduled – for a bean instance that was assigned a message after another instance was assigned a previous message to end up being executed first. The only way to ensure incoming messages are processed serially is to administratively configure the application server to limit the number of pooled message-driven instances to one.

Of course, you should always try to design your application in such a way that you can make full use of the application server's pooling capabilities by not requiring that messages must be processed strictly serially. You will achieve much higher message throughput and scalability if you do.

 Like stateless session beans, multiple instances of a message-driven bean may be active at the same time, but each individual instance is guaranteed to be allowed to complete its onMessage() method before receiving another message. In technical terms, the instances are *not* re-entrant.

Also, unlike a normal JMS consumer where you can use a single message listener object to handle messages from more than one destination and/or messages matching a variety of message selectors, it's likely that your application server will only let you tie one destination and message selector to any particular message-driven bean pool. This generally will not be something you need to be concerned with when developing your message-driven beans. It can, however, have some impact on the amount of resources your application ends up consuming. Be sure to consult your application server's documentation before engaging in any tuning exercise.

 As is usual with the first pass at a new EJB technology, Sun has deferred the specification of a service-provider interface for message-driven beans until a later time. There is currently no standard way to plug in an arbitrary vendor's JMS product into another arbitrary vendor's application server product. (If you're interested, this is being addressed by the *J2EE Connector Architecture 2.0*.) This does not mean it's not possible, it just depends on whether the vendor's application server you are using supports it or not. Before committing to an application server product, be sure to find out what vendor's JMS products are guaranteed to work with it and whether those JMS products have all the features you need.

Writing and Deploying Message-Driven Beans

In this section you'll see how easy it is to write a message-driven bean. We'll also look at a sample *deployment descriptor* that is used to, among other things, tell an application server which messages your bean is interested in receiving.

The bean code

Like a regular JMS message listener, a message-driven bean is very simple to write. The meat of the logic will be in, or called by, the bean's `onMessage()` method. Unlike regular EJBs, message-driven beans have no `EJBHome` or `Remote` interfaces that must be implemented because they cannot be looked up or invoked by any conventional client.

Also, like regular JMS listeners, an EJB `onMessage()` method has no return value and should never throw a `RuntimeException`. If the bean instance ever does throw an exception, it is immediately invalidated and removed from the container's pool of available beans.

Finally, because the container is solely responsible for receiving JMS messages and distributing them to the appropriate message-driven bean instance, your bean should never attempt to manipulate any JMS message listener objects directly by calling `javax.jms.MessageConsumer.setMessageListener()` or `javax.jms.MessageConsumer.getMessageListener()`.

Code Listing 7-1 shows an example of a simple message-driven bean.

TIP If you're using the ant build tool to compile your message-driven beans, be sure to check out the ant home page at `http://jakarta.apache.org/ant`. There are many task modules available for managing the creation and deployment of EJBs for the various application servers that might make your life easier. If there aren't any available for your vendor's product, remember that ant is extensible so you can always write your own modules.

Listing 7-1: A message-driven bean example

```
import javax.ejb.*;
import javax.jms.*;

public class TicketPurchaseService
            implements javax.ejb.MessageDrivenBean,
                       javax.jms.MessageListener
{
```

Continued

Listing 7-1 *(Continued)*

```
    MessageDrivenContext context;

    // A public no-args constructor is required
    public TicketPurchaseService() {}

    // All methods are required by the
    // MessageDrivenBean interface

    public void ejbCreate() {}

    public void ejbRemove() {}

    public void setMessageDrivenContext(MessageDrivenContext context)
    {
        this.context = context;
    }

    // This method is required by the javax.jms.MessageListener
interface
    public void onMessage(Message msg)
    {
        // Process the message as in normal JMS MessageListener.
        // Perhaps you'll want to examine the message and invoke
        // one or more other EJB services. Perhaps you'll want
        // to send out a JMS message somewhere. The full range
        // of EJB capabilities is available here.

        // Do not attempt to call msg.acknowledge() under
        // any circumstances. All messages will be automatically
        // acknowledged by the container in the manner specified
        // in the bean's deployment descriptor.

    }
}
```

The `javax.ejb.MessageDrivenContext` you see in the code sample from Listing 7-1 is similar to the standard `javx.ejb.EJBContext` supplied by the container to other enterprise beans. In fact, as of EJB 2.0, `MessageDrivenContext` is nothing more than an empty subclass of `EJBContext`. Note, however, that the methods `getCallerInRole()` and `getCallerPrinicpal()` cannot be used inside a message-driven bean because they refer to information about the client that invoked a bean. Since the container does not necessarily know anything at all about the client that sends a message to a message-driven bean, these context methods are useless.

What if you want to invoke your message-driven bean from another EJB? Message-driven beans have no `javax.ejb.EJBHome` interface so there's no way to look them up and call them as you would a normal enterprise bean. The answer is simple — just send it a message. As we saw in the last chapter, any EJB can easily use JMS to send a message anywhere. As long as you address the message properly, it will be picked up by the desired message-driven bean in your application server.

The deployment descriptor

As mentioned earlier in this chapter, the message-driven bean deployment descriptor has three main purposes:

◆ Associate a `Topic` or `Queue` and, optionally, a message selector with a particular bean class.

◆ Specify by what means the bean desires to receive messages: point-to-point, regular pub/sub, or durable pub/sub.

◆ Specify the transaction type or JMS acknowledgment mode for messages.

EJB deployment descriptors are simple XML-based files that get packaged up along with the bean `.class` files in a `.jar` archive file. This `.jar` file is then deployed as a unit to the application server. Message-driven bean deployments typically require two descriptor files: one called `ejb-jar.xml` and another with a proprietary name. The structure of the former file is governed by the EJB specification and is standard across application server vendors. The latter's structure is specific to a particular vendor.

Listing 7-2 shows an example of the portion of the standard `ejb_jar.xml` file descriptor that deals with message-driven beans.

Listing 7-2: A J2EE standard message-driven bean deployment

```
<?xml version="1.0"?>

<!DOCTYPE ejb-jar PUBLIC "-//Sun Microsystems, Inc.//DTD Enterprise
JavaBeans 2.0//EN" "http://java.sun.com/dtd/ejb-jar_2_0.dtd">

<ejb-jar>

  <enterprise-beans>

    <message-driven>
```

Continued

Listing 7-2 *(Continued)*

```
      <ejb-name>ticketService</ejb-name>

      <ejb-class>TicketPurchaseService</ejb-class>

      <transaction-type>Container</transaction-type>

      <message-driven-destination>

        <destination-type>javax.jms.Queue</destination-type>

      </message-driven-destination>

    </message-driven>

  </enterprise-beans>
```

Listing 7-3 shows an example of WebLogic's proprietary descriptor; it is used to associate the bean instance with a sample Queue destination that was previously configured to be looked up via the Java Naming and Directory Interface (JNDI).

Listing 7-3: A sample WebLogic 6.1 message-driven bean deployment descriptor

```
<?xml version="1.0"?>

<!DOCTYPE weblogic-ejb-jar PUBLIC "-//BEA Systems, Inc.//DTD
WebLogic 6.0.0 EJB//EN"
"http://www.bea.com/servers/wls600/dtd/weblogic-ejb-jar.dtd">

<weblogic-ejb-jar>

  <weblogic-enterprise-bean>

    <ejb-name>ticketService</ejb-name>

    <message-driven-descriptor>

      <pool>
        <max-beans-in-free-pool>50</max-beans-in-free-pool>
        <initial-beans-in-free-pool>10</initial-beans-in-free-pool>
      </pool>

      <destination-jndi-name>BUYTICKETS</destination-jndi-name>

    </message-driven-descriptor>
```

```
  </weblogic-enterprise-bean>

</weblogic-ejb-jar>
```

Notice the use of the `<pool>`...`</pool>` block to indicate how WebLogic should manage the number of instances of the `TicketPurchaseService` bean in the pool of objects it creates. You'll need to refer to your application server vendor's documentation for complete details on how to properly configure a deployment descriptor for their particular product.

Creating Message-Driven Architectures

Now that it's possible to create enterprise beans that are invoked asynchronously, it's reasonable to ask how you might leverage them in your system to create more efficient and functional architectures. We'll explore this area in example form later in Part III of this book, but for now I'll outline the three main ways in which you might design your system based on message-driven beans.

Queue-based architectures

Queues are valuable architectural devices that will likely serve in some capacity in any large-scale enterprise system. Often, queue technology provides data transfer services between a mainframe and a microcomputer environment because – due to the difference in data representation and networking technology – it's the only convenient software that understands both worlds. This is the main reason IBM's MQSeries technology has become so popular.

In more general terms, though, what a queue does is serve as a buffer between two environments. This buffer helps hide the difference between two systems or processes that operate at very different speeds. By buffering in this way, you enable each application to operate at its maximum speed without having to wait for the other one to complete each operation before proceeding to the next. Thus, at times it will make sense to incorporate a queue into your architecture even when the applications at each end of the queue are based on the same technology and running on the same machine.

Of course, buffering will do little good if the message sender is consistently faster than the receiver. The buffer will simply continue to grow indefinitely. Only when the average speed of each process is roughly equal, over whatever time period you deem appropriate, will the insertion of a queue between the sender and receiver prove to be useful. In other words, queues are good at evening out spurts of traffic.

For example, say you have an online store that is able to accept purchase requests in the Web tier at a maximum rate of 1,000 per minute. Your midtier order processing application server can only process orders – validate them, put them in the database, send them to the order fulfillment system, and so on – at the maximum rate of 500 per minute. Figure 7-4 shows a synchronous architecture for supporting this scenario.

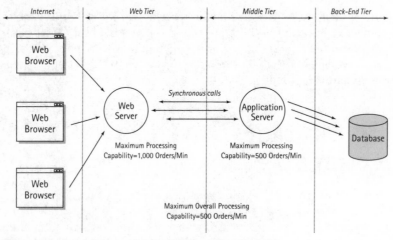

Figure 7-4: A synchronous architecture for online shopping

Because each order must be processed fully by the middle tier before proceeding with the next order, the maximum processing rate of this system is 500 per minute. If your daily load looks something like what appears in Figure 7-5, then clearly you will have to defer about 250 orders per minute to non-peak periods. Naturally, not all of those 250 customers will want to return to your site when the load is lower, and you will wind up losing business.

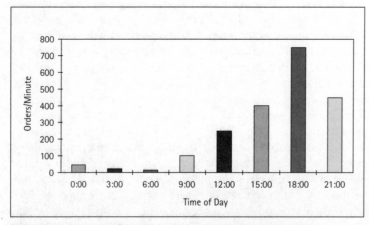

Figure 7-5: Average daily order volume of a sample online store

One solution to this problem, of course, is to upgrade your infrastructure – CPU, disk, database, network, and so on – to enable your midtier to support 750 orders per minute. On the other hand, had you inserted a queue between the Web tier and the application server tier in the first place, you'd be in a position not only to handle the current peak load of 750, but you could even handle the Web server's maximum load, which is 1,000, all without having to engage in a costly infrastructure upgrade.

As long as the peaks do not persist over long stretches of time, the queue will be able to safely hold the orders in nonvolatile storage outside the application server until it is capable of processing them. Figure 7-6 illustrates an application server front-ended by a queue. Note that until message-driven beans became available, it would not have been easy to implement a front-end buffering architecture like this.

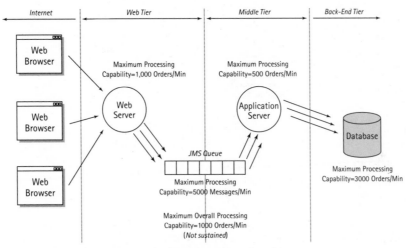

Figure 7-6: A queue-based architecture for online shopping

With a queue buffering architecture, a simple and useful performance analysis exercise is to chart queue size (the number of pending messages in the queue) over time to help determine when it becomes necessary to upgrade the middle tier. If the maximum average queue size is increasing over time, then that means the middle tier is not keeping up with the incoming messages as well as it used to and probably needs to have its operating environment enhanced. Many JMS providers supply tools that allow you to see the number of unprocessed messages sitting in the queue at any given time; charting the queue size over time will help identify any performance degradation.

An upgrade of the middle tier might involve hardware infrastructure, or it might involve employing additional application servers. Additional application servers could be added in a clustered manner if your vendor supports clustering, or in an unclustered manner because more than one program can read from a single queue at a time.

Because point-to-point messages are doled out on a first-come-first-served basis, it is easy to add additional processes — even ones running on separate machines — to increase the overall throughput of your system. Figure 7-7 shows a simple example of using multiple processes and machines in the middle tier to balance a load. As long as your design is tolerant of messages being processed out of order, this architecture will help to increase your system's scalability.

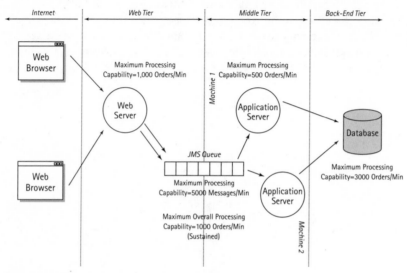

Figure 7-7: Using a queue to increase scalability

Note, of course, that your overall scalability is always going to be limited by whatever your slowest single point of contention is. For example, say you have a system that currently has a peak load of 500 transactions-per-minute (TPM) being fed to an application server on a single machine; the application server itself can handle at most 700 TPM and the back-end database it uses, 800 TPM. If the incoming message load were to jump to 1,000, then one way to tackle the problem would be to add another application server on a separate machine and have both application servers split the message load; each would process roughly a 500 TPM load. However, if both application servers still accessed the same back-end database, then the overall system will not be able to keep up with the incoming messages because the capacity of the database has not been increased to meet the new 1,000 TPM requirement.

Pub/sub architectures

As we saw in earlier chapters, (non-durable) pub/sub systems are generally geared toward super-high-volume messaging over a large number of consumers. This is usually achieved at the cost of some degree of delivery reliability. Middle-tier systems like application servers, on the other hand, are geared toward maximum reliability and are expected to properly field every request thrown at them. This is why pub/sub messaging is usually used at the periphery of an enterprise system, whereas queue-based messaging is used in the core.

Rules always have exceptions, though, and, given the right circumstances, a case can certainly be made for writing message-driven beans that respond to pub/sub messages. Just keep in mind that an application server is meant to support many different components simultaneously and you never want to be in the position of dragging down the performance of all applications because one of them is forcing the container to deal with the large number of pub/sub messages you might receive in some high performance messaging environments, such as trading floors. Figure 7-8 shows a pub/sub architecture using message-driven beans.

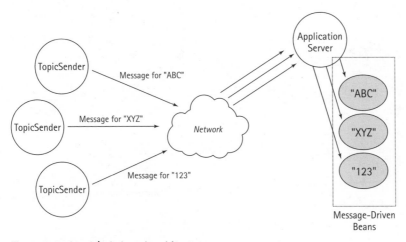

Figure 7-8: A pub/sub-based architecture

Request/reply architectures

You can use the request/reply messaging model to implement service-based architecture using message-driven beans. As we saw in the previous chapter, any EJB has the capability to send a message using JMS. Message-driven beans can be used to receive a message, do some processing, and then respond to the caller specified in the **JMSReplyTo** message property.

Because EJBs already provide a perfectly adequate RPC-style calling capability (that is, blocking), when might you prefer to use a message-driven bean to front-end your service as opposed to a session bean? There are two possible reasons:

◆ You want to offer your EJB-based service to clients who cannot make direct calls to your application server but do have access to your messaging bus.

◆ Your clients are making requests that are not particularly response-time-sensitive and you'd rather not have your application block while waiting for a long-running operation to complete.

The first case provides access to your EJB services by applications written in other languages such as COBOL, for example. The second case addresses clients that initiate long-running operations – for example, the generation of a PDF report file. From a client application perspective, a request/reply architecture in which message-driven beans fulfill the service request would look no different than if any other application provided the service. The client could use a `TopicRequestor` or `QueueRequestor` just as described in Chapters 5 and 6. Figure 7-9 illustrates request/reply using message-driven beans.

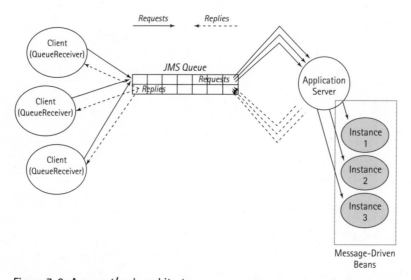

Figure 7-9: A request/reply architecture

 For the time being, message-driven beans are limited to being invoked in response to a JMS message. Future versions of EJB technology will likely allow for bean invocation based on other types of asynchronous messaging.

Summary

Hopefully, this chapter has given you a good taste of how asynchronous messaging can play a vital role in any enterprise architecture. If the service layer of such a system is EJB-based, then the message-driven bean will be the tool you need to messaging-enable your application server.

Another emerging J2EE technology in this same space is the *connector*. In some places, connectors complement JMS and in others you can use them instead of it to accomplish your inter-process communication goals. Because it is not a JMS technology, this book does not discuss connectors. However, you should become familiar with the technology and its capabilities before embarking upon a new architecture that interfaces with legacy systems. Connectors are also being used as a basis for providing a standard interface for JMS providers to integrate their products into application servers, thus improving the plug-and-play capability of the J2EE platform. You can find more information in the "J2EE Connector Architecture Specification" at the Java Community Process Web site (`http://jcp.org`).

Chapter 8

JMS Transactions

THIS CHAPTER COVERS THE SUBJECT OF JMS AND TRANSACTIONS. Understanding all the details of transactional behavior in any technology can be daunting. Fortunately, JMS has reduced to a bare minimum the amount of coding required to manage transactions – at least for the most common cases developers will encounter.

Even if the transaction-specific portions of the API are easily mastered, it is still critical to understand exactly what portions of the message's journey are protected by a transaction and which ones are not. It's sometimes too easy to assume in JMS that just by using the transactional API that nothing can go wrong with message delivery. We'll see why this is not the case and how best to plan for it.

Understanding JMS Transactions

In this section I'll cover some of the key issues pertaining to how JMS transactions behave and what you'll need to watch out for. We'll start by looking at how some of the various J2EE technologies make use of transactions and then move on to a discussion of how JMS uses transactions.

JTS, JTA, EJB, and connectors

Before getting into a discussion of JMS and transactions, let's first review a few concepts. From a technology point of view the J2EE platform has four main technologies supporting transactions in applications:

◆ Java Transaction Service (JTS)

◆ Java Transaction API (JTA)

◆ Enterprise JavaBeans (EJB)

◆ Connectors

JTS is an API that defines a Java language binding to products that are built to the Object Management Group's (OMG) CORBA Object Transaction Service (OTS) specification. As such, you can think of JTS as an API for a specific type of distributed transaction service.

JTA is more similar to other Java APIs in that it is an API that defines an abstraction to a generic distributed transaction service much in the same way that JMS is an API that defines an abstraction to a generic message service. JTA may use a JTS implementation as its underlying mechanism, or it may not. When programming with JMS, you do not need to be concerned with JTS, only JTA. Any JMS product that you buy may be using JTS under the covers but, as a developer, that will never be exposed to you.

EJB technology is designed to work with JTA. However, one of the services EJB containers provide for you is automated transaction management. Because transactional behavior can be configured administratively on a per-method basis using EJBs, it is entirely possible that you will never have to directly access JTA in your EJB code, either. Of course, it is still possible to manage your own transactions, if necessary, in EJBs.

Connectors are a relatively new addition to the J2EE platform. The main purpose of Connectors is to provide a platform-independent way of connecting a J2EE application server to an existing system, such as CICS, R/3, SAP, and so on. Connector-based software also provides support for JTA-based transactions. Connectors and JMS are not directly related, though each is often used to connect to legacy systems. When designing a system that will need to interface with legacy software, you should investigate the possibility of using both connectors and JMS in order to make an informed decision as to which is the best fit for your requirements and environment.

JMS transaction behavior

Regarding transactional behavior in JMS, the following sub-sections address a variety of issues that will be important for you to understand in order to design a completely safe and reliable system built using the transaction technology supported by JMS providers.

TRANSACTIONS ARE THREAD-CENTRIC

In JMS, transactions are managed on a per-session basis. This means that all activity related to a particular session object (that is, a `QueueSession` or a `TopicSession`) can be either committed or rolled back as a unit (we'll get into the specific method calls in the code examples later in this chapter), but you cannot combine operations from different sessions into the same transaction. It's therefore not possible, for example, to receive a point-to-point message and send a pub/sub message all in a single transaction because a topic session and a queue session can never be managed by the same session object. It is possible, however, to receive a point-to-point message and turn around and send another point-to-point message in the same transaction, provided you do so through the same session object.

To see why this is so, you have to understand how transactions based on JTA work. JTA defines a class called `javax.transaction.UserTransaction`. User transactions are managed on a per-thread basis; all JTA-aware activity in a given thread is automatically associated with whatever the current `UserTransaction` is, if any. While this is a dramatic simplification for the developer who no longer needs to write a lot of transaction housekeeping code, it does limit the scope of what can be included in a transaction to the current thread.

To make this discussion more concrete, remember from Chapter 4 that the receipt of a message occurs asynchronously via a JMS message listener – that is, using `MessageListener.onMessage()` – and always takes place in the context of the delivering session's thread. Naturally, a call to `QueueSender.send()` from a `TopicSubscriber`'s `onMessage()` callback, for example, would, by definition, be a call from a method running in one thread to a method executing in another thread. Because of the way JTA works, the transaction context in the `onMessage()` method could not be propagated across this boundary. Figure 8-1 depicts this concept.

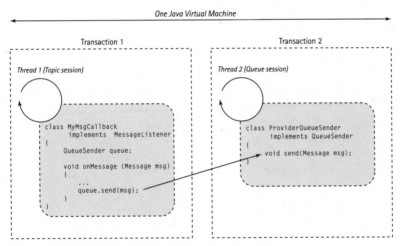

Figure 8-1: Transactions cannot span multiple thread

TRANSACTION BOUNDARIES

While it's important to understand the scope of what a transaction covers within your application, this only really comes into play if you're using multiple JMS sessions in your application. Unless you're transferring messages between JMS providers or between a single provider's pub/sub and point-to-point implementation, a single session is probably all most JMS developers will ever manipulate directly within a single application. In such a case, JMS transactions will work easily and fairly transparently for you.

With the advent of message-driven beans (discussed in Chapter 7), many developers are writing EJBs that access JMS as well. In this case, multiple sessions will exist at the same time, but you're generally still only going to be using one at a time (and, in any case, these sessions are managed for you by the EJB container).

While in most cases the JMS developer can sidestep the intricacies of low-level transaction behaviors, the architect cannot. As we've pointed out often, many points of possible failure exist in any distributed messaging system that could result in the loss of messages. One of the reasons for using transactions is, of course, to eliminate the possibility of lost information.

From an architectural perspective, however, it's very important to understand that JMS systems do not provide complete end-to-end message-delivery guarantees – at least not all within a single transaction. Messages are guaranteed to be delivered within the boundaries of the immediate transaction, but the process always requires more than one transaction for a message to be delivered to its ultimate destination. In other words, JMS transactional semantics are defined in terms of these boundaries, not in terms of the complete message transmission.

In the case of a point-to-point message or a durable topic subscription message, for instance, the following two transactions are required to get a message from the sender to the receiver:

1. Between the sender and the provider-managed queue

2. Between the queue and the receiver

Of course, it would be technologically possible to combine both operations into a single distributed transaction but to do so would violate the asynchronous nature of JMS delivery semantics. One advantage of asynchronous delivery is that senders do not need to be concerned with whether a message's recipient is available at the moment the message is delivered. On the other hand, the sender can never be sure the message ultimately made it to the destination or that it made it within any particular time frame.

This means that, from the sender's perspective, the successful completion of a send() call within a transaction has no meaning other than that the provider accepted the message and will make its best effort to deliver the message in the future. If the receiving application has failed or never existed, then the message either sits in the delivery queue forever or expires and is silently discarded.

Figure 8-2 shows the transaction boundaries for point-to-point message delivery.

There are always limits to what you can design into a system to enable it to adequately recover from all manner of possible failures. As anyone who has ever had to support a production system on a daily basis knows, a good understanding of where a system can fail is critical to the quick diagnosis and resolution of problems because those weaknesses are the first places to check when something goes wrong.

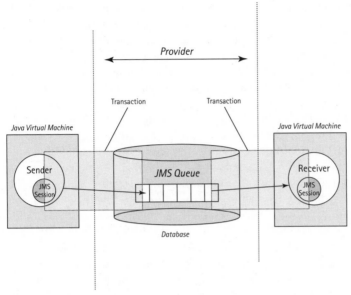

Figure 8-2: Transaction boundaries for a point-to-point message

 The procedures and processes required to support a production enterprise system are rarely included up front in the project plan because they just add time and cost to a system that everybody wants to be rolled out in a few months. But they are just as critical to the success of an application as the business logic and messaging components. For JMS-based systems, the most important maintenance feature is message traceability. Strategies for ensuring that all messages — even ones sent via transactionalized, persistent messaging — make it to their destination should perhaps include tasks such as the daily running of "break" reports of messages received on one system to those received on another, and the automatic analysis of your JMS provider's log files for anomalies such as expired messages and system errors.

COMBINING JMS TRANSACTIONS WITH OTHER TRANSACTIONS

For most server-based applications, receiving a message within the context of a transaction is ideal for ensuring the correct receipt of every message – but the story generally doesn't end there. Often a server application takes that message and creates a record in the database based on the information it contains. Database developers are used to employing transactions to ensure the relational integrity of the information in persistent storage. Consequently, the standard techniques using Java Database Connectivity (JDBC) are more than adequate for this purpose.

But as we discussed in the preceding section, two independent transactions are not better than one when it comes to reliability because you have no means to roll back the first transaction if the second one fails. Fortunately, JMS defines a way in which providers can expose their JMS activity as an XA operation, which means that you can use an external transaction manager to combine JMS activity with other XA-aware activity, such as database inserts and updates. For client-side JMS developers interested in using the XA capabilities of JMS, you will need to get a handle to the particular transaction manager object you are using and enlist the appropriate JMS session with the transaction manager. You will then need to explicitly demarcate the beginning and end of your transactions using the transaction manager. When using JMS XA sessions in this manner, you should create your sessions to be non-transacted because creating a transacted session implies that the JMS provider will be managing its own local transaction and this is not what you want. The `javax.transaction.TransactionManager` interface defines the API for an abstract transaction manager. The way in which you get a handle to a transaction manager will depend on the particular installation you are using, however.

For server-side developers writing message-driven beans, the situation is greatly simplified. Any enlistment of XA resources, including JMS sessions, will be handled at the administrative level so it will not be a concern for you as a developer—there's no special code you'll need to write to manage the activity of the transaction manager.

Using a global transaction manager based on XA, any activity that can be exposed as an XA resource (see the Javadoc for `javax.transaction.xa.XAResource`) activity can be included in the transaction that encloses a JMS send or receive operation. JDBC and JMS itself are just the two most prominent examples. Figure 8-3 illustrates this behavior.

Unfortunately, combining activities such as this into a single distributed transaction requires that your provider support XA—your sessions will be an instance of `javax.jms.XASession`—but JMS does not specifically require that they do so. If your provider does support XA transactions you'll probably need to enable this behavior on a per connection basis through your provider's administration tools (see Chapter 12 for an example of how to do this).

PUB/SUB MESSAGING AND TRANSACTIONS

Even if you've opted not to try to guarantee delivery of messages in your system — say, for example, you've chosen to implement pub/sub messaging because it's okay if you happen to lose a message every once in a while — JMS transactions can still be invaluable.

We can easily replace the point-to-point messaging in Figure 8-3 with pub/sub messaging, as shown in Figure 8-4.

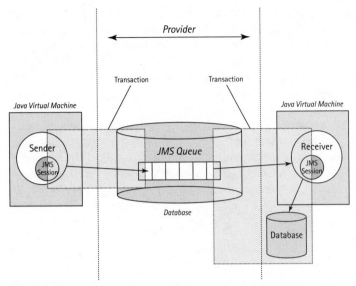

Figure 8-3: Non-JMS activity can be included in a transaction.

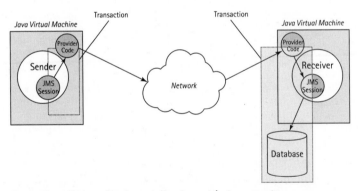

Figure 8-4: Transaction boundaries for pub/sub messaging

This alternative does not change much inside the sender or receiver code but we've now dramatically changed the system's failure characteristics. Whereas before we knew that a message would – short of an exceptional system failure – always make it to its destination, we have no such guarantee any more. With transactionalized point-to-point messaging, where each message is shepherded hop-by-hop en route to its destination within the safety of a transaction, transactionalized (nondurable) pub/sub messages are only ensured to make it to the provider's code – not across the network.

This situation opens up the question of what value transactions have when using nondurable pub/sub messaging. If you are not combining a message send or receive operation with another transactionalized operation, the answer is not much.

However, as previously mentioned, it is frequently a requirement that all received messages result in something being stored in the database. In this case, being able to include a database modification inside the same transaction that receives the message can be quite important – you may not be guaranteed to receive every message, but for each message you do receive, a transaction will ensure that all associated activity completes successfully.

Unlike many point-to-point scenarios where you're likely to incorporate transactions on both the sending and receiving ends to help ensure delivery, non-durable pub/sub scenarios generally don't require a transaction on the sending side (unless, of course, you have database activity related to the send), just the receiving one. Using a transaction on the sending side won't buy you much because, though you guarantee the provider has received the message properly, the provider itself makes no guarantee as to the message's ultimate delivery. Figure 8-5 illustrates a typical pub/sub scenario.

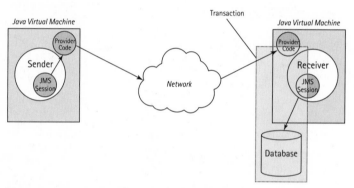

Figure 8-5: A better pub/sub transaction scenario

SENDS AND RECEIVES INCLUDED

All activity with a given JMS session can be transactionalized. It's important to remember that this includes both the receipt and sending of messages, as long as both are done via the same session. This is very valuable if your application is sending out messages based on the messages it receives – request/reply messaging is a prime example.

There's no requirement that a transaction be committed at the end of each message send or receive. The commit can be done in batch form after the receipt of several messages and/or several sends. But it's also important to think through the consequences of using a single session to send and receive messages if the outgoing messages bear no relation to the incoming ones. It may be better to use one session for sending and another one for receiving rather than tying up the outgoing messages with the incoming ones. This could particularly be a problem if one developer writes the sending code and another developer writes the receiving because each may not be entirely aware of how the other is using the transaction. The receiving code, for instance, may only commit a transaction after receiving X number of messages, which would have the effect of delaying the delivery of the sender's messages for some time.

IMPLICATIONS OF COMMIT()

A JMS session object has two methods that have meaning only for transacted sessions: commit() and rollback(). You must actively call the commit() method on the appropriate session object to conclude the transaction (see the following code examples). As soon as you do this, all pending activity is committed at once. In the case where you're sending several messages in the same transaction (i.e. the messages are batched), this means that all pending messages will be delivered to the provider only when commit() is called.

Because message acknowledgment (see Chapter 4) is automatic when using transactions, calling commit() also causes all messages received since the last call to commit() to be acknowledged to the provider. You should never try to explicitly acknowledge messages when using a transactioned JMS session. Your provider will not complain if you call acknowledge(), but messages will not truly be acknowledged until you call commit(). This will become apparent if you later roll back an uncommitted transaction when messages you thought you had acknowledged are retransmitted to you.

Committing the current transaction also has the effect of beginning a new transaction that all subsequent activity will be included in. You do not need to actively call a begin() method of any sort to start a new transaction; this is done automatically for you by the provider immediately after a commit().

Since JMS is not managing the transaction when it is part of an XA transaction, calling the normal commit() on a session that is part of a distributed transaction will cause a javax.jms.TransactionInProgressException to be thrown.

IMPLICATIONS OF ROLLBACK()

Should your application encounter a problem prior to or during a transaction commitment, it is possible to use the rollback() method — on the same session object on which you'd call commit() — to throw away all pending activity and start anew. If there are messages waiting to be sent, rolling back a transaction causes any such messages to be discarded.

Likewise, any previously received messages — because they will not have been acknowledged — will be redelivered to your application. For this reason, it's important to be sure that any and all activity that takes place in your application as the result of a message receipt takes place in the context of a transaction so it, too, can be rolled back.

To the extent you're executing business logic inside your application that cannot participate in a transaction, and thus cannot be automatically rolled back, you'll have to write explicit code to undo previous operations upon rollback or to examine the **JMSRedelivered** property on each message so as not to perform certain operations if a message is being received a second time. The Memento pattern from the *Design Patterns* book by Gamma, Helm, Johnson, and Vlissides may help you design your application in a way that allows certain operations to be undone (i.e. rolled back).

Writing Transactional Code

In this section we'll run through some sample source code that will help illustrate the behavior you'll see when using JMS's transactionalized sessions.

Receiving messages in a transaction

Receiving messages within a transaction is very similar to receiving them in a non-transacted session. The main difference stems from the need to keep a handle to the appropriate session object around in order to use it to commit the transaction. This make it difficult to use the same message listener instance to process messages received via two different sessions. Because you have no way to retrieve the session that produced a message from the message itself, it's best to store away the session handle inside the message listener object (see Listing 8-1 and Listing 8-4 for examples).

The other difference is the use of `Session.commit()` instead of `Message.acknowledge()`. This also makes it impractical to use the same message listener class for both transacted and nontransacted sessions, though of course you could call `Session.getTransacted()` and alter behavior in your message handler accordingly if you really want to use the same class for both types of sessions.

Remember that committing a transaction also has the side effect of acknowledging any unacknowledged messages the same as calling `acknowledge()` did in the examples in Chapter 4. In addition, rolling back the transaction results in the redelivery of all messages received since the last commit.

The JMS API makes the incorporation of transactional behavior very simple for the programmer. As previously mentioned, it all centers around a JMS session. All you need to do is be sure to specify that you want a session to be transactionalized when you create it using `TopicConnectionFactory` or `QueueConnectionFactory`.

Listing 8-1 shows a program that sets itself up as a listener for both pub/sub and point-to-point messages. As you can see, the difference in creating a nontransactionalized and transactionalized session is extremely minor; otherwise the code in `main()` looks very much like the code we've seen in other examples, such as those from Listings 4-5 and 4-6 in Chapter 4. The message handler in Listing 8-1 is slightly different from those shown previously, though; this one keeps track of the session object associated with the messages it is processing and replaces calls to `acknowledge()` with calls to `commit()`.

For illustrative purposes I've designed the message handler to arbitrarily roll back the current transaction for every third message it receives; otherwise, `commit()` is called after each message is received. If you run the Listing 8-1 program and send messages to it using either sample program from Chapter 3 (Listing 3-3 or 3-4), you'll see that after a roll back the last message received will immediately be redelivered to the handler. The **JMSRedelivered** property can be checked to verify that a message is being delivered for a second time.

Listing 8-1: A program illustrating the creation of transacted sessions and the effects of the rollback() method

```java
import javax.jms.*;
import javax.naming.*;
import java.util.*;

public class JMSTransaction
{
    public static class MessageHandler implements MessageListener
    {
        Session session;
        String id;

        int cnt=0;

        public MessageHandler(Session session, String id)
        {
            this.session = session;
            this.id = id;
        }

        public void onMessage(Message msg)
        {
            // If message type is unexpected, just ACK it
            if (!(msg instanceof MapMessage))
            {
                try { session.commit(); }
                catch (JMSException e) {}
            }

            MapMessage mm = (MapMessage) msg;

            try
            {
                System.out.println("New Message Received. Was
Redelivered? " +
                        msg.getJMSRedelivered());

                if (++cnt % 3 == 0)
                {
                    System.out.println("ROLLBACK");
                    session.rollback();
                    return;
                }
```

Continued

Listing 8-1 *(Continued)*

```
                System.out.println("Handler = " + id +
                        ";  ProductID = " +
mm.getString("ProductID") +
                        ";  Quantity = " +
mm.getInt("Quantity"));
            }
            catch (JMSException ex)
            {
                // Unexpected error encountered
                ex.printStackTrace();
                return;
            }

            System.out.println("COMMIT");
            try { session.commit(); }
            catch (JMSException e) {}
        }
    }

    public static void main(String[] args) throws Exception
    {
        try
        {
            // Context is loaded from the jndi.properties file
            Context context = new InitialContext();

            // Pub/sub set up
            TopicConnectionFactory tcFactory =
                    (TopicConnectionFactory)
context.lookup("TOPICFACTORY");

            TopicConnection topicConn =
                    tcFactory.createTopicConnection();

            // Use 0 instead of an acknowledgment constant
            TopicSession tcSession =
topicConn.createTopicSession(true, 0);


            // Point-to-point set up
            QueueConnectionFactory qcFactory =
                    (QueueConnectionFactory)
context.lookup("QUEUEFACTORY");
```

```
            QueueConnection queueConn =
                    qcFactory.createQueueConnection();

            // Use 0 instead of an acknowledgment constant
            QueueSession qcSession =
queueConn.createQueueSession(true, 0);

            // Create a pub/sub consumer
            Topic topic = (Topic) context.lookup("PUBSUBNAME");

            TopicSubscriber tsubscriber =
tcSession.createSubscriber(topic);

            tsubscriber.setMessageListener(
                    new MessageHandler(tcSession, "PUB/SUB
MESSAGES"));

            // Create a queue consumer
            Queue queue = (Queue) context.lookup("QUEUENAME");

            QueueReceiver qreceiver =
qcSession.createReceiver(queue);

            qreceiver.setMessageListener(
                    new MessageHandler(qcSession, "QUEUE MESSAGES"));

            // Allow messages to be delivered

            topicConn.start();
            queueConn.start();

            Thread.sleep(60 * 60 * 1000);
        }
        catch (NamingException ex)
        {
            ex.printStackTrace();
        }
        catch (JMSException ex)
        {
            ex.printStackTrace();
        }
    }
}
```

Listing 8-2 shows an ant build.xml file that can be used to compile and run the example from Listing 8-1; the run target is runtrantest. Listing 8-3 shows the output you would see after sending three messages – either pub/sub or point-to-point messages – to the program.

Listing 8-2: An ant build.xml file for Listing 8-1 using WebLogic 6.1

```xml
<project name="JMSTest" default="compile" basedir=".">

  <property name="WL_HOME" value="c:/wlserver6.1" />
  <property name="jmslib" value="${WL_HOME}/lib/weblogic.jar"/>

  <path id="runclasspath">
    <pathelement location="."/>
    <pathelement location="./classes"/>
    <pathelement location="${WL_HOME}/lib/weblogic.jar"/>
  </path>

  <target name="prepare">
    <mkdir dir="./classes"/>
  </target>

  <target name="compile" depends="prepare">
    <javac srcdir="." destdir="./classes" classpath=".;${jmslib}">
    </javac>
  </target>

  <target name="runtrantest" depends="compile">
    <java classname="JMSTransaction" fork="yes">
      <classpath refid="runclasspath"/>
    </java>
  </target>

  <target name="clean">
    <delete dir="./classes" />
  </target>

</project>
```

Listing 8-3: Sample output from sending three messages to the program in Listing 8-1

```
runtrantest:
    [java] New Message Received. Was Redelivered? false
    [java] Handler = ALL MESSAGES;  ProductID = JMO425;  Quantity =
50
    [java] COMMIT
```

```
[java] New Message Received. Was Redelivered? false
[java] Handler = ALL MESSAGES;  ProductID = JMO425;  Quantity =
50
[java] COMMIT
[java] New Message Received. Was Redelivered? false
[java] ROLLBACK
[java] New Message Received. Was Redelivered? true
[java] Handler = ALL MESSAGES;  ProductID = JMO425;  Quantity =
50
[java] COMMIT
```

Listing 8-4 presents an adaptation of an example from Chapter 4 (Listing 4-4), which showed how to use asynchronous message processing with a JMS MessageListener object. In this example, I've extended the MessageHandler class to accept a session handle when it's instantiated because it will need it during message processing to commit the transaction. The calls to acknowledge() have been replaced with calls to commit(), which produces one transactional commit per message received. Proper placement of commit() and rollback() is essential to ensure your application's internal state accurately reflects the content of the messages that have been safely received.

Listing 8-4: Properly executing business logic inside a transaction-aware message handler

```
public class MessageHandler implements MessageListener
{
    Session session;
    SomeBusinessObject someBusinessObject = new
SomeBusinessObject();

    public MessageHandler(Session session)
    {
        this.session = session;
    }

    public void onMessage(Message msg)
    {
        // If message type is unexpected, just ACK it
        if (!(msg instanceof StreamMessage))
        {
            try { session.commit(); }
            catch (JMSException e) {}
        }

        StreamMessage sm = (StreamMessage) msg;
```

Continued

Listing 8-4 *(Continued)*

```
        StockQuote quote = new StockQuote();

        try
        {
            quote.setSymbol( sm.readString() );
            quote.setBid( sm.readFloat() );
            quote.setAsk( sm.readFloat() );
            quote.setQuoteTime( new Date(sm.readLong()) );

            try
            {
                // Be sure not to commit until all business logic
has
                // successfully completed
                someBusinessObject.setQuote(quote);
                session.commit();
            }
            catch (SomeException e)
            {
                // If this is a recoverable problem maybe we'll
                // want to roll back the current transaction. The
                // message will be delivered and we can try again.
                try
                {
                    session.rollback();
                }
                catch (JMSException je) { je.printStackTrace(); }
            }
        }
        catch (JMSException ex)
        {
            // Unexpected error encountered
            ex.printStackTrace();
            return;
        }
    }
}
```

Sending messages in a transaction

Sending messages in a transactional context is virtually the same as sending them outside a transaction. The main difference, aside from the parameters you must pass to the session factory method, is the need to call commit() after each message or batch of messages is sent.

Listing 8-5 shows a code fragment for a transactionalized queue message send.

Listing 8-5: Sending messages within a transaction

```
QueueConnection qconn = (a previously created connection);

QueueSession qsession = qconn.createQueueSession(true, 0);

Queue queue = (a previously created queue);

QueueSender sender = qsession.createSender(queue);

TextMessage msg = tsession.createTextMessage();

// Send as many messages as you like ...
for (int i=0; i < 10; ++i)
{
    msg.setText("Hello World #" + i);
    sender.send(msg);
}

// Then call commit() to send them all at once
qsession.commit();
```

Transactions and message-driven beans

From a programming point of view, there's very little a developer needs to do to transaction-enable their message-driven beans. The main thing to know is that a standard EJB container-managed transaction must be used if you want to ensure the JMS message is received within a transacted session. Only by using container-managed transactions will the receipt of the JMS message be included in the same transaction as any transaction related activity in the onMessage() method itself (and in any methods called from within onMessage()). If you're performing any transaction-related activity (e.g. database updates) in response to a received message, you'll almost certainly want to use container-managed transactions, because failure to do so might result in the database activity succeeding but the message acknowledgement failing, potentially resulting in a message redelivery and then you performing the same operation over again.

It is possible to use bean-managed transactions in a message-driven bean's onMessage() method. A bean-managed transaction is a standard EJB technique where the developer is responsible for explicitly demarcating a transaction's boundaries (see Listing 8-8 for an example). Since bean-managed transactions do not include the receipt of the message being processed in the transaction, however, they are generally not desirable to use in message-driven beans.

Listing 8-6 shows a standard ejb.xml descriptor file for a sample message-driven bean with container-managed transactions. The two key lines you need to pay attention to are in bold type. The first tells the application server that you want the container to control the creation and committing of the transaction on your behalf (i.e. container-managed transactions). The second says that a transaction should be required for all methods in the bean (specified by the * in the <method-name> block). In the case of a message-driven bean, this can only be the onMessage() method since it is the only method that can be invoked by a client application (albeit indirectly).

Note that the only two choices for the <trans-attribute> block are Required or NotSupported. The other standard EJB transaction options (RequiresNew, Supports, Mandatory, Never) are not valid for message-driven beans because they presume a prior transactional context (one that existed from an invocation of a different bean) or that a client application is invoking a bean method. Since message-driven beans cannot be invoked by other EJBs or by client applications (at least not by a direct method call) it is not possible to have a pre-existing transaction context.

Listing 8-6: A sample ejb.xml file for a message-driven bean with container-managed transactions

```
<?xml version="1.0"?>
<!DOCTYPE ejb-jar PUBLIC "-//Sun Microsystems, Inc.//DTD Enterprise
JavaBeans 2.0//EN" "http://java.sun.com/dtd/ejb-jar_2_0.dtd">

<ejb-jar>

  <enterprise-beans>

    <message-driven>

      <ejb-name>ticketService</ejb-name>

      <ejb-class>TicketPurchaseService</ejb-class>

      <!-- transaction-type must be Container or Bean -->
      <transaction-type>Container</transaction-type>

      <!-- The message-selector block is optional.
           It's required only if there is a selector.
      -->
      <message-selector>ProductID LIKE 'JM%' AND Quantity > 20
      </message-selector>

        <!-- acknowledge-mode must be Auto-acknowledge or Dups-ok-
acknowledge
      -->
```

```
    <acknowledge-mode>Auto-acknowledge</acknowledge-mode>

    <message-driven-destination>

      <destination-type>javax.jms.Topic</destination-type>

      <!-- subscription-durability applies only to Topic-based
messaging.
          Use Durable for durable subscriptions, NonDurable (the
default)
          otherwise.
      -->
      <subscription-durability>NonDurable</subscription-
durability>

    </message-driven-destination>

  </message-driven>

 </enterprise-beans>

 <assembly-descriptor>

  <container-transaction>

    <method>

      <ejb-name>ticketService</ejb-name>

      <method-name>*</method-name>

    </method>

  <trans-attribute>Required</trans-attribute>

  </container-transaction>

 </assembly-descriptor>

</ejb-jar>
```

As we saw earlier in this chapter, it is possible to perform an explicit rollback on a JMS session in a normal (i.e. non-message-driven bean) client. Performing a rollback will cause any unacknowledged messages to be redelivered. Similarly, it is possible to roll back the current transaction from within a container-managed message-driven bean. Since a message-driven bean does not have access to the JMS session from which it is receiving messages, you would not use the `Session.rollback()` method as you would in a non-message-driven client. Rather, you use the `setRollbackOnly()` method on the `MessageDrivenContext` object that is passed to your bean — via the `setMessageDrivenContext()` method — when the bean is created.

`setRollbackOnly()` has essentially the same effect as `rollback()`: the current message will not be acknowledged and, consequently, will be redelivered to your bean (though not necessarily to the same instance of the bean). Of course, `setRollbackOnly()` also will cause any distributed transaction that is associated with the current JMS transaction to be rolled back as well.

The main problem with using `setRollbackOnly()` in a message-driven bean is that unless you know that the failure condition that caused you to roll back the transaction in the first place can be recovered from, there's not much point in rolling back the transaction. If the failure is not recoverable — such as you might get if there's a coding error somewhere — then you'll simply encounter the same error again when the message is redelivered. Some providers have an error queue facility that allows you to administratively configure a maximum number of times a message delivery is allowed to fail. If the failures reach this number, then the message is dropped and logged; this saves you the trouble of having to deal with the various types of possible failure modes in your code.

Listing 8-7 shows a sample message-driven bean that has a container-managed transaction and performs an explicit rollback on the transaction.

Listing 8-7: A message-driven bean that performs a transaction rollback

```
import javax.ejb.*;
import javax.jms.*;

public class TicketPurchaseService
              implements javax.ejb.MessageDrivenBean,
                         javax.jms.MessageListener
{
    MessageDrivenContext mdcontext;

    public TicketPurchaseService() {}

    public void ejbCreate() {}

    public void ejbRemove() {}

    public void setMessageDrivenContext(MessageDrivenContext
context)
    {
        this.mdcontext = context;
    }
```

```
    public void onMessage(Message msg)
    {
        try
        {
            // doBusinessLogic() may include transactional activity
            boolean recoverableError = doBusinessLogic();

            if (recoverableError) mdcontext.setRollbackOnly();
        }
        catch (Exception ex)
        {
            // Unexpected error encountered
            ex.printStackTrace();
            // Possibly might want to roll back here, too, if it is
possible
            // to recover from the exception condition
        }
    }
}
```

The trickiest part of getting transactionalized message-driven beans to work properly is not in the coding or the descriptors but in configuring your application server correctly. Administratively configuring the application server's JMS connections, transactional behavior, and data sources; ensuring you have the right JDBC drivers; and verifying your underlying database is capable transactional activity are all issues that can cause you to have to pore over many different vendor's documentation before everything works just right.

Sending messages from an EJB

Inside an EJB is probably the most common place you would combine a JMS send operation and a database operation in the same transaction. Because most J2EE applications encode their server-side business logic inside enterprise beans, this is also the most likely endpoint for sending messages to a back-end system over a persistent JMS pipe.

Application servers, of course, allow for container-managed transactions in which all activity inside a particular method call is automatically enclosed in a transaction. If you have administratively configured an EJB method to operate in container-managed mode, then you can write JMS and JDBC calls to your heart's content and all will be committed in a single transaction when the method completes. Bean-managed transactions, on the other hand, require the programmer to manipulate a `UserTransaction` object directly.

Listing 8-8 illustrates a bean-managed transaction example that combines a JMS send and a database insert into the same transaction. Removing the transaction and database code from the bean would result in an example of simply sending a JMS message from an EJB without involving a transaction.

Listing 8-8: Sending messages from within an EJB

```java
import java.sql.*;
import javax.transaction.*;
import javax.sql.*;
import javax.jms.*;
import javax.ejb.*;
import javax.naming.*;

public class OrderService implements SessionBean
{
    EJBContext ejbContext;

    public OrderService() {}

    public void ejbRemove() {}

    public void ejbActivate() {}

    public void ejbPassivate() {}

    public void setSessionContext(SessionContext sc)
    {
        ejbContext = sc;
    }

    public void placeOrder(Order order)
    {
        try
        {
            InitialContext context = new InitialContext();

            DataSource ds = (javax.sql.DataSource)
            context.lookup("java:comp/env/jdbc/SomeDataSource");

            java.sql.Connection dcon = ds.getConnection();

            Statement stmt = dcon.createStatement();

            QueueConnectionFactory qcf =
(javax.jms.QueueConnectionFactory)
            context.lookup("java:comp/env/jms/SomeQConnFactory");

            QueueConnection qcon = qcf.createQueueConnection();

            QueueSession qsession = qcon.createQueueSession(true,
0);
```

```
            Queue queue = (javax.jms.Queue)
                context.lookup("java:comp/env/jms/SomeJMSQueue");

            QueueSender qsender = qsession.createSender(queue);

            MapMessage message = qsession.createMapMessage();

            message.setString("OrderNum", order.getOrderNum());
            message.setInt("Quantity", order.getQuantity());
            message.setFloat("Price", order.getPrice());

            // Do a transaction involving both JMS and the DB
            UserTransaction userTran =
ejbContext.getUserTransaction();

            userTran.begin();

            stmt.executeUpdate("insert into table order values ("
                    + order.getOrderNum() + ","
                    + order.getQuantity() + ","
                    + order.getPrice() + ")"
            );

            qsender.send(message);

            userTran.commit();

            // cleanup
            stmt.close();
            qsender.close();
            qsession.close();
            dcon.close();
            qcon.close();
        }
        catch (JMSException e) { e.printStackTrace(); }
        catch (SQLException e) { e.printStackTrace(); }
        catch (NamingException e) { e.printStackTrace(); }
        catch (NotSupportedException e) { e.printStackTrace(); }
        catch (RollbackException e) { e.printStackTrace(); }
        catch (SystemException e) { e.printStackTrace(); }
        catch (HeuristicMixedException e) { e.printStackTrace(); }
        catch (HeuristicRollbackException e) { e.printStackTrace();
    }
    }

    }
```

Summary

While in the majority of cases transactions are simple to use in your JMS messaging, failure to understand the exact behavior of the behind-the-scenes transaction activity might lead you to think your messaging and business operations are protected when, in fact, they are not. As usual, thorough testing is essential. But since transactions are meant to protect against spurious error conditions – conditions that may be hard to create during a controlled test – it's extremely important during the design phase to explicitly chart out your messages' flow through the system to see where transactions are required to ensure the correct behavior of the system and where they are not. Transactionalizing everything may not always be the best answer since it will impact the overall performance.

Since JMS does not mandate support for transactions (local or distributed) at all, you should always be sure to thoroughly determine your transaction-based needs prior to evaluating vendors' JMS products.

Chapter 9

Securing JMS

IN THIS CHAPTER

◆ Reviewing authentication, authorization, and encryption

◆ Possible attacks on a JMS system

◆ Protecting messages with encryption and authentication codes

WHEN SECURING JMS IT'S IMPORTANT TO REALIZE, as with any network-based messaging system, that several layers are involved, each of which has its own peculiar security needs and models. As we will see, there are a number of reasons JMS systems can be problematic to secure. This is not to say that one cannot secure a JMS-based system – you'll just need to approach the problem from a variety of angles.

This chapter primarily covers the threats posed by employees of a corporation or others who have access to an enterprise network running a JMS messaging system. Firewalls are pretty effective at barring hackers from the outside world. If the many reports are to be believed, however, the far greater threat is posed by a person who has already been granted access to the network. Financial companies, for example, certainly need to be on constant guard against the possibility of an internal employee stealing or misusing data. But any company or government entity that is serious about protecting their customer's personal information – and we hope this is all of them – must be on guard as well.

Too often, messages passed around on an internal LAN or extranet are assumed to be safe because the transmission occurs completely on equipment owned and managed by the corporation. Even when developers and management are aware of potential security problems, solutions tend to be put on the back burner because implementing them only adds to a project's budget and duration. Unfortunately, like most things that have an impact on system's architecture, if it doesn't make it into the initial design, it tends not to make it in at all.

Reviewing Security Concepts

Security is, in reality, too generic a term to be useful. Before discussing how JMS deals with security issues, let's first review the main features of a secure system. For the most part, security can be broken down into three categories:

◆ Authentication

◆ Authorization

◆ Encryption

Let's briefly review each.

Authentication

Authentication is the process of identifying a particular user or application. This user or application entity is also known as a *principal*. The most common form of authentication is, of course, the password, or PIN. In security parlance, a *credential* is the information that a system uses to validate that you are the user you claim to be. A password is just one form of credential, although by far the most common.

Another type of credential is the *digital certificate*, which is essentially a file containing information that uniquely identifies a principal. The file's contents must be certified (that is, digitally signed) by a trusted third party so that its contents cannot be faked. The certificate file also contains a principal's *public key,* which can be used to sign and encrypt messages (see `http://www.rsasecurity.com/rsalabs/faq/2-1-1.html` for a quick overview of public key cryptography).

Digital certificates are commonly used to securely identify users of some desktop-based applications. Corporations sometimes assign certificates to users of Internet browser-based applications, for instance; the browser program is responsible for sending the certificate to the server whenever a new secure session begins. The certificate file resides on the computer's local hard drive or on a smart card.

Of course, more exotic types of authentication exist that are based on biometrics and other technologies, but we don't need to be concerned with them here.

Authorization

Controlling access to a system is but the first level of security. For example, once you've identified yourself and gained entry to an environment, there are things that you can and cannot do in that environment: you can modify certain files but only read others; you can enter your expense report but you cannot approve it, and so on. This is the domain of *authorization*. Authorization components provide a yes/no answer to the question "can principal P perform action A?" If yes, the application will allow the activity. If no, it will either prevent the activity or not even make the activity available to the user in the first place – for instance, by graying out a menu item. A principal/action pair is called a *permission*.

From an API point of view, authorization is very simple. However, the underlying mechanisms that support the assignment and querying of permissions can be quite complicated. A flexible and comprehensive authorization scheme should have the following features:

◆ Allows for the grouping of principals into *realms* that share a common set of permissions.

- ◆ Ability to define *roles* that can be assigned to individuals en masse.

- ◆ Hierarchical permissioning so that permissions can be inherited and do not need to be explicitly assigned to each individual or role.

- ◆ Ability to temporarily transfer or revoke permissions.

- ◆ Ability to reconfigure a principal's permissions on the fly in a running system.

There are many third-party products on the market that can help you manage your system's authorizations but the most common enterprise solutions still seem to be developed in-house.

Enterprise JavaBeans technology defines a very simple, declarative way of specifying permissions inside the EJB XML-based descriptor file. Application servers use these permissions to enforce access control at the EJB method level. Defining permissions with this method tends to be too rudimentary and inflexible for sophisticated applications, but you should certainly take advantage of it where it makes sense for your application. Any JMS activity that takes place inside an access-controlled bean method will, of course, be access-controlled as well. It is also possible to implement more fine-grained permissioning in EJBs by directly using the `EJBContext.isCallerInRole()` and `EJBContext.getCallerPrincipal()` methods. Remember, though, from Chapter 7 that these two methods are not available to message-driven beans because there is no "caller" known to the application server. Non-message-driven EJBs that happen to make use of JMS messaging can use these two methods to enforce permissioning as usual (refer to the EJB documentation and your vendor's product manuals for full details on how to administer permissions for your non-message-driven beans).

 Though it has no direct bearing on JMS (at least not yet), Sun has a specification called the Java Authentication and Authorization Service (JAAS). JAAS has no direct link to JMS currently, but that is likely to change in the future. Even if you just have a general interest in security — and every good architect should — it would be worth your while to review JAAS and other security-related APIs in order to have a good understanding of the basic terms used in the Java security model and how they apply to your application. See `http://java.sun.com/products/jaas` for more information.

Encryption

The final element of security is *encryption*. Encryption is the process of encoding a message in a way that it can only be read by an application that holds the right decryption key. An everyday use of encryption is the HTTPS protocol, which is used to encrypt the Internet traffic of browser-based applications such as home banking and online trading. HTTPS is simply the normal HTTP Web protocol running over a secure sockets layer (SSL) connection instead of a vanilla socket.

Many encryption technologies are available today. Which one, if any, you decide to use in your application depends on your needs. As with many software systems, the various encryption packages generally differ in the trade-offs they make between higher security and higher performance.

The Java platform supports encryption through the Java Cryptography Extension (the `javax.crypto` package), which I'll show some JMS-related uses for later in this chapter. You can read more about Java Cryptography at `http://java.sun.com/products/jce/index.html`.

As we saw in earlier chapters, many JMS implementations make heavy use of sockets. Some of the JMS vendors that utilize socket-based messaging allow you to use SSL sockets instead of regular sockets so that all your messaging traffic will be encrypted.

Security and JMS

Interestingly enough, the current version of the JMS specification has no direct support for security, even though security and privacy is becoming more and more of a hot-button issue these days. The reason for this lies in what we said about the origins of JMS back in Chapter 1. JMS was designed from the beginning to work primarily with a variety of enterprise messaging systems that already existed in the marketplace. Because these systems almost universally were designed to run exclusively on an internal corporate network – this was, after all, before the explosion in popularity of the Internet – there was no need for tight security. Or, more correctly, there was no *perceived* need for tight security.

If the majority of the malicious activity pertaining to data theft and corruption occurs inside the corporate walls, one would think that large corporations would invest significant time and money into securing their enterprise data as much as possible. Rarely is this the case, even though large amounts of sensitive data – stock trading activity, banking records, personal customer information – is shipped in the clear over internal networks every day.

Most corporations do an excellent job of keeping the outside world at bay through the judicious use of firewalls, but the network inside the firewall is a far different story. Certainly, basic password technology is routinely used to prevent access by unauthorized employees to the various internal systems and databases, but messaging systems such as JMS present a unique security challenge because their distributed nature results in messages travelling over large portions of the network, often in broadcast mode.

Types of attack

Any employee who has access to an internal network has the potential to cause mischief – or worse. A malicious person might want to attempt any of three types of attack on a JMS system:

- ◆ Reading messages
- ◆ Altering messages
- ◆ Sending false messages

The following sections talk about each type of attack and describe the steps you might employ in your system to defend against them. For the purposes of our discussion, we'll make the assumption that a pub/sub system is implemented on top of a broadcast technology such as UDP running over Ethernet and that all pub/sub messages do not pass through a central server. Conversely, we'll assume that point-to-point systems (as well as durable pub/sub subscribers) are implemented on top of TCP sockets and that all messages get routed through a central server. Though these are not the required implementations by any means for pub/sub and point-to-point messaging, the distinction will allow us to better explore the security issues associated with each type of implementation. See Chapters 5 and 6 for detailed discussions of the ways in which these types of messaging can be implemented.

Furthermore, let's assume that an attacker has access to the internal LAN but cannot log in as a user to any of the machines participating in the JMS messaging. Clearly, security can be subverted in many ways by someone with privileged access to a critical machine – by altering code, for instance – but this can be controlled by other security techniques that are not the subject of our discussion here.

One step that corporations can take to limit the range of potential attackers is the deployment of internal firewalls. Just as the commonplace Internet firewall only allows certain users through to the internal network, so too can internal firewalls be used to keep out employees who don't need access to certain systems and networks. Perhaps there's no reason for the analyst department to have access to the investment banking department's network, for instance; a firewall could be used to keep them separate. Though effective, internal firewalls are generally not used extensively due to the increase in network management costs and the inconvenience they cause to some users.

READING MESSAGES

Reading messages without permission is probably the most common desire of an attacker. Perhaps attackers want to collect insider information that would give them an advantage in the stock market; perhaps they are looking for the salary or other personal information about a coworker; there are many reasons someone might want to illicitly view internal messages.

In some ways this is also the most dangerous attack because, depending on the JMS implementation used, it can be conducted passively and undetectably.

A person has two ways he or she might try to gain unauthorized access to JMS messages. The first is to access the network directly with a sniffer or other device; the second is to simply write an application that is a JMS client, and then attempt to receive messages.

One of the nice features of JMS is how it enables applications to communicate without any *a priori* knowledge about who they are communicating with. This anonymous participation, however, can be a problem from a security perspective — more so with pub/sub messaging than point-to-point. A distributed pub/sub installation that does not require its messaging participants to supply any credentials or to obtain its connection factories and destinations from a central directory provides ample opportunity for someone to surreptitiously monitor traffic.

Figure 9-1 shows a decentralized JMS installation accessed by an unknown attacker.

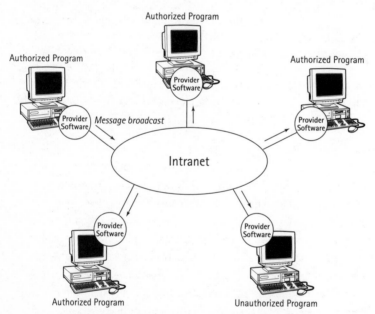

Figure 9-1: An internal network with an unknown attacker

You can take a couple of steps to make it harder for an attacker to receive messages. Remember first that JMS connection factories and JMS destinations are intended to be administered objects. This means that a client should look them up in a JNDI directory service in order to receive messages from a provider. Fortunately, many directory services can limit access to only authorized users by requiring the client applications to supply their credentials before being allowed to look up anything from the JNDI directory.

You can supply a credential to the JNDI API's InitialContext inside your program just as you supply other initialization parameters such as the provider's URL: either directly in the code or by putting them in a jndi.properties file as we've seen in previous examples, such as Listing 3-5 in Chapter 3.

Listing 9-1 shows how to supply your authorization information to the directory service prior to getting the initial JMS connection factory.

Listing 9-1: Authenticating a JMS client with JNDI using WebLogic 6.1

```java
import javax.jms.*;
import javax.naming.*;
import java.util.*;

public class JMSSecurityCredentials
{
    public static void main(String[] args)
    {
        try
        {
            Hashtable hash = new Hashtable();
            hash.put(Context.INITIAL_CONTEXT_FACTORY,
                "weblogic.jndi.WLInitialContextFactory");
            hash.put(Context.PROVIDER_URL, "t3://localhost:7001");
            hash.put(Context.SECURITY_PRINCIPAL, "a_user_name");
            hash.put(Context.SECURITY_CREDENTIALS, "a_password");

            // Could also use InitialContext() and a jndi.properties
file
            Context context = new InitialContext(hash);

            TopicConnectionFactory tcFactory =
                (TopicConnectionFactory)
context.lookup("TOPICFACTORY");
        }
        catch (AuthenticationNotSupportedException e)
        {
            // This type of authentication is not supported
            // by the directory service
        }
        catch (AuthenticationException e)
        {
            // The principal could not be authenticated
            // with the given credentials.
        }
        catch (NamingException e)
        {
            // A general error
        }
    }
}
```

Listing 9-2 shows how to specify a principal and credentials in a `jndi.properties` file should you choose to have your JNDI `InitialContext` get the information it needs from an external file instead of hard-coding the information in your application.

Listing 9-2: A sample jndi.properties file with security credentials

```
java.naming.factory.initial=weblogic.jndi.WLInitialContextFactory
java.naming.provider.url=t3://localhost:7001
java.naming.security.principal=guest
java.naming.security.credentials=guest
```

Examining other possible lines of attack

Using the directory service to prevent an attacker from even creating a JMS connection or from looking up a destination is a good first start and you should definitely use it. There are, however, a few other questions you'll need to answer:

◆ Does your provider actually *require* JMS connection factories and destinations to be looked up from a JNDI directory in order to communicate with the messaging bus? An attacker with enough knowledge about the provider's Java JMS implementation classes might simply be able to instantiate the appropriate connection factory and destination objects needed to receive messages, thereby bypassing the directory service's security altogether. Some providers even have officially supported API for defining connection factories and destinations. Whether you can stop an attacker from bypassing the lookup process – either through hacking or using a supported API – depends on the specific implementation of the provider and the administrative controls it provides.

◆ Is it possible for an attacker to simply replicate the entire JMS provider's installation on his or her own machine so that it looks like the installation being attacked? By installing their own copy of your provider's software and creating their own directory of administered objects, an attacker might simply be able to look up all the required objects in the local directory service – one without access controls – and start receiving messages from the original JMS installation. To prevent this, a provider would need to ensure that all connection factories and destinations accessing a particular bus were originally retrieved from a specific, secure JNDI directory.

◆ Does access to one entry in the JNDI tree imply access to all entries? Most directory services are fairly dumb about how they implement access control. What if, for instance, an attacker is a legitimate consumer of JMS messages but you only want them to receive messages sent to Destination A, not Destination B? If the directory service lets you control access at the directory entry level then you're all set. If not, then there's nothing to stop the Destination A receiver from also getting Destination B messages. Of course, even if your directory service does support entry-level access control, you as an administrator have to ensure that you require the appropriate credentials for the appropriate destinations. If there are a lot of destinations and a lot of different categories of users, this can obviously be quite a hassle to manage and maintain.

ENCRYPTING MESSAGES

Even if you can (and have) adequately limited the ability to look up connections and destinations through the directory service, the problem always exists of someone using a sniffer to read the messages directly off the network. The only sure way to prevent this from happening is to encrypt the contents of your messages.

Unfortunately, encrypting is easier said than done in most cases. Certainly, if you are sending a JMS `BytesMessage` or an `ObjectMessage`, you have the opportunity to use the Java cryptography package to encode the information before sending the message. However, JMS expects other types of messages, such as the `MapMessage`, to be populated using real, unencoded data, so there is no point at which you can encrypt the message prior to its being sent. The same is true with the headers and properties of any JMS message type.

The ultimate solution will require an extension to the JMS specification that allows for pluggable security modules. These could be used by client applications to encrypt the bytes that comprise a JMS message just before they are sent over the wire, and to decrypt them after they are received on the destination machine but before they are delivered to the receiving application.

As mentioned earlier in the chapter, some providers allow you to do all your messaging over a secure channel such as HTTPS — though not necessarily for all messaging modes. If, for whatever reason, you cannot transmit your messages over a secure channel, or you'd simply prefer to limit your encryption of messages to a relative few that really require being hidden, then you certainly can do so. You will just have to limit yourself to sending an encrypted `BytesMessage` or `ObjectMessage`, which will hold the encrypted data. (Encryption for other message types could be done but only on a field-by-field basis.) And be sure to keep sensitive information out of the message's properties.

You will also have to be prepared to pay the associated encryption/decryption performance penalty that, in a high-volume system, can be a significant factor. This is especially true if you do not have hardware-based encryption support.

Another method of securing message traffic that could be implemented without any specific configuration of your JMS provider or manipulation of your messages is the *virtual private network,* or VPN. A VPN can be useful because it automatically encrypts all traffic traveling over it without the knowledge or intervention of any particular application that transmits information over it, including a JMS provider. However, a VPN is like a firewall; it keeps out a large percentage of attackers but does nothing to prevent attacks by people who already have authorized access to the network. By all means, use a VPN where appropriate, but be sure to keep in mind that all the same issues we discussed in this chapter regarding access to JMS connection factories and destinations still apply.

Listing 9-3 shows how to use the SealedObject class from the Java cryptography package to encrypt a JMS ObjectMessage (or, more correctly, to encrypt the object *inside* an ObjectMessage). Decrypting the object on the receiver's side is shown in the message handler in Listing 9-5 later in this chapter. Refer to the Java Cryptography Extension (JCE) API for full details on how to use the crypto package.

Listing 9-3: Using javax.crypto.SealedObject to encrypt an ObjectMessage

```
import java.security.*;
import javax.crypto.*;
import javax.crypto.spec.*;
import javax.jms.*;

String skey = "A NOT SO SECRET KEY";
char[] cbuff = new char[skey.length()];
skey.getChars(0, cbuff.length, cbuff, 0);

// PBE = "Password Based Encryption"
PBEKeySpec spec = new PBEKeySpec(cbuff);

SecretKeyFactory skf =
SecretKeyFactory.getInstance("PBEWithMD5AndDES");
Key key = skf.generateSecret(spec);

Cipher cipher = Cipher.getInstance("PBEWithMD5AndDES");
cipher.init(Cipher.ENCRYPT_MODE, key);

Serializable objToSend = "THIS STRING IS A PLAINTEXT MESSAGE";
SealedObject so = new SealedObject(objToSend, cipher);
```

```
ObjectMessage om = session.createObjectMessage();
om.setObject(so);

publisher.publish(om);
```

ALTERING MESSAGES

What if, instead of just passively observing the messages flowing through the network, an attacker wishes to alter a message in some way? Perhaps an attacker has a checking account at the bank where he or she works and would like to alter the "DEPOSIT_TO_ACCOUNT" message they know is transmitted at the close of business each day to increase the dollar amount of a deposit he or she made at a local ATM machine that morning.

This is actually the least feasible of our three scenarios due to the way in which JMS pub/sub messaging — and the underlying UDP-based messaging it is built on top of — is implemented. Because a pub/sub message is essentially a broadcast to every machine on the network, there is no opportunity for an interloper to alter the content of a message. By the time this can be done, the original message will already have been received.

For queue-based messaging it is possible to alter the content of a message while it resides in the permanent store, of course, but this requires authorized access to the file or database where the message is held. Since we've said we're assuming an attacker cannot get access inside the system housing the JMS provider, then it wouldn't be possible for them to manipulate the queue. This possibility does, however, point out how important standard system access controls and privilege limitation are as a part of any comprehensive enterprise security model.

SENDING FALSE MESSAGES

What if instead of trying to alter a message an attacker simply decided to generate a bogus "DEPOSIT_TO_ACCOUNT" message indicating a large deposit to his or her account and send it over the LAN? This is a much harder event to defend against.

In this case we have all the same issues regarding unauthorized access to JMS factories and destinations that we had in the scenario discussed in the preceding "Reading Messages" section. For the sake of argument, let's assume that the attacker has defeated any bus access controls we might have in place and devised a way to send an arbitrary message to the JMS destination of their choice. How can we ensure the fake message is detected and not processed?

One way to accomplish this is through the use of a *message authentication code,* or MAC. Whereas encryption is used to hide the contents of a message from prying eyes, a message recipient uses a MAC to verify that a message has not been altered in transit and that it was sent by whoever claims to have sent it. This is accomplished by using a secret key and the contents of the message together to generate a value that is unique for all messages. This is known as a *secure hash.*

Unlike encryption, the use of a MAC does not require the original contents of a message to be altered. The message is sent in the clear as usual but it is accompanied by a code — a sequence of bytes — that the sender has generated for it using a predetermined secret key. For the system to be effective, only the sender and receiver of the message can know the key. When the message arrives at its destination, the receiver generates its own MAC for the message using the same secret key the sender used. If the resulting MAC does not match the one that came with the message, then the message is not valid and should be discarded. In a JMS installation where there is a lot of peer-to-peer traffic, you'd probably want to make the same secret key available to all applications participating in the messaging.

For our example case of an internal employee attempting to send a false deposit message, we can easily prevent this deception by tagging all deposit messages with MACs. As long as the key used to generate the MAC remains safely behind the security barrier of the sending and receiving environments, then the attacker has no way of generating a valid message. A MAC also enables us to detect if a message has been somehow altered in transit because the MAC in the message would not match the contents of the message. It is possible to use a MAC over any mode of message transport — pub/sub or point-to-point — and over any underlying implementation — queue or broadcast.

MACs have several advantages over encryption in JMS systems:

1. They are easy to generate and generally have less of a performance impact than full-blown encryption.

2. A MAC can be applied to the entire message — properties and contents — or to any subset of a message.

3. Because they are passed as a non-intrusive addition to a message, MACs can be used with JMS `MapMessages`, which normally can't be encrypted easily.

Generally speaking, the most likely candidate for a false message attack is, of course, a developer who worked on, or is working on, the system in question because he or she knows the internal operation of the system and could easily generate any message they desired. As long as the keys used to generate the MAC are safely stored on the production system, however, even specialized knowledge about a system's operation would not be enough to allow a person to send a false message. Only those relatively few people who manage the production system will have access to the secret keys and thus have the opportunity for abuse. (Granted, in many environments the developers are the ones running the production system — but that's a different story.)

Listing 9-4 shows a utility class that uses the `javax.crypto.Mac` class to tag a JMS `MapMessage` with a MAC code. This class does not consider a message's properties when generating the MAC, but you could easily modify it to do so.

A sender should call the `tagMessage()` method immediately prior to sending the message because any alteration of the message fields after tagging would invalidate the MAC. The receiver calls `isValid()` to verify that the message is legitimate. The assumption is made that the sender and receiver have access to the same `javax.crypto.SecretKey` object.

Listing 9-4: A utility class for generating message authentication codes for a MapMessage

```java
import java.security.*;
import javax.crypto.*;
import java.util.*;
import javax.jms.*;

/**
 * This class can be used to tag JMS MapMessages with a message
authentication
 * code (a MAC). A MAC is a byte[] value that is the calculated
secure MD5 hash
 * of all the fields in the message, not including the message's
properties.
 */
public final class MACUtil
{
    /**
     * Generate a MAC for the given JMS MapMessage by calculating a
     * MD5 hash of all the fields in the message.
     *
     * @param      msg    A JMS MapMessage
     * @param      key    The key to use to generate the MAC
     * @param      fieldsToExclude
     *                    A list of MapMessage fields that should NOT
be
     *                    considered when generating the MAC; or null
     * @return     The generated MAC
     */
    public static byte[] generateMac(MapMessage msg, SecretKey key,
                                                    List
fieldsToExclude)
        throws NoSuchAlgorithmException, InvalidKeyException,
JMSException
    {
        // Get instance of Mac object implementing HMAC-MD5, and
        // initialize it with the above secret key
        Mac mac = Mac.getInstance("HmacMD5");
        mac.init(key);


        // The order in which the fields of the message is processes
is
        // very important to the final calculated MAC. Since JMS gives
```

Continued

Listing 9-4 *(Continued)*

```
        // no guarantee that a field name Enumeration performed on the
        // sender's side will return field names in the same order
that
        // an Enumeration on the client's side will, we'll have to
create
        // our own list of field names and alphabetize them before
        // generating the MAC.

        List alphaNames = new LinkedList();

        for (Enumeration en=msg.getMapNames();
en.hasMoreElements();)
        {
            alphaNames.add((String) en.nextElement());
        }

        Collections.sort(alphaNames);


        for (Iterator it=alphaNames.iterator(); it.hasNext();)
        {
            String fieldName = (String) it.next();

            if (fieldsToExclude != null &&
                fieldsToExclude.contains(fieldName)) continue;

            Object fieldValue = msg.getObject(fieldName);

            if (fieldValue instanceof byte[]) mac.update((byte[])
fieldValue);

            else if (fieldValue instanceof Byte)
                mac.update(((Byte) fieldValue).byteValue());

            // The Mac class requires input in bytes so if a
            // field name is not a byte[] or byte field then
            // we'll retrieve it as a String first (all JMS
            // MapMessage fields except byte[] can be retrieved
            // as Strings) and then convert the String to a
            // byte[].
            else mac.update(msg.getString(fieldName).getBytes());
        }

        return mac.doFinal();
```

```
        }

    /**
     * Generates a MAC for the supplied MapMessage and adds the MAC
to the
     * same message as a field with the supplied name. The field to be
     * added should not already exist in the message.
     *
     * @param     msg       A JMS MapMessage
     * @param     key       The key to use to generate the MAC
     * @param     macField  The name of the field the MAC should
be added as
     * @return    void
     */
    public static void tagMessage(MapMessage msg, SecretKey key,
                                              String macField)
        throws NoSuchAlgorithmException, InvalidKeyException,
JMSException
    {
        msg.setBytes(macField, generateMac(msg, key, null));
    }

    /**
     * Checks the supplied MapMessage to see if it has been tampered
with.
     * The supplied key must be the same key used to generate the MAC
     * that is in the supplied message. A MAC is expected to be in the
     * message at the supplied field name prior to calling this
method.
     * If no MAC exists, the message is considered to be invalid.
     *
     * @param     msg       A JMS MapMessage
     * @param     key       The key to use to generate the MAC
     * @param     macField  The name of the field the MAC should
be added as
     * @return    true/false
     */
    public static boolean isValid(MapMessage msg, SecretKey key,
                                              String macField)
        throws NoSuchAlgorithmException, InvalidKeyException,
JMSException
    {
        // To see if a message is unaltered we need to generate
        // our own MAC for it and compare it to the one that came
```

Continued

Listing 9-4 *(Continued)*

```
        // along with the message.

        byte[] msgMac = msg.getBytes(macField);

        if (msgMac == null) return false;

        List excludeFields = new ArrayList(1);

        excludeFields.add(macField);

        byte[] localMac = generateMac(msg, key, excludeFields);

        return Arrays.equals(msgMac, localMac);
    }


    // For testing
    public static void main(String[] args)
    {
        try
        {
            // Context is loaded from the jndi.properties file
            javax.naming.Context context = new
javax.naming.InitialContext();

            TopicConnectionFactory tcFactory =
                    (TopicConnectionFactory)
context.lookup("TOPICFACTORY");

            TopicConnection topicConn =
                    tcFactory.createTopicConnection();

            TopicSession tcSession =
topicConn.createTopicSession(false,

Session.AUTO_ACKNOWLEDGE);

            MapMessage msg = tcSession.createMapMessage();

            msg.setLong("OrderNumber", 12345);

            msg.setInt("Quantity", 50);

            msg.setFloat("Price", 65.88f);
```

```
                msg.setString("ProductID", "JMO425");

                msg.setObject("CustomerNumber", new Long(4563345));

                msg.setBytes("SourceIP",
                      java.net.InetAddress.getLocalHost().getAddress());

                String skey = "A NOT SO SECRET KEY";
                char[] cbuff = new char[skey.length()];
                skey.getChars(0, cbuff.length, cbuff, 0);

                javax.crypto.spec.PBEKeySpec spec =
                               new javax.crypto.spec.PBEKeySpec(cbuff);

                SecretKeyFactory skf =

SecretKeyFactory.getInstance("PBEWithMD5AndDES");
                SecretKey key = skf.generateSecret(spec);

                // Tag the message with the MAC

                MACUtil.tagMessage(msg, key, "MAC");


                byte[] mac = msg.getBytes("MAC");

                System.out.println("The generated MAC is " +
                                           new String(mac));

                System.out.println("The message is " +
                        (MACUtil.isValid(msg, key, "MAC") ? "" : "not
") +
                        "valid");
        }
        catch (java.security.spec.InvalidKeySpecException e) {
                                          e.printStackTrace();
}
        catch (NoSuchAlgorithmException e) { e.printStackTrace(); }
        catch (InvalidKeyException e) { e.printStackTrace(); }
        catch (JMSException e) { e.printStackTrace(); }
        catch (javax.naming.NamingException e) {
e.printStackTrace(); }
        catch (java.net.UnknownHostException e) {
e.printStackTrace(); }
    }
}
```

TIP   Java provides several classes that could be used to verify a message's source and content; `java.security.Signature`, for instance, can be used to digitally sign a message. Signing is very similar to generating a MAC. `java.security.Signature` operates much like `javax.crypto.Mac` but utilizes public and private keys rather than shared keys.

Listing 9-5 shows a message handler that illustrates how to validate `MapMessage`s with MACs in them and how to decrypt `ObjectMessage`s that contain `SealedObject`s. The key used by the handler must, of course, be the same key that was used to process the message when it was sent. Keys can be created and serialized to a file or database where they can be used by more than one application. Keys can also be instantiated on the fly by an application from a predetermined piece of information — such as a password — to ensure both the sender and receiver have the same key.

Listing 9-5: A message handler for receiving MapMessages with MACs and ObjectMessages with SealedObjects

```
public class MessageHandler implements MessageListener
{
    String id;
    Key key;

    public MessageHandler(String id, Key key)
    {
        this.id = id;
        this.key = key;
    }

    public void onMessage(Message msg)
    {
        if (msg instanceof MapMessage)
        {
            MapMessage mm = (MapMessage) msg;

            try
            {
                boolean isValid = MACUtil.isValid(mm, (SecretKey)
key, "MAC");

                System.out.println("Msg is valid? " + isValid);

                if (!isValid)
                {
```

```
                    // If an invalid message is received we would
                    // want to be sure not to process it and to
                    // save it somewhere for later examination.
                    try { msg.acknowledge(); }
                    catch (JMSException e) {}
                    return;
                }
            }
        catch (Exception e) { e.printStackTrace(); }

        System.out.println("Handler = " + id + " Msg = " + mm);

        try { mm.acknowledge(); }
        catch (JMSException e) {}
    }
    else if (msg instanceof ObjectMessage)
    {
        ObjectMessage om = (ObjectMessage) msg;

        try
        {
            Serializable ser = om.getObject();

            if (!(ser instanceof SealedObject))
            {
                System.out.println("ERROR: Expecting a
SealedObject");

                try { om.acknowledge(); }
                catch (JMSException e) {}

                return;
            }

            SealedObject so = (SealedObject) ser;
            Object obj = null;

            try
            {
                obj = so.getObject(key);
            }
            catch (Exception e) { e.printStackTrace(); }
```

Continued

Listing 9-5 *(Continued)*

```
                System.out.println("Handler = " + id + ";  Object =
" + obj);
            }
            catch (JMSException ex)
            {
                // Unexpected error encountered
                ex.printStackTrace();
                return;
            }
            finally
            {
                try { om.acknowledge(); }
                catch (JMSException e) {}
            }
        }

        // If message type is unexpected, just ACK it
        else
        {
            try { msg.acknowledge(); }
            catch (JMSException e) {}
        }
    }
}
```

The JCE package is integrated into JDK1.4 but is available only as a standard extension to JDK1.3.1, which means the libraries needed to compile are different depending on which JDK you're using. Listing 9-6 show an ant `build.xml` fragment that should help get you started compiling and running Java crypto applications. Be sure to read the JCE installation documentation thoroughly, especially for JDKs prior to 1.4, to be sure you've set up your JCE installation properly.

Listing 9-6: Specifying JCE libraries for JDK1.4 and JDK1.3.1 using ant

```
<!-- For JDK1.4->
<property name="jcelib" value="c:/jdk1.4/jre/lib/jce.jar"/>


<!-- For JDK1.3.1 -->
<property name="jcelib"
value="c:/jce1.2.1/lib/jce1_2_1.jar;c:/jce1.2.1/lib/sunjce_provider.
jar;c:/jce1.2.1/lib/local_policy.jar"/>
```

Summary

A computer system can be compromised in many ways. Full protection of your enterprise system is a much more extensive exercise than what we've talked about here.

To adequately protect your JMS infrastructure you'll need to take as many scenarios as possible into account while always keeping in mind the realistic risks faced and the cost/benefit tradeoffs of implementing countermeasures.

One of the reasons people don't pay enough attention to internal security issues is because they haven't encountered problems in the past. But if you don't control the integrity of your messages, how do you know your system hasn't been victimized by receiving false messages? If you don't encrypt messages, how do you know your messages aren't being read without authorization? Waiting until it's obvious your security has been compromised before realizing there is a danger is, of course, waiting too long.

Chapter 10

Maximizing JMS Performance

IN THIS CHAPTER

◆ Using JMS performance-related features

◆ Environmental factors affecting performance

◆ Writing optimized code

◆ A sample benchmarking application

FOR ARCHITECTS CONSIDERING THE INCORPORATION of JMS products into their design, the number-one question is often, "How's the performance?" As we'll see in this chapter, there's no easy answer to this question. JMS performance depends on many variables, such as the type of messaging, the size of the messages, the provider configuration, the system resources available, the network speed, the efficiency of the application code, and more. As a result, achieving optimal performance is a problem best tackled from various angles.

Using JMS Performance-Related Features

The performance of any computer software is, naturally, determined by how that software is implemented and the hardware enironment it runs in. Since JMS specifies an API only, not an implementation, you won't find many references to performance-related issues *per se* in the JMS specification. Even so, the designers of JMS were hardly performance-unaware. There are ample opportunities for third party providers to optimize their proprietary JMS implementations as well as opportunities for you to architect your system so that it operates efficiently.

Designing for performance

In JMS systems, overall message throughput primarily results from the design choices you make regarding the type of messaging you use and how that messaging is configured.

183

As we saw in Chapters 5 and 6, JMS topic messaging is often implemented on top of a broadcast technology such as UDP or IP Multicast. Queue-based messaging, more likely than not, uses a central server with the transport based on TCP stream sockets.

Given the same number of messages being sent to the same number of clients, broadcast messaging typically performs much better and is more scalable than centralized (hub and spoke) messaging for the following reasons:

♦ A single copy of a message can be sent to all applications at once instead of serially delivering a message to each client.

♦ Processing is pushed to the edges of the network, alleviating the load on the central server if one is even required.

♦ Client and server applications do not need to maintain open, long-lived socket connections.

For these reasons, applications that require super-high-performance messaging usually are based on broadcast technologies. There are tradeoffs in reliability and other factors, however, that make broadcast messaging inappropriate for some applications.

As usual with JMS, much depends on the underlying provider implementation. Topic-based messaging that is not based on a broadcast technology will not likely perform any better than queue-based messaging, for instance. To be able to make intelligent architectural decisions, be sure to find out how your provider has implemented its messaging solution for the various types of messaging.

Performance-related APIs

Not too many features supported by the JMS API specifically address performance-related factors. The following are a few tips you can consider using to squeeze some extra performance out of your messaging.

USE DUPS_OK_ACKNOWLEDGE ACKNOWLEDGMENT

If possible, use the DUPS_OK_ACKNOWLEDGE acknowledgment mode when receiving messages. Because this mode does not require the provider to ensure that each message is delivered no more than once, it is the lightest weight acknowledgment mode. In the vast majority of cases, your application will still only receive each message once anyway. If you can live with the occasional duplicate delivery or if you can implement a quick check of the **JMSRedelivered** property and throw out duplicate messages in your code, then DUPS_OK_ACKNOWLEDGE is the way to go.

TURN OFF MESSAGE IDS

Message IDs are unique strings that identify a particular message (via the JMSMessageID property). Ensuring that a string is unique can cause a provider to incur a fair amount of overhead, relatively speaking. If you don't need them, the generation of IDs can be disabled using the following API call:

```
MessageProducer producer = ...;

producer.setDisableMessageID(true);
```

Message IDs are generally not useful, anyway. (See Chapter 2 for more information on this topic.) JMS does not require that a provider honor this command — it's just a hint — so be sure that yours does before you attempt to turn off message ID generation. You may not see any change in performance.

TURN OFF TIME STAMPING

Asking a provider to generate a timestamp for each message-sent message (via the **JMSTimestamp** property) is not likely to impact your throughput much, but if you're not using the timestamp, you might as well turn this feature off using the following call:

```
MessageProducer producer = ...;

producer.setDisableTimestamp(true);
```

Timestamps are often not useful if messages travel between machines unless you make considerable effort to ensure that the clocks on those machines are synchronized. (See Chapter 2 for more information on the problems associated with timestamps and inter-machine message delivery.) As with message ID disabling, JMS providers are not required to honor this request.

Environmental Factors Affecting Performance

Many factors help determine the overall performance of any application. Among the key environmental factors (that is, ones not affected by application code or design) that affect the messaging throughput of a JMS system are the following:

- ◆ Network configuration
- ◆ Database configuration
- ◆ Operating system configuration
- ◆ Java virtual machine configuration
- ◆ Provider implementation and configuration

Many books and articles are dedicated to the subject of system performance tuning. Serious, high-end performance tuning requires a good grounding in a number of topics related to operating systems, hardware, networking, and application software.

Naturally, not every application requires a huge performance tuning effort. Here are a few quick points to keep an eye on in each of the preceding categories when attempting to improve the performance of your JMS system.

Network configuration

As a developer, the main piece of information you need to worry about is the network's Maximum Transfer Unit (MTU). This value varies from network to network but is typically on the order of 1 to 10 kilobytes. The MTU is the maximum size of a message (a network message, not a JMS message) that can be sent in a single transmission. Messages larger than this value must be broken up, sent in pieces, and then reassembled by the receiver. Naturally, all this activity is hidden from your application code by the protocol stack, but forcing the network to handle too many large messages negatively impacts performance, particularly if your provider uses UDP.

If the vast majority of the messages delivered are under the MTU, then you probably don't have anything to worry about. On the other hand, if you're routinely sending large numbers of messages whose size exceeds the network's MTU, then you should seriously consider reducing their size. You could also try to get your network administrator to increase your network MTU, but unless the network you're running your JMS system on is entirely dedicated to your application, it's unlikely you'll be able to convince them to tune it specifically to your needs.

Unfortunately, it's hard to know exactly the size of the JMS messages your provider sends over the network. You can add up the bytes that you put in the message, but headers and other information that get tacked onto the message are usually beyond your reach. Some OSes may provide utilities to help you, but in many cases you'll just have to estimate.

Database configuration

You can optimize databases in far too many ways than we can cover here. But if you send a lot of persistent JMS messages and use a database to store them, then it would be beneficial to get your database administrator involved early in the physical infrastructure configuration process. Your provider documentation may also give some hints about how best to configure and optimize your database.

Operating system configuration

Low-level operating system tuning is generally beyond the boundary of where application developers care to go. Hopefully, you won't need to resort to mucking around with lots of OS parameters in order to get your JMS provider to perform at the desired level but many OSes, particularly Unix-based ones, have myriad configurable parameters. Thus, you may find it profitable to spend at least a little time explaining your application to an OS engineer to see if they have any suggestions for ways in which the OS can be tuned to allow your JMS application to run faster, or *vice versa*. A couple of examples are:

CONFIGURE YOUR OS TO SUPPORT LARGE NUMBERS OF CONNECTIONS

With the rise of the Internet, most OSes are now being optimized to better support large amounts of network traffic and large numbers of simultaneous socket connections. JMS servers that handle many clients will certainly benefit from this. Whether you're using a brand-new version of your OS or an older version, be sure that your system administrator has configured it for maximum communications performance. The best way to do this will heavily depend on your provider's specific architecture (for example, some are more connection-oriented and some are more broadcast-oriented) so be sure to find out what's best for your particular provider.

MAKE THE MOST OF AVAILABLE CPUS

If the system on which you are running your JMS application – particularly one running a JMS server – has more than one CPU installed, be sure to take maximum advantage of as many of them as you can. Running your JMS server on one processor and its associated database server on another processor, for instance, can definitely improve performance. In addition, most high-end operating systems will let you configure an application so that the threads it creates are distributed over a predetermined range of CPUs. Because JMS servers tend to make heavy use of threads, this is an option worth looking into if your OS architecture allows it.

Java virtual machine configuration

Most newer Java virtual machine implementations have a large number of parameters that you can set when running a VM. Some are fully documented, while others are somewhat hidden. The Sun J2SE 1.3 (HotSpot 2.0) VM for Solaris, for example, has the following categories of options that might make your JMS systems run faster:

JVM OPTIONS -XMS, -XMX

These flags control the initial (-Xms) and maximum (-Xmx) amount of memory available to the JVM. Generally speaking, making more memory available to the VM is a good idea because, among other reasons, it causes the garbage collector to run less frequently. This is especially important in high-volume messaging situations because the more CPU cycles the garbage collector consumes, the fewer that are available to process messages. Typically, you'll want to set the initial and maximum values to the same amount to prevent the JVM from having to resize its heap while running. For example, use the following command line options to set the initial and maximum values to 128 megabytes:

```
java -Xms128m -Xmx128m
```

Keep in mind that increasing the heap increases the amount of memory that has to be scanned for unreferenced objects, so be sure not to set these values to unnecessarily large values (otherwise, you could just set it to 4 gigabytes and forget about it!). You should also avoid setting these numbers to be larger than the amount of physical RAM available in order to avoid excessive paging and/or swapping.

JVM OPTIONS -CLIENT, -SERVER

The -client and -server flags are mutually exclusive; you can only use one or the other. The default is -client. Unfortunately, the names of these flags, -client and -server, are a bit of a misnomer and exist primarily for historical reasons. The -server flag is generally appropriate for any long-running application, even GUI-based ones. The -client option is generally appropriate for applications where a minimal memory footprint is critical because this flag causes the adaptive compiler to be turned off. With JMS, it is probably almost always better to use the -server option because most applications can benefit from use of the adaptive compiler.

JVM OPTIONS -XX:+USEBOUNDTHREADS, -XX:+USELWPSYNCHRONIZATION, -XX:THREADSTACKSIZE=#

On the Solaris version of the HotSpot VM (Version 2.0), it is possible to specify that the VM always allocate a Lightweight Process (LWP) for each java.lang.Thread object. For systems that have multiple CPUs, this helps applications that create many threads run much more efficiently. In fact, even on machines that have only a single CPU, use of the -XX:+UseBoundThreads flag often improves performance because the kernel's thread management is more efficient than the Solaris user-level thread libraries.

   -XX:+UseLWPSynchronization is another Solaris-specific option that causes the VM to use the LWP synchronization primitives directly. Again, the kernel's locking primitives are more efficient than the user-level libraries. A side-effect of using this flag is that more LWPs will be created. Generally, this is not an issue and may, in fact, cause LWPs to be created in a more efficient fashion (for example, only when an existing LWP is blocking).

   Finally, it may be desirable to tune the amount of memory allocated for each thread's stack space. The default is 512 kilobytes. You should definitely consider reducing this number if you know that your application creates lots of threads and does not require this much stack space per thread. In particular, it is possible that your server may page and swap excessively when large numbers of threads are created. Setting the per thread stack can be done using the -XX:ThreadSize flag. This flag is available on all platforms.

   See http://java.sun.com/j2se/docs/VMOptions.html for more details and the latest information regarding these and other related parameters. Note that the -XX flags are not guaranteed to be supported from release to release of the VM, so be especially careful when upgrading to a new version of the J2SE platform (the features are likely to be preserved, but the exact flags may differ).

Provider implementation and configuration

There's not much you can do about a vendor's JMS product that is implemented poorly with respect to performance – short of switching vendors that is, which JMS makes relatively easy to do. However, before tossing one vendor for another, be sure you've taken full advantage of the tunable parameters a vendor provides through its administrative capabilities. This way, you can ensure that its product is configured optimally for the environment in which it is running and for the types of messaging for which you are using it. Also, be sure to follow a vendor's guidance for configuring any operating system, database, or other parameters that might influence their product's performance and reliability.

Writing Optimized Code

This section covers a few of the best practices you should follow when writing JMS client code. As with all best practices, these are merely recommendations, not hard and fast rules. It's up to you to decide if a particular best practice is worth the extra time and effort to follow given your particular environment, system requirements, and time constraints.

For example, the "internal queue" best practice presented later in this chapter can be difficult to implement properly but can be a lifesaver for high-volume, high-processing messaging systems. On the other hand, if you have a low-volume system that has no trouble keeping up with the influx of messages, then it may not be worth implementing. In the latter case, there's no point in spending the extra time and effort to implement and debug a solution to a problem that doesn't exist. The tricky part is being knowledgeable and experienced enough to know not only when a problem does not exist but also when it *will not exist* for the foreseeable future.

Minimize time in onMessage()

When processing incoming messages, it's generally not a good idea to linger in any of your `MessageListener.onMessage()` callbacks for too long. Remember that JMS sessions are single-threaded (see Chapter 4), so even if you have multiple message listeners registered with a single session — say, one per destination you are receiving messages for — all messages received through that session are processed sequentially. Until you return from the current call to `onMessage()`, no other messages can be processed by any other message handler object.

If you are familiar with Swing programming, this situation is analogous to the one that exists when you've registered a listener on a GUI component. Because the listener is executed in the context of the GUI thread, all GUI activity is suspended for the duration of the listener method call. This can cause the user interface to appear frozen or sluggish if listener methods are taking up more than a reasonable amount of processing time.

In JMS systems, however, it is sometimes difficult to make your `onMessage()` methods short and fast. This is especially true if you are using an XA session and need to include the receipt of a message in a distributed transaction involving other resources such as a database. Any database-related activity that results from the receipt of a message definitely has a negative impact on message throughput rates, but if you have to do it then you have to do it. You'll just have to be sure that your callback method is optimized as much as possible and that your application is running in an environment that will enable it to process messages quickly enough to keep up with the number of incoming messages.

The following three sections cover design ideas that will help you avoid making `onMessage()` calls a gating performance factor:

USE MULTIPLE JMS SESSIONS

Because a JMS session is single-threaded, one obvious solution to achieving greater throughput in your application is to design some parallel processing into your application by creating multiple sessions. This is perfectly acceptable and you can achieve great increases in throughput this way, especially if the environment in which your application is running is optimally configured for threading.

Using multiple sessions is going to require a bit more up-front design time, however. Some of the things you need to keep in mind are:

◆ Each destination you receive messages for should only receive them through one session. For example, registering a consumer for the same JMS topic destination with two sessions results in the message being received twice in your application. You need to figure out how best to divide up the messages.

◆ Transactions cannot cross session boundaries (see Chapter 7 for more information on how JMS sessions and transactions are related).

◆ Messages processed in separate threads are not necessarily handled in the order in which the provider delivered them to your application. This may or may not be a problem depending on how your application is designed.

Keep in mind, also, that sessions are not lightweight constructs. If you have too many, you'll certainly reach a point of diminishing returns where the resources required for the provider to manage all the sessions is greater than would be used to process the messages with fewer sessions. Generally speaking, the overhead associated with managing a large number of threads in a JVM can be greater sometimes than the benefit achieved by multithreading in the first place. So if you do use multiple sessions it's best to keep the number relatively low.

CONFIGURE SESSIONS FOR THE MINIMUM FUNCTIONALITY NEEDED

Always create a JMS session with the minimum functionality required. This means you shouldn't bother creating a transacted session if you don't require transactions. Also, as previously mentioned in this chapter, use the lightest weight acknowledgment mode you can get away with.

USE AN INTERNAL QUEUE TO SEPARATE INTAKE FROM PROCESSING

A frequent mistake designers make is to try to update many different parts of an application with the information received in a single message. The problem is that if it takes longer to update an application's internal components for each message than the average rate of incoming messages, then messages will start to back up, possibly resulting in dropped messages and definitely resulting in stale information being used or displayed. This is a common occurrence in some desktop financial applications that must cope with a high volume of incoming quote and trade messages. Usually what a programmer will do upon receipt of a new message is to extract the relevant information and then sequentially update the set of components that are interested in that information (graphs, tables, and so on). This updating can be done in a custom fashion or via some standardized mechanism that delivers its messages serially, such as InfoBus (`http://java.sun.com/products/javabeans/infobus`). Unfortunately, graphical components tend to be the slowest parts of a system, and the time it takes to update even a few of them can easily be longer than the average time between incoming messages.

One solution to this problem is to use an internal queue or other buffering construct to deliver messages to the various graphical components. One of the advantages of using a JMS queue is that it lets separate applications run at their own speed, thereby preventing one portion of a system from inordinately holding up another. Likewise, an internal application queue can accomplish the same thing. The basic principle is to separate the intake portion of the application, which tends to operate quickly, from the presentation portion of the application, which tends to operate slowly. If an `onMessage()` method immediately places the received message (or relevant information from the message) in an internal buffer without waiting for all interested components to be updated, then it is free to return and process more messages. You can find a more detailed description of this technique in Chapter 13.

Use message selectors with caution

The ability to filter incoming messages using message selectors is a unique and useful feature of JMS (see Chapter 4 for a description of message selectors). Unfortunately, using selectors can negatively affect your performance in some circumstances.

Whether you should be concerned about selectors depends on the specifics of your provider's implementation, which can be a very hard thing to decipher. The WebLogic documentation, for instance, directly recommends against using message selectors at all. But this is far too strong a blanket statement to make.

As a rule of thumb, you can probably assume that message selection operations that take place on the client side are more of a concern than server-side selections because client-side selections take place inside the client application's JVM using an SQL engine incorporated into the provider's client-side code. This is typically the case for topic-based messaging. Because generic SQL evaluation can be CPU-intensive, it's not something you want to be doing for every message – unless, of course, you have a low-volume system.

On the other hand, message selection that takes place on the server may not have as much of a performance impact. This is especially true of queue-based systems built on top of a standard database package because it's easy to imagine a provider simply taking the JMS message selector and, with slight modifications, handing it off to the database as an SQL statement for it to evaluate. Because databases are designed to handle SQL very efficiently, you might not notice much of a performance degradation.

In any case, the only way to know for sure what the impact of using message selectors is in your application is to benchmark it. You should measure how long it takes to process a message using the selector versus how long it takes if you simply hard-code the required logic into your onMessage() method. Figure 10-1 illustrates client-side versus server-based message filtering.

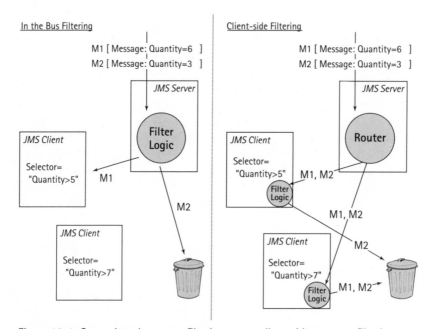

Figure 10-1: Server-based message filtering versus client-side message filtering

Reuse TopicRequestor and QueueRequestor instances

When implementing request/reply messaging, you can use the TopicRequestor and QueueRequestor classes to simplify the process (see Chapter 5 and Chapter 6 for descriptions of the TopicRequestor and QueueRequestor classes). If your application is routinely making use of request/reply messaging, then it's best to keep a single instance of the requestor class available to reuse rather than creating a new one each time. In this way you'll avoid the overhead of creating a new temporary topic for each message.

Use XML-based messaging only when necessary

XML is here to stay, there's no doubt about it. However, in the mad rush to XML-ize the entire world, designers sometimes lose sight of the big picture. XML-based messages have many advantages, but increased performance is definitely not one of them. The overhead associated with formatting outgoing messages and parsing incoming ones can be substantial, so it's worth asking yourself exactly why you want to employ XML messaging in the first place.

XML has two main advantages over traditional message formats. One is platform neutrality; XML messages are text-based, so they are easily processed on any computer architecture. Another is that XML messages are not fixed-format so they can be modified and extended without having to recode every application that processes them so that they understand the new format.

In a JMS system, the first advantage is a non-issue because any JMS provider that supports clients running on a particular platform will automatically convert data formats from one platform's internal representation to another, and likely in a much more efficient way than does XML (because not every type of data will need to be converted to a string and back). This is true even if, for example, the sender of a message is written in Java and the receiver is written in COBOL. Thus, XML offers no advantage in this case. (See the "Interplatform message delivery" section in Chapter 2 for a discussion of XML messaging.)

As for the second XML advantage, there's no denying that flexible message formats enable systems to be more loosely coupled, which in turn reduces the maintenance required to keep all applications up to date with the latest format of each particular message. JMS already defines a message type (`MapMessage`) that supports flexible format messaging, thus XML isn't buying you much in this case either.

Flexible formatting is much less of an advantage in practice than it is in theory anyway, especially for in-house enterprise systems where you generally have control over the release cycle and versioning of the applications participating in messaging. If, for instance, you're adding a new field to a message, chances are it's because you want your applications to do something with that field so some or all of your applications are going to have to be updated anyway.

XML messaging has its place, especially when exchanging messages with foreign systems (that is, systems outside the corporate firewall) and with systems that you don't have direct control over. But, it's less likely that you would be using JMS as the transport mechanism in such scenarios.

If you do decide to go with XML as a message interchange format between your internal applications, be sure to start benchmarking early in the development process so that you're fully aware of the performance impact it will have on your system.

Don't use persistent messaging if you don't need to

It may seem obvious, but be sure not to use persistent messaging if you don't need it. The cost of storing a message on disk is much higher than if the entire operation can be handled in memory. If losing some messages in the rare event of a complete system failure is acceptable in your environment, then you don't need to send those messages in a persistent manner.

Even if losing some messages is not acceptable, you may want to consider other alternatives to using persistent messaging. For example, if in your particular application it's possible to reconstruct any lost messages from some other data source, then it may be worthwhile to write a recovery program that can figure out what messages never made it to their destination and then resend them. In the event of a major system failure, you could then run this application as part of the restart process. Using the recovery technique, your system can adequately compensate for the rare failure and you do not have to pay the persistent messaging penalty for each message sent during the long stretches of normal operation.

Performing low-level optimizations

When discussing performance-related issues, keep in mind that it's often the lowest-level code that causes the biggest problems. A small block of code, if written inefficiently and executed repeatedly, can have a negative impact on performance disproportional to the size of the code itself. Since such blocks of code are notoriously difficult to track down after a system is in production, it's always best to write them optimally in the first place. In addition to the best practices we just covered, you should also consider a million and one generic Java best practices as well, such as the following:

♦ Using unsynchronized collections (such as `ArrayList`) instead of synchronized ones (such as `Vector`)

♦ Using `StringBuffer`s instead of extensive string concatenations using +

♦ Consider declaring classes, methods, and variables `final`; in some case the VM can optimize accesses to `final` elements.

♦ Reuse objects instead of allocating new ones where possible to reduce the load on the garbage collector

These and other techniques need to be employed to get the best performance out of your Java application. The Internet is peppered with white papers and articles about how to optimize your Java code. When looking for small code optimization opportunities, however, the best place to start in an application is simply to have an experienced person or team conduct a thorough code walkthrough. Many lower-level inefficiencies in both source code and design can be detected and corrected this way.

Working with vendors

Optimizing the code for any application is a painstaking and time-consuming process but well worth the effort. Human nature being what it is, however, it's usually easier for development teams to point the finger at their software infrastructure vendors or hardware manufacturers as the main cause for their application's poor or limited performance.

Could the performance of a product you're using be better? Of course! Do a few vendors sell products with rotten internal implementations? Some do. However, in general, it's safe to say that the majority of software and hardware vendors have put a lot more thought into how to best optimize their products than any given development team has to a system it just finished writing.

It is not realistic to expect a vendor to somehow improve the performance of its product enough (and in a reasonable amount of time) to offset the implementation inefficiencies in your application. The vendor will not be able to do it and you will still be left with the problem of management breathing down your neck to make the system faster.

First be sure you've thoroughly optimized your design and code. In conjunction with this, you should have some way of measuring the various parts of your application to find out exactly where the hot spots are. After doing this, you'll not only have a much faster application, you'll have a much better idea of what specifically you'd like to be done by the vendor of whatever product you are using to improve the performance of its piece of the puzzle.

Benchmarking JMS Applications

To properly performance-test an application, you must take a layered approach. Like any good experimenter, you should control various factors so that you can properly test each layer.

The best performance analysts are multidisciplinary people who have a good understanding of operating systems, networks, and databases and who understand how an application is designed and coded. In addition, and perhaps most important, they should understand how to go about dividing up a system in a way that enables each major component to be isolated and measured. I'll talk about techniques for benchmarking JMS applications in this section.

Approach benchmarking in a layered manner

It's not always possible to rip out various pieces of an application so they can be benchmarked in isolation. Looking at an application as a series of layers, however, and benchmarking from the inside out will enable you to determine the performance characteristics of each layer by subtracting the speed measured at a given layer from the speed measured at the layer below it. If your application is designed well, it should not be difficult to conduct performance testing in this manner. Figure 10-2 shows a sample of how to conduct layered performance benchmarking.

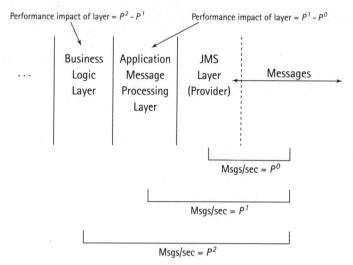

Figure 10-2: Benchmarking an application layer by layer

Consider changes over time

If you plan on running your system for long periods of time without a system restart — and who doesn't these days? — then it only makes sense to run your benchmark over a long period of time as well. It's clearly not practical to run a benchmark for months on end, but running one for a few days is not so unreasonable.

When conducting this type of benchmark, it's not the final performance numbers (such as messages per second) that are most important; it's the trend over the life of the test. If, for instance, message throughput is decreasing steadily over the life of the benchmark, then this is not a good sign that a system will be able to run smoothly for long stretches of time. Your benchmark program should report its values periodically — say, every half hour — when running a long-term test. Graphing these results will help you quickly discover whether your system will hold up over the long run.

Make your benchmarking comprehensive

Don't just measure basic JMS message throughput in your application. This is important information but not all you need to be concerned about. The rate of increase in resource consumption for a variety of system components should be measured as well, including the following:

- ◆ Disk usage
- ◆ Memory consumption
- ◆ CPU load

An application that consumes more and more memory over time, for example, may have a memory leak that would preclude it from being run over long periods of time without a restart. Memory usage for Java applications can be measured using the following call:

```
long memBytes = Runtime.getRuntime().freeMemory();
```

 Long-term benchmarking should not just be reserved for preproduction testing. Automated, routine measurement of key performance-related factors in a live system can help spot problems long before they result in a system failure. Such information can also be valuable in planning for future system upgrade requirements. Just be sure the measurement activity in your production systems doesn't overly degrade their performance!

A sample benchmarking application

This section includes a sample JMS benchmarking application to help you get started on your performance-testing effort. A single program handles both the sending and receiving side of the benchmark but not in a single instance. You should run two instances of the program, one in "send" mode and one in "receive" mode. They do not, of course, have to be run on the same machine. There's also no reason that more than one sender or more than one receiver can't be run at the same time; sometimes you want to do exactly this to generate a realistic load on the system. The following are examples of how to run the "receive" and "send" sides of the benchmark program.

```
command% java JMSPerformanceTest receive
```

```
command% java JMSPerformanceTest send
```

The receiving instance should be run before the sending. The sender should not be executed until the receiver reports that it is ready to receive messages.

The constructor for the `JMSPerformanceTest` class is where to create a `TestParams` object that contains the parameters to be used when running the test. The `TestParams` class contains the following fields you can use to control the test:

- ◆ int `spinUpMessages` — The number of messages to send before beginning performance timing. This field ensures that the application and JMS server are fully initialized and ready.

- ◆ int `benchmarkMessages` — The number of messages to send/receive.

- ◆ int `messageSize` — The size of each message sent.

- ◆ String connFactory — The Java Naming and Directory Interface (JNDI) name of the connection factory to use.

- ◆ String destination — The JNDI name of the destination to use.

- ◆ boolean transacted — Should the session be transacted?

- ◆ int ackMode — The JMS acknowledgment mode to use.

- ◆ int deliveryMode — The JMS delivery mode to use.

- ◆ boolean disableTimestamp — Should timestamp generation be disabled?

- ◆ boolean disableMsgID — Should message ID generation be disabled?

Listing 10-1 shows the source code for the JMS benchmark application.

Listing 10-1: A JMS benchmarking application

```
import java.util.*;
import java.text.*;
import java.io.*;
import javax.transaction.*;
import javax.naming.*;
import javax.jms.*;


/** A benchmark program that runs in send or receive mode and
 *  records the elapsed time.
 *  Be sure to run the program in "receive" mode first and wait
 *  for the "Ready" message before running the "send" mode
 *  instance.
 */


public class JMSPerformanceTest
{
    static public final int SEND = 0;
    static public final int RECEIVE = 1;

    List results = new ArrayList();

    public JMSPerformanceTest(Context ctx, int typeOfTest,
TestParams params)
        throws JMSException, NamingException
    {
        if (typeOfTest == SEND)
        {
            if ("TOPIC".equals(params.type))
                results.add( topicSendBenchmark(ctx, params) );
            else
```

```
                results.add( queueSendBenchmark(ctx, params) );
    }
    else
    {
        if ("TOPIC".equals(params.type))
            results.add( topicReceiveBenchmark(ctx, params) );
        else
            results.add( queueReceiveBenchmark(ctx, params) );
    }
}

public List getResults()
{
    return results;
}

TestResults queueSendBenchmark(Context ctx,
    TestParams params)
    throws JMSException, NamingException
{
    // Lookup the queue connection factory
    QueueConnectionFactory qcf =
        (QueueConnectionFactory)
            ctx.lookup(params.connFactory);

    QueueConnection qc = qcf.createQueueConnection();

    // Register a listener for server errors
    qc.setExceptionListener(new ExceptionListener()
    {
        public void onException(JMSException e)
        {
            e.printStackTrace();
        }
    });

    QueueSession qs =
            qc.createQueueSession(params.transacted,
                params.ackMode);

    // Lookup the queue destination
    javax.jms.Queue queue =
        (javax.jms.Queue) ctx.lookup(params.destination);
```

Continued

Listing 10-1 *(Continued)*

```
        QueueSender qsend = qs.createSender(queue);

        qsend.setDisableMessageTimestamp(params.disableTimestamp);
        qsend.setDisableMessageID(params.disableMsgID);

        Message msg = createBenchmarkMessage(qs, params);
        msg.setJMSDeliveryMode(params.deliveryMode);

        for (int n=0; n < params.spinUpMessages; ++n)
        {
            qsend.send(msg);
        }

        TestResults result = new TestResults();

        result.params = params;

        result.timeBegin = System.currentTimeMillis();
        result.memoryBegin = Runtime.getRuntime().totalMemory() -

Runtime.getRuntime().freeMemory();

        for (int n=0; n < params.benchmarkMessages; ++n)
        {
            qsend.send(msg);
        }

        result.timeEnd = System.currentTimeMillis();
        result.memoryEnd = Runtime.getRuntime().totalMemory() -

Runtime.getRuntime().freeMemory();

        result.numMessages = params.benchmarkMessages;

        // Clean up

        qs.close();
        qc.close();

        return result;
    }

    TestResults queueReceiveBenchmark(Context ctx,
        TestParams params)
```

```
    throws JMSException, NamingException
{
    // Lookup the queue connection factory
    QueueConnectionFactory qcf =
        (QueueConnectionFactory)
            ctx.lookup(params.connFactory);

    QueueConnection qc = qcf.createQueueConnection();

    // Register a listener for server errors
    qc.setExceptionListener(new ExceptionListener()
    {
        public void onException(JMSException e)
        {
            e.printStackTrace();
        }
    });

    QueueSession qs =
            qc.createQueueSession(params.transacted,
            params.ackMode);

    // Lookup the queue destination
    javax.jms.Queue queue =
        (javax.jms.Queue) ctx.lookup(params.destination);

    QueueReceiver qrecv = qs.createReceiver(queue);

    TestResults result = new TestResults();

    result.params = params;

    ReceiveListener rlistener =
        new ReceiveListener(this, params, result);

    qrecv.setMessageListener(rlistener);

    result.numMessages = params.benchmarkMessages;

    qc.start();

    System.out.println("Ready to receive messages");

    try
```

Continued

Listing 10-1 *(Continued)*

```
    {
        synchronized (this) { wait(); }
    }
    catch (InterruptedException e) { e.printStackTrace(); }

    System.out.println("Done");

    // Clean up

    qs.close();
    qc.close();

    return result;
}

TestResults topicSendBenchmark(Context ctx,
    TestParams params)
    throws JMSException, NamingException
{
    // Lookup the topic connection factory
    TopicConnectionFactory tcf =
        (TopicConnectionFactory)
            ctx.lookup(params.connFactory);

    TopicConnection tc = tcf.createTopicConnection();

    // Register a listener for server errors
    tc.setExceptionListener(new ExceptionListener()
    {
        public void onException(JMSException e)
        {
            e.printStackTrace();
        }
    });

    TopicSession ts =
            tc.createTopicSession(params.transacted,
                params.ackMode);

    // Lookup the topic destination
    javax.jms.Topic topic =
        (javax.jms.Topic) ctx.lookup(params.destination);

    TopicPublisher tsend = ts.createPublisher(topic);
```

```
        tsend.setDisableMessageTimestamp(params.disableTimestamp);
        tsend.setDisableMessageID(params.disableMsgID);

        Message msg = createBenchmarkMessage(ts, params);
        msg.setJMSDeliveryMode(params.deliveryMode);

        for (int n=0; n < params.spinUpMessages; ++n)
        {
            tsend.publish(msg);
        }

        TestResults result = new TestResults();

        result.params = params;

        result.timeBegin = System.currentTimeMillis();
        result.memoryBegin = Runtime.getRuntime().totalMemory() -

Runtime.getRuntime().freeMemory();

        for (int n=0; n < params.benchmarkMessages; ++n)
        {
            tsend.publish(msg);
        }

        result.timeEnd = System.currentTimeMillis();
        result.memoryEnd = Runtime.getRuntime().totalMemory() -

Runtime.getRuntime().freeMemory();

        result.numMessages = params.benchmarkMessages;

        // Clean up

        ts.close();
        tc.close();

        return result;
    }

    TestResults topicReceiveBenchmark(Context ctx,
        TestParams params)
        throws JMSException, NamingException
```

Continued

Listing 10-1 *(Continued)*

```java
{
    // Lookup the topic connection factory
    TopicConnectionFactory tcf =
        (TopicConnectionFactory)
            ctx.lookup(params.connFactory);

    TopicConnection tc = tcf.createTopicConnection();

    // Register a listener for server errors
    tc.setExceptionListener(new ExceptionListener()
    {
        public void onException(JMSException e)
        {
            e.printStackTrace();
        }
    });

    TopicSession ts =
            tc.createTopicSession(params.transacted,
                params.ackMode);

    // Lookup the topic destination
    javax.jms.Topic topic =
        (javax.jms.Topic) ctx.lookup(params.destination);

    TopicSubscriber trecv = ts.createSubscriber(topic);

    TestResults result = new TestResults();

    result.params = params;

    ReceiveListener rlistener =
        new ReceiveListener(this, params, result);

    trecv.setMessageListener(rlistener);

    result.numMessages = params.benchmarkMessages;

    tc.start();

    System.out.println("Ready to receive messages");

    try
    {
```

```
        synchronized (this) { wait(); }
    }
    catch (InterruptedException e) { e.printStackTrace(); }

    System.out.println("Done");

    // Clean up

    ts.close();
    tc.close();

    return result;
}

static Message createBenchmarkMessage(Session session,
        TestParams params)
        throws JMSException
{
    BytesMessage msg = session.createBytesMessage();

    byte[] data = new byte[ params.messageSize ];

    msg.writeBytes(data);

    return msg;
}

public static void main(String[] args) throws Exception
{
    if (args.length != 1 ||
        !("send".equalsIgnoreCase(args[0]) ||
          "receive".equalsIgnoreCase(args[0])))
    {
        System.out.println(
            "Usage: java JMSPerformanceTest { send | receive }");
        System.exit(1);
    }

    boolean isSend = "send".equalsIgnoreCase(args[0]);

            // Test params can be hardcoded
    /*
    TestParams params = new TestParams(
            100, 1000, 512,
```

Continued

Listing 10-1 *(Continued)*

```
                "TOPIC", "TOPICFACTORY",
                "PUBSUBNAME",
                false, Session.AUTO_ACKNOWLEDGE,
                DeliveryMode.NON_PERSISTENT, true, true);
        */


        // Or read from a properties file like this
        Properties props = new Properties();
        props.load(new FileInputStream("testparams.properties"));
        TestParams params = new TestParams(props);



        // Context is loaded from the jndi.properties file
        Context ctx = new InitialContext();

        JMSPerformanceTest jpt =
            new JMSPerformanceTest(ctx, isSend ? SEND : RECEIVE,
params);

        DecimalFormat df = new DecimalFormat("0.###");
        DecimalFormat dfmem = new DecimalFormat("###,###");

        for (Iterator it=jpt.getResults().iterator();
                it.hasNext();)
        {
            TestResults result = (TestResults) it.next();

            System.out.println(result.params);
            System.out.println();
            System.out.println("\tNumber of messages " +
                (isSend ? "sent" : "received") +
                " = " + result.numMessages);
            System.out.println("\tTotal Time = " +
                toDuration(df, result.timeEnd-result.timeBegin));
            System.out.println("\tRate = " +
                df.format(result.numMessages /
                ((result.timeEnd - result.timeBegin)/1000.0)) +
                " msgs/sec");
            System.out.println("\tMemory used at start of test = " +
                dfmem.format(result.memoryBegin / 1024) + "k");
            System.out.println("\tMemory used at end of test = " +
                dfmem.format(result.memoryEnd / 1024) + "k");
            System.out.println();
            System.out.println();
```

```
        }
}

static String toDuration(DecimalFormat df, long ms)
{
    if (ms < 1000) return ms + " milliseconds";

    if (ms < 60*1000)
        return df.format(ms / 1000.0) + " seconds";

    String s = (ms / (60*1000)) + " minutes, ";
    ms %= 60*1000;
    return s + df.format(ms / 1000.0) + " seconds";
}

/* This class is the listener object for "receive" mode
 * benchmarking. It read the required number of "spin-up"
 * messages and then notifies the main thread when the
 * right number of benchmark messages have been received.
 */
static class ReceiveListener implements MessageListener
{
    Object caller;
    TestParams params;
    TestResults result;
    int msgsReceived = 0;
    boolean spinUpDone = false;

    ReceiveListener(Object caller, TestParams params,
        TestResults result)
    {
        this.caller = caller;
        this.params = params;
        this.result = result;
    }

    public void onMessage(Message msg)
    {
        try
        {
            msg.acknowledge();
        }
        catch (JMSException e) { e.printStackTrace(); }

        // First read all the spin up messages
```

Continued

Listing 10-1 *(Continued)*

```
            if (!spinUpDone)
            {
                if (++msgsReceived == params.spinUpMessages)
                {
                    msgsReceived = 0;
                    spinUpDone = true;
                }
                return;
            }

            // Start the timer on the receipt of the
            // first message
            if (msgsReceived == 0)
            {
                result.timeBegin = System.currentTimeMillis();
                result.memoryBegin =
Runtime.getRuntime().totalMemory() -

Runtime.getRuntime().freeMemory();
            }

            // End the test if we've received all the messages
            if (++msgsReceived == params.benchmarkMessages)
            {
                result.timeEnd = System.currentTimeMillis();
                result.memoryEnd =
Runtime.getRuntime().totalMemory() -

Runtime.getRuntime().freeMemory();

                // Notify the main thread that the test is over
                synchronized (caller) { caller.notify(); }
            }
        }
    }

    /* This class holds the results of the test run
     */
    static public class TestResults
    {
        TestParams params;

        // Total messages sent or received
        long numMessages;
```

```
        // Duration of the test in milliseconds
        long timeBegin, timeEnd;

        // Beginning and end memory usage
        long memoryBegin, memoryEnd;
    }


    /* This class is used to specify the parameters the benchmark
     * should be executed with. The parameters can be hardcoded or
     * loaded from a properties object.
     */
    static public class TestParams
    {
        // The number of messages required to warm up the server
        int spinUpMessages;

        // The number of messages to benchmark
        int benchmarkMessages;

        // The size of the message to send
        int messageSize;

        String type; // "TOPIC" or "QUEUE"
        String connFactory;
        String destination;
        boolean transacted, disableTimestamp, disableMsgID;
        int ackMode;
        int deliveryMode;

        public TestParams(Properties props) throws Exception
        {
            this.spinUpMessages = Integer.valueOf(
                    props.getProperty("spinupmsgs")).intValue();
            this.benchmarkMessages = Integer.valueOf(

props.getProperty("benchmarkmessages")).intValue();
            this.messageSize = Integer.valueOf(

props.getProperty("messagesize")).intValue();

            this.type = props.getProperty("type");
            this.connFactory = props.getProperty("factory");
            this.destination = props.getProperty("destination");
            this.transacted =
```

Continued

Listing 10-1 *(Continued)*

```
Boolean.valueOf(props.getProperty("transacted")).booleanValue();
          this.ackMode =

ackModeFromString(props.getProperty("acknowledgment"));
          this.deliveryMode =
            deliveryModeFromString(props.getProperty("delivery"));
          this.disableTimestamp = Boolean.valueOf(

props.getProperty("disabletimestamp")).booleanValue();
          this.disableMsgID = Boolean.valueOf(

props.getProperty("disablemessageid")).booleanValue();
       }

     public TestParams(int spinUpMsgNum, int benchmarkMsgNum, int
msgSize,
          String type, String connFactory,
          String destination, boolean transacted,
          int ackMode, int deliveryMode,
          boolean disableTimestamp, boolean disableMsgID)
     {
       this.spinUpMessages = spinUpMsgNum;
       this.benchmarkMessages = benchmarkMsgNum;
       this.messageSize = msgSize;

       this.type = type;
       this.connFactory = connFactory;
       this.destination = destination;
       this.transacted = transacted;
       this.ackMode = ackMode;
       this.deliveryMode = deliveryMode;
       this.disableTimestamp = disableTimestamp;
       this.disableMsgID = disableMsgID;
     }

     public String toString()
     {
       return "Messaging Type = " + type +
         "\nDestination = " + destination +
         "\nTransacted = " + transacted +
         "\nAck Mode = " + toAckMode(ackMode) +
         "\nDelivery Mode = " +
            (deliveryMode == DeliveryMode.PERSISTENT ?
            "PERSISTENT" : "NON_PERSISTENT") +
```

```
                          "\nDisabled Timestamp = " + disableTimestamp +
                          "\nDisabled MessageID = " + disableMsgID;
        }


        static String toAckMode(int mode)
        {
            if (mode == Session.AUTO_ACKNOWLEDGE)
                return "AUTO_ACKNOWLEDGE";
            if (mode == Session.CLIENT_ACKNOWLEDGE)
                return "CLIENT_ACKNOWLEDGE";
            if (mode == Session.DUPS_OK_ACKNOWLEDGE)
                return "DUPS_OK_ACKNOWLEDGE";
            return "UNKNOWN";
        }


        static int ackModeFromString(String s)
        {
            s = s.toUpperCase();

            if ("CLIENT_ACKNOWLEDGE".equals(s))
                return Session.CLIENT_ACKNOWLEDGE;

            else if ("DUPS_OK_ACKNOWLEDGE".equals(s))
                return Session.DUPS_OK_ACKNOWLEDGE;

            return Session.AUTO_ACKNOWLEDGE;
        }


        static int deliveryModeFromString(String s)
        {
            s = s.toUpperCase();

            if ("PERSISTENT".equals(s))
                return DeliveryMode.PERSISTENT;

            return DeliveryMode.NON_PERSISTENT;
        }
    }
}
```

Rather than hard-coding the values you need to drive the benchmark test, the TestParams class from the JMSPerformanceTest program in Listing 10-1 also has a constructor that accepts a Java Properties object that has the required values. Naturally, these properties can be loaded from a file so that you do not have to recompile the benchmark program before every run. A sample of the properties file is shown in Listing 10-2.

Listing 10-2: A sample properties file holding parameters for the benchmark program

```
spinupmsgs=1000
benchmarkmessages=30000
messagesize=512
type=TOPIC
factory=TOPICFACTORY
destination=PUBSUBNAME
transacted=false
acknowledgment=AUTO_ACKNOWLEDGE
delivery=NON_PERSISTENT
disabletimestamp=true
disablemessageid=true
```

Listings 10-3 and 10-4 show the sample output you'd see from the "receive" and "send" sides of the benchmark program, respectively.

Listing 10-3: Sample output from the "receive" side of the benchmarker

```
Ready to receive messages
Done
Messaging Type = TOPIC
Destination = PUBSUBNAME
Transacted = false
Ack Mode = AUTO_ACKNOWLEDGE
Delivery Mode = NON_PERSISTENT
Disabled Timestamp = true
Disabled MessageID = true

    Number of messages received = 30000
    Total Time = 7 minutes, 33.57 seconds
    Rate = 66.142 msgs/sec
    Memory used at start of test = 1,946k
    Memory used at end of test = 1,703k
```

Listing 10-4: Sample output from the "send" side of the benchmarker

```
Messaging Type = TOPIC
Destination = PUBSUBNAME
Transacted = false
Ack Mode = AUTO_ACKNOWLEDGE
Delivery Mode = NON_PERSISTENT
Disabled Timestamp = true
Disabled MessageID = true

Number of messages received = 30000
    Total Time = 7 minutes, 33.63 seconds
```

```
Rate = 66.133 msgs/sec
Memory used at start of test = 1,485k
Memory used at end of test = 1,431k
```

In the case where the sender and receiver are running on the same box, you'll generally see a message throughput rate roughly the same for the send and receive side of the benchmark, as in the preceding samples. However, if, for instance, a receiver is running on a platform with fewer resources in comparison to the sender, you may see a big difference in the measured rate at each end. You may need to address this problem somehow because it could mean, for example, that a sender is filling a JMS queue at a faster rate than it can be read by the receiver. Over time, this situation might cause the queue to grow to unmanageable proportions.

Implementing a performance optimization strategy

As with security, performance tends to get short shrift in most applications. Adequate time and procedures are rarely built into a new system's project plan. Unlike security, however, everybody recognizes that efficient, high-performing systems are extremely desirable. Unfortunately, most people seem to think that performance is somebody else's responsibility, which results in a lot of unproductive finger pointing.

Achieving optimal performance with a complex enterprise system is only possible through a coordinated effort by all the major players: software vendors, hardware vendors, database vendors, applications developers, and internal systems administrators. Such a team needs a strategy. You should settle on a performance management plan and set it in motion as early as possible in the development process — ideally before coding begins. Some key elements of this strategy should be as follows:

◆ Realistic performance analysis of JMS (and other) products — prior to a final selection, if possible.

◆ Team whiteboard walkthroughs of high- and low-level designs focusing on functionality, maintainability, extensibility, *and* performance.

◆ Regular code reviews of some sensible percentage of the code base by experienced developers.

◆ Instrumentation of application components and layers to allow for performance testing.

◆ Beginning minimal performance testing early in the development process; increasing the scope of testing as the project progresses.

◆ Use of third-party tools for analyzing applications, systems, networks, and databases.

- ◆ Long-term performance testing prior to a production rollout.

- ◆ Routine analysis of live production systems.

Summary

After you follow all the right development processes, correctly configure your JMS provider, and thoroughly optimize your code, the sad truth is that you might not end up with a system that performs as well as you'd like. Every system — hardware and software — has its limits and you have to be reasonable about what you're expecting to be able to accomplish given the infrastructure available to you.

No one wants to implement a system that does not perform as well as you or management expects. Avoiding this painful (and career limiting) predicament begins at the beginning of the development process during the architecture phase. Knowing the performance you can realistically expect from the various systems components you're planning on using helps you design a system that is more likely to meet its performance goals. If you can make these decisions based on experience, then great. If not, you should at least be sure to get the information you need through early and targeted performance testing.

When it comes to JMS products, architects too often assume they can just stick any old JMS provider in the middle of their system and get infinite throughput out of it. Certainly this is not the case with a JMS (or any other) product. On a properly configured, top-of-the-line machine running a JMS provider, you're probably look-ing at a peak capacity of *around* a few hundred messages/second in an unclustered configuration. You can achieve higher rates through clustering and generally throwing hardware at the problem, but in the end you may also have to design your application to distribute traffic across several independent JMS instances. Refer to the "Creating Message-Driven Architectures" section of Chapter 7 for a discussion of the advantages of distributing your messaging traffic over several JMS instances.

Part II

JMS Administration

Chapter 11

Administering JMS

IN THIS CHAPTER

◆ Administration and the JMS specification

◆ Administered objects and directories

◆ Product-specific administered features

◆ Administration tools

◆ Role of the administrator

HOW BEST TO ADMINISTER A SYSTEM is certainly not the first task a developer or architect thinks of when starting to pick up a new technology. In fact, "administering" a messaging system such as JMS is, if not an entirely new concept, at least one that JMS has tried to push more to the forefront of activities. In JMS systems, administration is not just about getting an installation up and running; it's a process entwined on some levels with development. However, no longer do you completely configure and control a product's behavior from within your code or with simple, unmanaged configuration files as has been the traditional way of administering a product. Rather, most JMS vendors provide some means of configuring their product's runtime behavior using rich, graphical tools that store your configuration choices in a directory service.

For this reason, developers and architects must be aware of the administrative capabilities and requirements of their JMS server. Developers need to know which behaviors (such as transactions, timeouts, and so on) should be specified in the source code and which should not. Architects need to know what features of their JMS installation can be tuned to squeeze maximum performance out of it.

And, of course, there's the most prosaic reason of all for understanding JMS administration: you just downloaded a new JMS product and need to be able to get it up and running so you can play with it.

Administration and the JMS Specification

A reading of the JMS specification reveals that very little has been nailed down with respect to administrative capabilities, though it is clear that the designers' intent is that administration (and administrators) play a key role in the management and operation of JMS installations. The vast majority of the specification provides details on what's required of a JMS-compliant system from an API and behavior point of view, and includes only suggestions for how an administrator might actually go about manipulating the required features.

This is by design, of course, because JMS recognizes that numerous provider solutions are implemented in a variety of ways. Consequently, each vendor's product has its own peculiar set of tunable parameters for the system administrator. As we'll see later in this chapter, these tunable parameters will address the following important factors:

- Connection factories

- Destinations

- Directory management

- Queue management

- Persistent storage

- Security

- Performance

Of these factors, only connection factories and destinations are generally assumed – but not technically required – by the JMS specification to be managed by an administrator. JMS objects such as connection factories and destinations that can be configured externally are called *administered objects*.

The main idea behind having an administered object is that it provides the opportunity for a central system administrator to provide both default and required configuration parameters to objects that are used by JMS client applications. To some extent, this lets the behavior of a JMS messaging system be manipulated without rewriting any client code. It also has the advantage of enabling the system to be tuned and reconfigured while it is running, though with practical limits in many cases.

Administered Objects and Directories

JMS strongly recommends that all vendors provide a facility for managing JMS connection factories and destinations. The reason why these two elements are key is that one of each is required to create the object necessary to do any JMS messaging: either a consumer or a subscriber (review Chapters 3 and 4 for full details). Controlling the configuration of both – and access to both, as we saw in Chapter 9 – also gives an administrator control over the gateway that all clients must use to talk to the messaging subsystem.

In addition, because JMS message objects can only be created by one of the factory methods available in a JMS session object – and remember, JMS session objects can themselves only be created from a connection factory object – the ability to control the parameters of a connection factory gives the administrator control over the properties (**JMSDestination**, **JMSExpiration**, etc.) associated with a JMS message object. Because many of these properties affect how a message is delivered, as well as how long it lives, this is an important feature (see Chapter 2 for more on message properties and their effects).

The UML (Unified Modeling Language) diagram in Figure 11-1 shows the relationship of JMS's administered objects to each other.

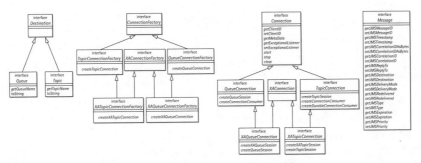

Figure 11-1: JMS-administered objects and their relationships

Preconfiguring objects

The ability to preconfigure or prepopulate connection factories, destinations, and messages is valuable for managing message flow through the system because it keeps the developer from having to hard-code such information in the source code. It also removes the need to write custom code to look up the appropriate parameters from a separate data source such as a database or property file; when a developer instantiates (via the lookup process) an administered object in their program, the object is already pre-populated with the necessary configuration. Finally, administration also facilitates the configuration of some parameters that might not be accessible through the normal JMS API. We'll discuss this further in the next section.

For example, a common JMS message property that you might want to set on an installation-wide basis is the time-to-live (TTL) property (the **JMSExpiration** property). The traditional way of setting a global parameter for an application entailed using solutions such as a Java property file that all client applications could read and making it a policy that all developers had to process this file during their application's start-up phase so that they could configure their application's behavior accordingly. This would look something like the following in a file called, say, `appconfig.properties`:

```
myapp.messaging.timetolive=60000
```

It would look something like this in application pseudo-code:

```
java.util.Properties props = new java.util.Properties();
props.load(new FileInputStream("config.properties"));

long ttl =
    Long.parseLong(
        props.getProperty("myapp.messaging.timetolive", "120000")
    );

...

Message msg = jmssession.createMessage();
msg.setJMSExpiration(ttl);

send message . . .
```

While this method has the advantage of enabling the value for time-to-live to be specified externally to any specific application, it still requires the proper encoding of the system-wide TTL policy inside the application source code. Not only is this a real pain to program, it is prone to error and not enforceable in any sort of centralized way. Aside from thorough testing, you have no way to be sure each developer has implemented the TTL policy properly or that the code was not broken accidentally at some point during the system's life.

Using the administration facilities provided by the vendor, a typical JMS product enables an administrator to centrally specify that all JMS messages created by a particular connection factory will automatically have their time-to-live property set to a standard value. In the preceding example, this would be 60 seconds (60,000 milliseconds). Clearly this is an advantage over the traditional method of requiring each application to set the appropriate values themselves because it requires no extra code to be written. The developer can simply create JMS messages as normal with the expectation that the **JMSExpiration** property is already set as desired.

Adapting the preceding example, we're simply left with:

```
Message msg = jmssession.createMessage();
```

A call to `msg.getJMSExpiration()` would return 60000.

Regardless of how a JMS connection is configured, you still need to ensure that the client application gets a handle to the right connection factory to begin with. Because this is controlled by a JNDI lookup using a plain string identifier, you may not want to hard-code this string inside the application but rather store it in an external source — ironically perhaps, in a common properties file. Another possibility is to utilize whatever directory service you have available to you — ideally the same one your JMS product stores its administered objects in — to store (as part of a user profile) the strings that identify the connection factories and destinations your application will need.

Generally speaking, a vendor's JMS product will enable you to administratively set all JMS message properties that the JMS specification allows to be set by a client application. Thus, for example, the **JMSExpiration** property can typically be configured administratively but the **JMSDestination** property cannot.

ENFORCING POLICIES

Suppose instead of just specifying a default value for the time-to-live property, we want to also ensure that developers cannot change this value to something else by overriding it in their code. When might we want to prevent developers from overriding administered values? Envision, for example, some futuristic automated system where spare CPU cycles from vast banks of computers are auctioned off round-the-clock every 60 seconds. JMS messages containing bids for the cycles are received over the course of one minute and the cycles are then sold to the highest bidder for that round; a new round begins every minute. Clearly messages that don't make it to the auction server within 60 seconds would be stale, so we've probably administratively configured a default **JMSExpiration** for all messages to be 60,000 milliseconds.

What if a new developer does not realize the JMS bid messages have been pre-configured with a time-to-live and they explicitly call the `setJMSExpiration()` method with a value that is too low or too high? What if a developer violates the policy on purpose because there's an advantage to be gained by changing the TTL to a higher number so that a bid carries over into the next round? If the auction system's design depends on messages living no longer than 60 seconds, then we need to enforce the pre-configured TTL somehow in order to preserve the integrity of the auction. Whether there is a way or not to tell our JMS bus to enforce the 60 second rule, however, depends on the particular JMS product being used.

Some JMS products not only let you set a default value for a message property, they also let an administrator enforce this value by saying that any attempt by a developer to set a value different than the preconfigured one will result in a `JMSException` being thrown. Because vendors write the implementation code to create an actual `javax.jms.Message`, they are free to do this or anything else behind the scenes, whether it's required by the JMS specification or not. Configuration enforcement features such as this are not universal, however.

Again, because the JMS specification says nothing about what parts of an administered object are explicitly configurable, or how that configuration should be enforced, controls such as this are handled on a product-by-product basis. If the ability to prevent changes to pre-configured values is important to you, it's just something you'll have to add to your checklist when evaluating competing JMS products.

Administered objects and JNDI

When we talk about an object being "preconfigured," what exactly does that mean? Precisely what object is being configured? All the JMS specification says is that an administered object should be retrievable via a JNDI lookup. There's no reason, given a custom JNDI provider, that each JNDI lookup in your application actually must retrieve an object from a directory service somewhere. All the provider's implementation really needs to do is create a new JMS object, set the pre-configured values appropriately on it and hand it back to the client.

Clearly, however, the specification's intent is that administered objects should be maintained in a standard directory service of some sort. These days, this typically means a directory service based on LDAP (Lightweight Directory Access Protocol), but it could also be something else, such as a file system-based directory. To be compatible with a directory service, a configured object will typically be implemented by a vendor so that it's serializable. In this way, a JMS administrative tool can pre-populate an object in the way the administrator desires and then store the bytes representing the serialized object in the local directory service. Thus, when you look up an object, you're just getting a deserialized version of a previous object. Of course, from an application point of view, a deserialized object and a newly instantiated object are indistinguishable.

For the most part, though, JMS products give you the option of storing your administered objects in a LDAP server or on the local disk. Vendors realize that not everybody has an LDAP server available and that, even if they do, people often don't want to be bothered to use one during the project's development phase so they often provide a basic, low-end directory service with their product that can be used in lieu of a more heavy duty enterprise directory.

LIMITATIONS TO REAL-TIME ADMINISTRATION

It's nice to be able to administratively pre-configure a client application's messaging behavior, but don't assume that any values you specify using a provider's administrative tools will be dynamically propagated to running applications that have already looked up an administered object such as a connection factory. This is particularly true of JMS message properties. In environments where many clients run for long stretches at a time, it may be difficult to change a message property and expect to see the new value take effect in every client within a reasonable amount of time – at least not until all clients have restarted or otherwise reestablished their JMS connections. In particular, JMS does not provide any facility to force clients to re-obtain administered objects from JNDI, so if this feature is required by your application, you will have to build it yourself (fortunately, this is a straightforward operation using JMS itself to deliver instructions to your applications).

On the other hand, some vendor-specific features may apply directly to the JMS server itself and will take effect immediately. It all depends on the specific feature and the vendor's particular implementation. As usual, you'll need to consult the vendor's documentation to find out exactly what's going on under the covers.

MESSAGE-DRIVEN BEANS

In many ways, the message-driven bean is a special case because it's not really part of JMS per se; it's part of EJB. For this reason, a JMS administration tool typically will not say anything about message-driven beans. Message-driven beans will, instead, be configured and administered using whatever tool a vendor provides for administering and configuring any Enterprise JavaBean. At a minimum, this involves the creation of an XML-based descriptor file – as described by the EJB specification – and a procedure for deploying the bean to the application server (refer to Chapter 7 for details about message-driven bean deployment descriptors).

Product-Specific Administered Features

Aside from the objects the JMS specification specifically mentions that should be administered, it's entirely possible (and likely) that a particular vendor has its own proprietary set of administered features as well. Such parameters would be provider-specific, of course, but because the JMS specification makes no claims regarding what types of things are administratively configurable, or defines any sort of administration API, this is all perfectly kosher.

In general, product-specific administered features fall into two main categories:

♦ Extensions to standard objects

♦ Non API–related server-specific behavior

Extensions to standard objects

As is true with any specification, the JMS specification is far from complete. Vendors have many good (and sometimes bad) ideas about desirable features that JMS should support and, in many cases, they've gone ahead and added them to their product. To a small degree, the JMS specification anticipates this by describing the way in which vendor-specific properties can be added to the standard properties already associated with a message. On the one hand, there are many other non-standard features vendors might want to support that do not fit into the message property model very easily and require specific, custom API support.

STANDARD PROPERTIES

In the JMS specification, properties that start with the prefix JMS_<vendor_name> are reserved for vendor-specific properties that are shipped along in a JMS message. To the extent a vendor defines and supports any such properties, they probably will also provide a way to administratively configure them using whatever their standard administration tool is (if it makes sense to do so).

CLIENT-SIDE EXTENSIONS

In addition, a vendor may add extended features to a standard administered object. Suppose, for example, a JMS vendor, UltraMessaging Corp., writes a `com.ultra.jms.UltraTopicConnectionFactory` class that is its implementation of the standard interface `javax.jms.TopicConnectionFactory`. Let's say that UltraMessaging Corp. thinks it a good idea to be able to gather performance metrics related to `TopicConnection` by logging the processing time related to each message that passes through the connection.

Naturally, you'd want to have the ability to turn on and off this client-side performance logging but no standard JMS API exists for doing so. UltraMessaging Corp. probably included a `void setPerformanceLogging(boolean)` method on its implementation of `TopicConnectionFactory`, but to access it, a JMS client would need to cast the `javax.jms.TopicConnectionFactory` it received via the JNDI lookup to the UltraMessaging Corp.–specific class, as follows:

```
TopicConnectionFactory tcf =
        (TopicConnectionFactory) context.lookup("TopicConn");

((UltraTopicConnectionFactory) tcf).setPerformanceLogging(true);
```

While easily done, manipulation of behavior using proprietary classes eliminates one of JMS's prime advantages (vendor-neutrality) by introducing provider-specific code into the source. Should you ever want to change providers, this and any other code like it would have to be hunted down and expunged.

A better way to handle this situation is to give the JMS system administrator the ability to simply check off a box that says he or she wants logging enabled at the time of defining or reconfiguring a connection factory using the vendor's admin tool. This way, the logging can be turned on or off without the knowledge of the client-side application or its developers.

Some typical, non-standard connection-related parameters a JMS administration tool will let you configure are as follows:

- How long before a transaction times out
- What is the time frame in which a message must be acknowledged?
- How big an internal buffer should be allocated to hold incoming messages
- Are distributed (XA) transactions allowed?
- Should the connection to the server be encrypted using SSL?

And, of course, depending on the particular product, there can be many more.

Non API–related server–specific behavior

A whole host of configurable parameters might be available in a JMS product that are related specifically to the operation of the JMS server. Mention of any of these is usually not found in the JMS specification because this is an area far removed from the programmer's API, which is the main focus of the specification. However, proper configuration of the server parameters exposed by a vendor is important to the smooth running, fast operation, and scalability of any JMS installation.

Of course, because such parameters are not governed by JMS, the particular features and available values can vary widely from product to product. Most of the common ones pertain to permanent queue-based messaging – both regular queues and durable topics – because these involve the use of persistent storage of some sort. Most products let you use any JDBC-compliant data source or the file system to store unread messages.

Some typical queue-based messaging parameters that products let you configure are as follows:

◆ What persistent storage should be used: database or file system?

◆ What's the maximum queue size?

◆ What's the maximum message size?

◆ What's the consumer model (one only or many) for messages?

Administration Tools

There are two broad areas of JMS messaging that a vendor's administration will cover:

◆ General configuration

◆ Queue maintenance

The bulk of any administrative tool is going to be related to the process of configuring your JMS provider in the ways that are outlined in the JMS specification: factories, destinations, transactions, messaging modes, etc. Higher-end vendors that support queue-based messaging often also provide tools that help you manage the content of your queues. Queue management is not addressed by JMS at all but can be a critical feature because of the long-lived nature of messages in queues.

General configuration

Usually, commercial products provide some sort of graphical tool that an administrator can use to manage a JMS installation based on that vendor's product. Some vendors accomplish this through the use of browser-based technologies (HTML interfaces, Web server scripts, and so on) while others employ a more traditional standalone GUI application.

As you well know, there are trade-offs between the two approaches. The browser-based interface is clunkier than a rich GUI, but it allows for ease of access from a wider variety of locations and machines than the rich interface, which must be installed locally on whatever machine the administrator is using.

Of course, the lower-end JMS packages – particularly the open source ones – frequently give you no graphical tools at all. In such a case, your main admin tool might be *emacs, vi,* or *WordPad,* which you will use to edit any configurations files by hand. (Which is not to say that it's not possible to hand edit high-end vendors' config files as well in many cases, should you prefer that method.)

In any case, the administrative tools' interfaces are less important than the functionality and breadth of features the product supports. As long as the interface is logically organized, both approaches should suffice.

Queue maintenance

One oft-neglected area of administration is queue maintenance. It's one thing to get your queue configured properly and up and running, but the persistent nature of the messages in a queue means that it will likely need ongoing maintenance to keep your messaging operating smoothly.

As we've noted many times already, JMS messaging is asynchronous. One of the implications of this is that messages can be blithely sent even if there is no reader waiting or available to consume them. For nondurable topic messaging this is not a problem because messages for which there is no reader at the time they are sent are simply dropped on the floor. Queue-based messages are another matter entirely. A message in a queue can linger for quite a long time if no application is interested in the destination it was sent to or if the durable subscriber it was meant for never comes to life to read it.

If a large number of unread messages exist in the queue, over time the overall throughput of the system can drop due to the increased use of system resources. This is somewhat analogous to a memory leak in a program: it won't prohibit the program from running properly, but over time it can cause performance degradation and system failures.

To some degree you can control this situation through the judicious use of the **JMSExpiration** property, which will enable the JMS server to discard expired messages and free up the resources associated with them after their time-to-live has passed. This can be tricky because you have to be sure all JMS connection factories are configured with an appropriate expiration value – one that is not excessively long but also one that will not confuse any application that expects to receive messages no older than some particular time period.

Something can always go wrong, however, so you will still likely require some sort of tool for examining the contents of your queues and administratively expunging any old or unwanted messages, even if you have to write that tool yourself. This is particularly true during development where rapid changes to applications and program failures can lead to stale information stored in the queue.

Queue management is an area where some vendors provide excellent graphical tools for administrators to use in order to browse the contents of a queue, search for particular messages, and remove anything unwanted. Other vendors provide nothing beyond the standard JMS APIs that you can use to write your own tool to perform the same tasks.

The Administrator's Role

One of the unique features of the J2EE approach to system deployment and maintenance is the prominent role given the administrator in the application of these processes. The EJB and JMS specifications have both carved out a separate and distinct role for the administrator — separate, that is, from the developer — but they have also defined the model and support structures to enable the administrator to play an important role in the management of a production enterprise system. With JMS in particular, this extra-development role is comprised of a few main tasks:

◆ Configuring connection factories and destinations

◆ Tuning the JMS server application

◆ Implementing security controls

◆ Ongoing queue maintenance

Though this all sounds fine in theory, it's hard to see in practice how some of these tasks can be accomplished without tight coordination with the development team. Let's examine each of these categories briefly with respect to the interplay between the administrator (or administration team) and the developer (or development/ design/architecture team).

Configuring connection factories and destinations

Configuring connection factories and destinations is one area where it's hard to see the administrator acting too independently from the developer. After all, the developer determines what destination names must be created administratively.

The developer also determines which messages should be sent via pub/sub and which should be sent point-to-point; determines which operations need to be transactionalized and which don't; and determines the appropriate default values of the various JMS message properties (**JMSExpiration**, **JMSTimestamp** disabling, and so on). In short, almost anything that affects the configuration of a connection factory is specified by the development team and not by an administrator working semi-independently.

Tuning the JMS server application

This is an area where an administrator can work fairly independently from the development team. Much as a database administrator (DBA) is responsible for determining how best to configure persistent storage (raw disk usage, RAID levels, replication strategies, and so on) to achieve optimal performance and reliability for an application, so too can a JMS administrator fulfill this role for a messaging system by manipulating the underlying persistent storage and other parameters of a JMS server (although for much of the database-related work they'd probably rely on a DBA anyway).

Implementing security controls

As we saw in Chapter 9, messages that are secured on a per-message basis (that is, by manipulating the contents of the message) must generally be taken care of by the development team. To the extent there is a need to manage the distribution of the keys that are required to accomplish secure messaging the JMS administrator can take control that process, however.

Some JMS products enable connections to be configured to run over SSL (for complete traffic encryption). Since applications would not require any changes to utilize SSL connections, such configuration can be done by a JMS administrator without the intervention of the development team. Keep in mind, though, that the performance hit that would likely be taken when a system running everything over SSL indicates that the development team should be consulted to help assess the impact to the application of such a move.

When it comes to securing access to the JMS server itself, however, the administrator need consult no one. It is his or her responsibility to ensure that only authorized users are allowed to get a handle to the administered JMS connection factories and destinations that are kept in the server's JNDI directory.

Ongoing queue maintenance

Clearly an administrator can and should operate independently to make sure any message queues used by the JMS server are kept free of dead messages. An administrator should be responsible for periodically examining the JMS queues – either manually or via automated script – and purging any unneeded messages. Reports of such activity should be provided to the development team because the existence of dead messages may indicate a problem with the application.

The same can be said of messages that are allowed to expire on their own and are automatically cleaned up by the JMS server. In most systems, it makes little sense to design a system where messages routinely are lost through expiration, particularly when messages are delivered using JMS's persistent delivery mode. Systems with a high rate of message expiration may have a design or operational flaw.

Summary

In most enterprise environments, a JMS administrator probably doesn't have enough to do to warrant a full-time employee. This is why the members of the development team still perform these tasks in many environments. Certainly if an enterprise already has administrators responsible for the health and well-being of other software, then adding JMS to their responsibilities would not overly burden them while helping to ensure the smooth operation of the messaging infrastructure.

Don't take any of this argument against the need for a separate and distinct administrator to mean, however, that there's no value in the administrative capabilities that JMS provides. There is, because these administrative capabilities help tune a system and adapt it in small but important ways without having to change any of your various application's source code. This is an important advantage over the state of affairs as they've traditionally existed, where every little change to a system required the developer's intervention. Though we haven't arrived at the point where a system can be tuned and maintained much as a mechanic keeps a car running smoothly, the J2EE administrative model is a definite step in the right direction.

Large enterprises already maintain dedicated system administrators to keep their production computer installations running smoothly and there's no reason to think that those teams cannot eventually start to take over some of the J2EE-related administrative tasks. The nascent administrative capabilities in JMS systems at least enable us to start moving in that direction.

This chapter took a high-level look at JMS's administrative capabilities and showed that little has been standardized. To the extent that all JMS systems must do similar tasks, the administrative tools available from each vendor enable you to configure much the same types of behavior in each. On the other hand, the JMS specification leaves much room for vendors to compete with each other on the basis of their underlying implementation, and the differences in what product A does compared to product B will often be reflected in the administration procedures supported by each. In fact, administrative capabilities and tools themselves are fertile ground for competition in the JMS server market, especially because most are still fairly weak.

The next chapter closely examines two real-world JMS products – WebLogic Server and iPlanet Message Queue – and explores how the issues we discussed in this chapter are manifested in their administrative tools. If you find yourself using either product, then the walkthroughs in Chapter 12 will be a great starting tutorial. If you are using another product or just evaluating products, it is still worthwhile to see how two of the market leaders operate. This can only help you when doing product comparisons and in understanding JMS better.

Chapter 12

Sample Administration of Real JMS Products

IN THIS CHAPTER

- ◆ Administering and configuring WebLogic 6.1 for JMS
- ◆ Administering and configuring iPlanet Message Queue 2.0

THIS CHAPTER GIVES YOU SOME HANDS-ON EXPERIENCE using the administration tools that come with two real-world JMS products: BEA WebLogic 6.1 and iPlanet Message Queue 2.0. Both products are written in Java and thus run on any number of platforms, including, as you'd expect, two of the leading ones: Sun's Solaris and Microsoft's Windows 2000.

We'll focus on how to use the GUI-based administration and configuration tools that come with the products as opposed to delving into the details of the underlying files they use to store their configurations, which are themselves editable manually. There are two reasons for this. First, the administrative capabilities of JMS products have come a long way in the past couple of years and the need to directly manipulate the configuration files has, in general, been greatly reduced. Second, the industry generally is moving toward storing most system configuration information in XML-format files. And while one of the big selling points of XML is that it's human-readable, it's really not a good idea to be routinely hand editing such files. Even with a generic XML editor, it can be a complex task – though, of course, it is perfectly acceptable for the occasional quick fix, especially during the development cycle.

Administering BEA WebLogic 6.1

In this section we'll walk through the essentials of setting up a WebLogic server so that you can use its JMS capabilities, plus message-driven beans. As we do so you'll begin to see how most of the main JMS features discussed so far in this book are reflected in the WebLogic administration facilities.

Overview of WebLogic 6.1 and JMS

The first thing to know about WebLogic and JMS is that BEA does not sell its JMS product as a standalone offering. It is tightly integrated into the WebLogic Server, or WLS (and its high-end cousin, WebLogic Enterprise, or WLE) product. WLS supports the entire J2EE suite (and then some), including JMS, and you get it in one all-or-nothing package. The latest version as of this writing is 6.1. While the bundling of the entire J2EE suite may be an issue for you from a cost perspective (you can't just buy the parts you need), it is great from a technology perspective as all the pieces come in one tightly integrated package. (BEA does sell a standalone product called MessageQ that does messaging but it does not support JMS.)

Traditionally, BEA has done a great job of keeping WLS right up to date with the latest J2EE standards. They participate actively in the J2EE standards development process (see http://www.jcp.org for more on the Java Community Process) so they are always very aware of what's coming down the pike. Often they have a downloadable add-on package available to upgrade your system to the latest standards as soon as a proposed API is released to the public.

While this is great for developers who want to try out the latest and greatest technologies, it can lead to a lot of rewriting if the final APIs deviate significantly from the initial release. Even worse, BEA has a tendency to simply add to a standard whatever features it thinks are useful. In most cases, they probably are, but if your application comes to depend on them, then you've got a case of vendor-lock that perhaps you were hoping to avoid by using a standards-based technology. A good example of this problem is its JMS offering, which faithfully supports the 1.0.2 specification but augments it with features such as XMLMessage and the NO_ACKNOWLEDGE acknowledgment option.

In any case, because WLS incorporates a full application server, you can expect not only a complete JMS product that supports topic-based messaging, queue-based messaging, *and* transactions (the three main components that JMS declares optional), but you will also be able to write message-driven beans, which are not part of the JMS specification but rather the EJB 2.0 specification.

Most WebLogic configuration and administration can be performed using a standard Web browser. This is very nice because it's a familiar interface for most people and, more importantly, allows you to access a server from a variety of locations.

For the examples in this section we'll assume that you already know how to log on to the WebLogic console (that is, to your WebLogic server's administration home page) and that you have the appropriate administrative privileges.

Administering your JMS server

If you've just installed a new WebLogic server and want to set it up to handle JMS messaging, you need to perform the following steps:

- ◆ Create a new JMS server instance
- ◆ Create a JMS connection factory

- Create a JMS destination

- Define permanent storage

- Define security

The following sections walk through how to set up a new JMS server and a sample topic connection factory and topic destination. We make the assumption that you already have a WLS domain and server configured properly and running. In the examples, the domain name is "galaxy" and the server name is "saturn." Review the appropriate WebLogic documentation if you do not know how to get to this point.

This walkthrough was derived from an installation on a Solaris box, though you'll encounter few differences, if any, on other platforms.

CREATING A JMS SERVER INSTANCE

To create a new JMS server instance, first log on to the WebLogic console home page. Look for a "JMS" section in the middle of the page. Select any subheading.

A typical WebLogic console page is divided into two browser frames. On the left is a tree structure that follows the directory/folder paradigm. The "directories" and "folders" are logical units of the current WebLogic domain, which is the root element. In our case, this is "galaxy."

Go to the Servers folder by following this pathway:

```
/galaxy/Services/JMS/Servers
```

Right-click the Servers folder and select "Configure a new JMS Server" from the pop-up menu. A tabbed folder panel appears on the right-hand side of the browser window (see Figure 12-1). Click the General tab, which contains the fields used to define a new JMS server instance. For our purposes, just leave the defaults in place, as follows:

Name	MyJMSServer
Store	(none)
Temporary Template	(none)

After reviewing the entries, click the Create button at the lower-right corner of the panel.

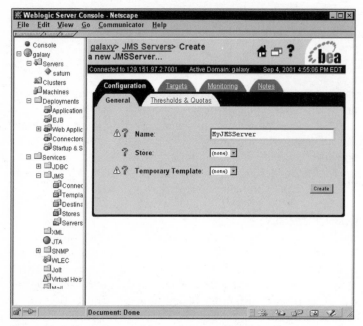

Figure 12-1: The main panel to create a new JMS server instance

Note that the Temporary Template field is used to configure the server so that temporary JMS destinations can be generated. Setting this field to something is required if you plan on using the TopicRequestor or QueueRequestor classes. The template specified on the screen in Figure 12-1 does not have to have any special configuration but you must create one first as follows:

1. Right click on the folder at /galaxy/Services/JMS/Templates

2. Select the menu item Configure a new JMSTemplate . . .

3. Enter any unique name for the template and click Create

The template name you choose will appear in the Temporary Template field when you go to create a new JMS server as specified in this section.

ASSIGNING A JMS SERVER TO A WEBLOGIC SERVER

When a WebLogic JMS instance is created, it is initially inactive because it must be created independently from any particular WebLogic server instance. The next step to perform is to assign our new JMS instance to a server instance.

In the same right-hand side panel shown in Figure 12-1, select the Targets tab. You will see all the servers in your domain listed in the Available list box. Highlight the server to which you want to assign your JMS instance – in our example it is "saturn" – and move it over to the Chosen list by clicking the right-pointing arrow button. Figure 12-2 shows the state of the panel after doing this.

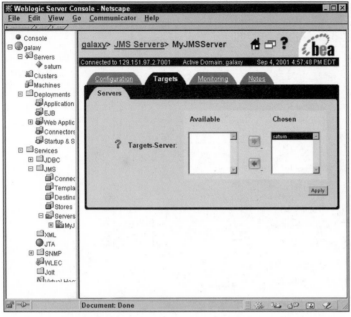

Figure 12-2: Assigning a JMS instance to a WebLogic server instance

Click the Apply button and the assignment takes place. A JMS server can only be assigned to one WebLogic server.

CREATING A JMS CONNECTION FACTORY

Recall from Chapter 11, that JMS defines two administered objects: the connection factory and the destination. First, let's define a new connection factory.

Find the Connection Factories folder via the following pathway:

```
/galaxy/Services/JMS/Connection Factories
```

Right-click the Connection Factories folder and select "Configure a new JMS ConnectionFactory" from the menu. You'll see numerous fields, but the three most important fields and values for our example are as follows.

Name	MyJMS Connection Factory
JNDIName	JMSConn
Default Delivery Mode	Non-Persistent

Figure 12-3 shows the basic connection factory screen. Enter the information for the three fields just listed and click the Create button to define your new connection factory.

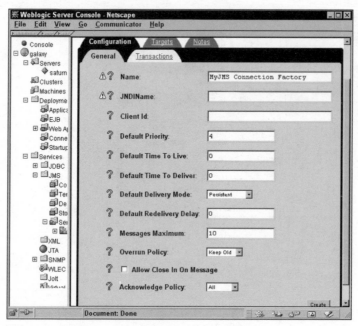

Figure 12-3: Defining a new JMS connection factory

You can leave the other fields on the screen with their default values but notice that the Default Priority and Default Time To Live values on the panel correspond to JMS message properties (see Chapter 2). Any values you configure here will be the default values a JMS message has when a client creates one using this connection factory. Clients, however, can override these values if they desire. The Client Id field is the unique identifier you give a connection when using durable topic subscription messaging. If you do not specify a client identifier when defining the connection factory, you can (if necessary) do so in the client code using the `javax.jms.Connection.setClientID()` method. (See Chapter 5 for more information about client identifiers.)

The remaining fields in the new connection factory panel pertain to WebLogic's underlying JMS message delivery implementation. They are not directly reflected in any JMS APIs. You should consult WebLogic's documentation to get a full explanation of what effect each field has on messaging (you can get a description of any field by clicking on the question mark symbol) before attempting to set a value in any of these fields.

In the vast majority of cases, you're probably better off leaving all the fields with their default values except for the Messages Maximum field. The Messages Maximum field determines how many messages are held in client-side memory while waiting delivery to your application's message handler. If you have a high-volume messaging system, a larger Messages Maximum number will likely give you better performance since the messages will be available as soon as the client is ready to process them without requiring any action on the part of the JMS server. You can also specify a value of –1 to indicate that as many messages as possible (up to available memory limitations) should be held in the client-side delivery queue. Note that whatever value you pick for Messages Maximum, the delivery semantics determined by the selected JMS delivery mode (i.e. Persistent or Non-Persistent) remain in effect.

From a client developer's point of view, the only name we really care about is the JNDI name because that's the logical name we will use to retrieve the initial connection factory instance. Review Chapter 3, "Sending Messages" for details.

One detail that might be confusing for someone who's administered other JMS products is how WebLogic fails to distinguish between topic connection factories and queue connection factories. Remember that in a JMS client application when we use JNDI to look up a connection factory, we must do so using the logical name – in our example, "JMSConn" – and cast the result to a `javax.jms.TopicConnectionFactory` or a `javax.jms.QueueConnectionFactory`. Because we haven't told WebLogic which type we want when we defined the connection, how does it know which to return to us when we do the lookup?

The answer is it doesn't care. Under the covers, WebLogic has created an implementation of a connection factory class that implements both the `TopicConnectionFactory` and `QueueConnectionFactory` interfaces. Because of this, it can successfully be cast to whichever you please.

TRANSACTIONALIZING A CONNECTION FACTORY

If you're just doing an initial test configuration of your JMS server as we are here, you don't really need to address the transaction parameters located under the Transactions tab. However, when you begin to do real work, you'll need to be sure the connection factories you create are configured appropriately with the desired transaction capabilities. The two configuration options are these:

◆ User Transactions Enabled

◆ XAConnection Factory Enabled

Enabling user transactions configures your connection factory for local transactions and ensures that all JMS traffic occurs within a transaction context. Enabling XA transactions enables you to combine other, non-JMS activity in the same transaction as the JMS activity, as we discussed in Chapter 7, "JMS Transactions." Do not set up a connection to be transactionalized if you don't need it because it's a performance drain. Figure 12-4 shows what the transaction setup panel looks like.

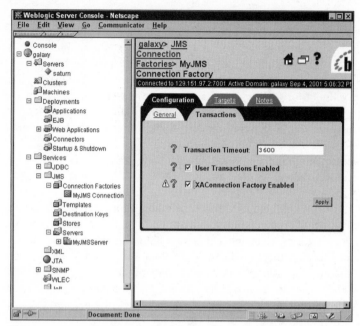

Figure 12-4: Configuring a connection factory for transactions

ASSIGNING A CONNECTION FACTORY TO A SERVER

With WebLogic, connection factories need to be assigned to server instances just as JMS servers do. To do so, select the Targets tab and move the desired server name (in our case "saturn") over from the Available list to the Chosen list, and then click the Apply button. A connection factory can only be assigned to one server.

CREATING A DESTINATION

To create destinations (topics and queues) you first need to find the home folder in the left panel for the new JMS server we created. Find the MyJMSServer folder via the following pathway:

```
/galaxy/Services/JMS/Servers/MyJMSServer
```

Right-click the "Destinations" entry. For testing purposes we'll create a topic destination, but the procedure is identical for a queue destination. Select "Configure a new JMS Topic" from the menu and enter the following values:

Name   MyJMSTopic [this is the default]

JNDIName   TestTopic

Figure 12-5 shows the General panel for the new topic destination after clicking the Create button. Note that you can use the Monitoring tab to track activity related to the destination after it has become active.

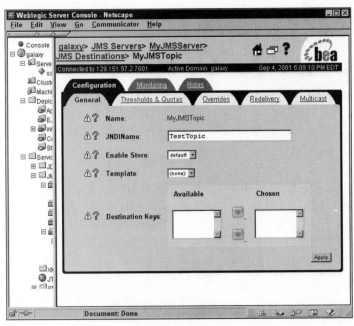

Figure 12-5: Creating a new topic destination

VERIFYING THE CONFIGURATION

If you've been watching your WebLogic server log while running through the steps, so far you'll have seen that the server has dynamically enabled the various services as required (if not, a "therapeutic" restart of the server may clear things up).

To verify that our new connection factory and destination are available for clients to start using, we can use the WebLogic feature that lets us view the contents of its JNDI directory. To do this, right-click the saturn entry under the Servers folder (/galaxy/Servers/saturn). Select View JNDI Tree from the menu. Verify that JMSConn (our topic connection JNDI name) and TestTopic (our topic destination JNDI name) are in JNDI tree for the server. You should also have a "weblogic.jms.backend.MyJMSServer" entry. Navigate the tree as required to see it. The directory should look something like Figure 12-6.

Finally, you may also want to review WebLogic's primary configuration file, config.xml, located in the home directory of your WebLogic server instance ($WL_HOME/config/galaxy in our case). All the information pertaining to the configurations we performed will be in this file. It is hand-editable but you should never do so while the WebLogic domain is active because your changes may be silently overwritten.

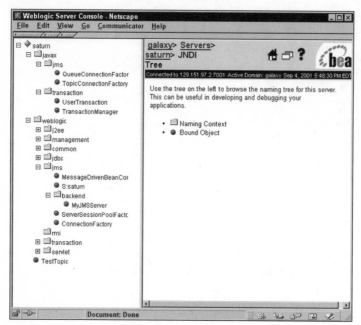

Figure 12-6: WebLogic JNDI directory entries

WRITING A TEST CLIENT

The ultimate determination of whether your configuration was a success is to send and receive messages, of course. Listing 12-1 shows a complete code example for sending and receiving a test message using the connection factory and topic that we created previously. The same program handles the sending and receiving side of the messaging. Two instances of the program should be run at the same time, one with a single parameter of "receive" and the other with a single parameter of "send."

Listing 12-1: A sending and receiving test program for the TestTopic topic

```
import java.util.*;
import javax.naming.*;
import javax.jms.*;

/* This program will send a simple "Hello World" text message
 * if the parameter passed it is "send". If it is "receive" it
 * will receive what it presumes to be a TextMessage and exit.
 */

public class TopicTest
{
    static final Object exitobj = new Object();
```

```
public static void main(String[] args) throws Exception
{
    if (args.length != 1 ||
        !("send".equalsIgnoreCase(args[0]) ||
        "receive".equalsIgnoreCase(args[0])))
    {
        System.out.println(
            "Usage: java TopicTest { send | receive }");
        System.exit(1);
    }

    Context ctx = null;
    Hashtable env = new Hashtable();

    env.put(Context.INITIAL_CONTEXT_FACTORY,
            "weblogic.jndi.WLInitialContextFactory");
    env.put(Context.PROVIDER_URL, "t3://localhost:7001");

    ctx = new InitialContext(env);

    // Lookup the topic connection factory
    TopicConnectionFactory tcf =
        (TopicConnectionFactory) ctx.lookup("JMSConn");

    TopicConnection tc = tcf.createTopicConnection();

    // Register a listener for server errors
    tc.setExceptionListener(new ExceptionListener()
    {
        public void onException(JMSException e)
        {
            e.printStackTrace();
        }
    });

    TopicSession ts = tc.createTopicSession(false,
                        TopicSession.AUTO_ACKNOWLEDGE);

    // Lookup the topic destination
    javax.jms.Topic topic = null;
    try
    {
        topic = (javax.jms.Topic) ctx.lookup("TestTopic");
    }
```

Continued

Listing 12-1 *(Continued)*

```java
catch (Exception e)
{
    e.printStackTrace();
}

/* This way of looking up destinations will also work but
 * is non-standard. It uses the real (i.e. non-JNDI) name
 * of the topic as defined in the WebLogic destination
 * administration panel.

try
{
    topic = ts.createTopic("MyJMSServer/MyJMSTopic");
}
catch (Exception e)
{
    e.printStackTrace();
}
*/

// RECEIVE SECTION
if (args[0].equalsIgnoreCase("receive"))
{
    TopicSubscriber tsub = null;

    try
    {
        tsub = ts.createSubscriber(topic);
    }
    catch (Exception e)
    {
        e.printStackTrace();
    }

    tsub.setMessageListener(new MessageListener()
    {
        public void onMessage(Message msg)
        {
            try
            {
                TextMessage tmsg = (TextMessage) msg;
                    System.out.println(
                        "Got message: " + tmsg.getText());

                synchronized (exitobj)
```

```
                    {
                        exitobj.notify();
                    }
                }
            catch (JMSException e)
            {
                e.printStackTrace();
            }
        }
    });

    tc.start();

    System.out.println("Waiting to receive messages."
              + " Will exit after receiving a message.");

    synchronized (exitobj)
    {
        exitobj.wait();
    }

    System.out.println("Cleaning up and exiting.");

    tsub.close();
    ts.close();
}

// SEND SECTION
else
{
    TopicPublisher tsend = null;

    try
    {
        tsend = ts.createPublisher(topic);
    }
    catch (Exception e)
    {
        e.printStackTrace();
    }

    TextMessage msg = ts.createTextMessage();
    msg.setText("Hello World");

    System.out.println("Sending message " + msg);
```

Continued

Listing 12-1 *(Continued)*

```
        tsend.publish(msg);

        tsend.close();
    }

    // Clean up
    ts.close();
    tc.close();
  }
}
```

Listing 12-2 shows an ant `build.xml` file that can be used to compile and run the test program. The "runsend" and "runreceive" targets can be used to execute the send and receive sides of the test program, respectively.

Listing 12-2: An ant build.xml for compiling and running Listing 12-1

```
<project name="JMSTest" default="compile" basedir=".">

  <property name="WL_HOME" value="c:/wlserver6.1" />
  <property name="jmslib" value="${WL_HOME}/lib/weblogic.jar"/>

  <path id="runclasspath">
    <pathelement location="." />
    <pathelement location="./classes" />
    <pathelement location="${WL_HOME}/lib/weblogic.jar" />
  </path>

  <target name="prepare">
    <mkdir dir="./classes"/>
  </target>

  <target name="compile" depends="prepare">

    <javac srcdir="." destdir="./classes" classpath=".;${jmslib}">
    </javac>

  </target>

  <target name="runsend" depends="compile">
    <java classname="TopicTest" fork="yes">
        <classpath refid="runclasspath"/>
        <arg value="send"/>
    </java>
  </target>
```

```
<target name="runreceive" depends="compile">
  <java classname="TopicTest" fork="yes">
      <classpath refid="runclasspath"/>
      <arg value="receive"/>
  </java>
</target>

<target name="clean">
  <delete dir="./classes" />
</target>
```

```
</project>
```

This program is pretty straightforward and if you have set up your WebLogic JMS server properly, it produces the desired result if you run one instance of it in "send" mode and another in "receive."

Pay attention to the commented-out section in the middle of Listing 12-1, however. In WebLogic's implementation of JMS passing a string of the format `JMS_Server_Name/Internal_Topic_Name` to the `TopicSession.createTopic()` method enables you to bypass the JNDI destination lookup and access the topic via the internal name used when you defined the topic administratively—in our case, that would be MyJMSTopic, the topic destination we created earlier in the chapter.

Though the WebLogic documentation asserts this is the behavior mandated by the JMS specification, this is not true. The JMS specification and API documentation say that `createTopic()` is meant for clients who wish to define topics on the fly (that is to say, unadministered destinations), though it does encourage developers and administrators to use only administered topics. In any case, to remain as standards-compliant as possible, you're better off using the JNDI lookup. If your system does need to create topics dynamically, however, you will unfortunately have to resort to using a proprietary WebLogic API, which you can find details for in their documentation.

Defining permanent storage

When defining the preceding TestTopic topic, we did not need to worry about any storage options because we defined the topic to be nonpersistent. In WebLogic's JMS, if we want to use nonvolatile storage for a destination, then we first need to define what WebLogic calls a *store* and then assign it to a destination. You can define two types of stores:

◆ A JDBC-compliant database

◆ A file

To use a JDBC data source as the nonvolatile storage for a message queue, you must first define a JDBC data source as you normally would (refer to the WebLogic documentation). Let's run through an example using a queue destination and a simple file store. We will execute the following steps:

- ◆ Defining a store
- ◆ Assigning it to a server
- ◆ Creating a new destination that uses the store

DEFINING STORES

Our first step is to define a new store. From the main console window, select the "Stores" hyperlink under the "JMS" section. Then click the "Configure a new JMSFile Store" hyperlink in the right-hand panel, which brings up the panel used to create a new store. Enter a logical name for the store in the Name field (we'll use the default of "MyJMSFile Store"). Enter the directory where the file will be created. Let's call it `queuefile`. This directory can be absolute or relative. If you do not specify a full system path, then it will be relative to the WebLogic server's home directory.

Note that the directory you select is not created for you automatically. You must explicitly create it and ensure it has the appropriate read/write permissions for the WebLogic server – and, for security reasons, *only* the WebLogic server – to access it. The directory does not have to exist at the time you define the store, so long as it's there prior to the next restart of the server.

Figure 12-7 shows the panel's state after you click the Create button.

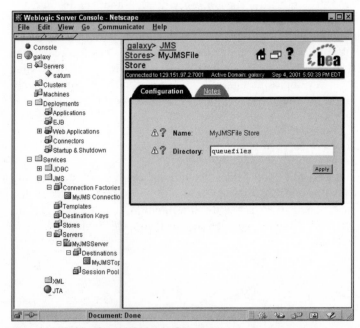

Figure 12-7: Creating a WebLogic file store

ASSIGNING A STORE TO A SERVER

Once you've defined the store, you just need to assign it to the JMS server. First, open the Servers folder via the following pathway:

`/Services/JMS/Servers`

Click MyJMSServer to bring up its configuration page. Select the newly defined store, MyJMSFileStore, from the Store option menu. Figure 12-8 shows the panel after you click the Apply button.

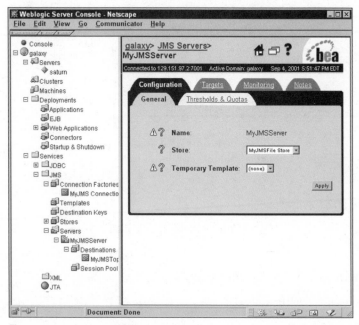

Figure 12-8: A store assigned to a server

CREATING A NEW DESTINATION WITH STORAGE

The last step is to create a new queue destination that makes use of MyJMSFileStore. As before, to create a destination, follow the pathway `/galaxy/ Services/JMS/Servers/MyJMSServer` and right-click the Destinations entry in the MyJMSServer folder. Then select "Configure a new JMSQueue" from the menu.

Let's stick with the default queue name MyJMSQueue and give it a JNDI name TestQueue. For the Enable Store field, select "true" from the pull-down menu.

You can assign only one store to a JMS server so there's no need to specify the store name when creating the destination. Simply enabling the use of a store for the destination is sufficient. This implies, however, that you must create multiple JMS server instances if you want to use multiple stores.

Figure 12-9 shows how the panel appears before you click the Create button.

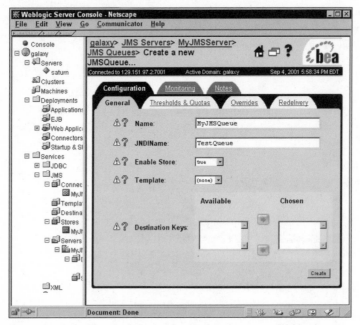

Figure 12-9: Creating a new queue destination that uses a WebLogic store

Defining security

With WebLogic JMS, access to JMS facilities can be controlled at three points, as follows:

1. Access to WLS itself via initial authentication

2. Access to the entire JNDI context

3. Access to JMS destinations

Because setting up logins to the WebLogic server itself is not a JMS-related feature *per se*, we will not discuss it here. We will, however, discuss how to control access to the two types of administered JMS objects. First we'll show how to define authentication parameters for an administered topic or queue destination, and then we'll see how to limit access to an administered connection factory.

The WebLogic documentation says that their JMS implementation supports encrypted connections via the HTTPS protocol. To use it you would connect to the WebLogic server using a provider URL starting with the `t3s://` prefix or `https://` prefix. While it seems obvious that all traffic over the connected socket would be secure, it is less clear what happens to unconnected traffic, such as when you use WebLogic's IP multicast "message delivery" option. Be sure you are satisfied that WebLogic is appropriately encrypting all your message traffic before relying on this feature.

CREATING A NEW ACL

WebLogic controls access to administered JMS destinations (and other WebLogic features) through the use of *access control lists* (ACL). An ACL is simply a permission that defines a particular operation and a list of users or user groups that are allowed to perform that operation.

Using the WebLogic console, creating a new ACL consists of these two steps:

◆ Defining the ACL (that is, the security category)

◆ Assigning users and groups to a permission in the category

To define an ACL, select ACL under the Security section on the main console window (this is not JMS-specific). You will be presented with a list of existing ACLs. If we want to create an ACL for the sample MyJMSTopic topic destination we created earlier in this chapter, then the appropriate ACL will not exist; we must create it. To do this, select the "Create a New ACL" link and enter **weblogic.jms. topic.MyJMSTopic** in the New ACL Name field. Then click the Create button.

Figure 12-10 shows what the panel should look like prior to creating the ACL.

Figure 12-10: Creating a new ACL for a JMS topic

CREATING A NEW PERMISSION   After creating the ACL you'll need to map a permission to a list of users and groups. You will be presented with the panel in Figure 12-11 after creating the ACL. You must restrict the value entered in the Permission field to either "send" or "receive" because these are the names WebLogic understands. The program will not complain, however, if you enter some other arbitrary value. As you'd expect, users who have "send" permission are allowed to send messages to the MyJMSTopic destination. Users who have "receive" permission are allowed to receive messages from it. If you want a user to be able to do both, you must repeat the permission creation process twice, once for the send permission and once for the receive. You cannot simply enter "send,receive" as a permission name.

Enter one or more comma-separated user names in the Grant to Users field (create a user first if needed by clicking the Users link). Enter any group names in the Grant to Groups field. Any users and groups entered must already be known to WebLogic and, of course, must be able to log in to the WebLogic server and have sufficient privileges to query the JNDI directory for the appropriate JMS connection factory.

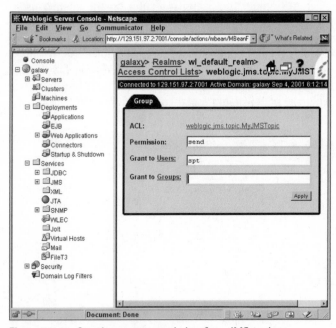

Figure 12-11: Creating a new permission for a JMS topic

Enter **send** for a Permission name and enter a valid user name — we'll use **spt** for this example. Then click the Apply button. Repeat this process for the "receive" permission.

TESTING THE ACL

In the code sample in Listing 12-1 we made the assumption we could log into WLS with "guest" privileges because we did not specify any authentication information when we accessed the server's JNDI tree.

Now that we have controlled access to the MyJMSTopic by using an ACL, if we were to execute the same code, we would receive the following exception when running the program:

```
java.lang.SecurityException: User "guest" does not have Permission
"receive" based on ACL "weblogic.jms.topic.MyJMSTopic".
```

This is because the default user ("guest") is not explicitly granted access to the receive permission in the ACL. To access the controlled JMS destination now we will simply need to augment the code from Listing 12-1 with the lines in bold, as follows:

```
Context ctx = null;
Hashtable env = new Hashtable();

env.put(Context.INITIAL_CONTEXT_FACTORY,
                "weblogic.jndi.WLInitialContextFactory");
env.put(Context.PROVIDER_URL, "t3://localhost:7001");
env.put(Context.SECURITY_PRINCIPAL, "spt");
env.put(Context.SECURITY_CREDENTIALS, "spt"); // password
```

The principal should be the user we assigned in the ACL ("spt"), and the credential is spt's password, the incredibly unsecure "spt". The user name and password must have been created already using WebLogic's user administration facilities.

After adding these two lines of code, run the program again. This time you will be able to create a TopicSubscriber object for MyJMSTopic (which you refer to in your program by its JNDI name, TestTopic).

CREATING A JNDI ACL

Notice how in our sample program from Listing 12-1 that without any login info (for example, with simple "guest" privileges) you can still view the available topics. Because this can be valuable information to an attacker, a properly configured production system would not allow it. We can limit access to the JNDI tree by creating an ACL for the JNDI context.

Your WebLogic installation should by default have an ACL named weblogic. jndi.weblogic already defined.

The WebLogic JNDI ACL has the following three permissions:

- ◆ list
- ◆ lookup
- ◆ modify

Each of these permissions does what you would expect based on the name. You can assign users to each individual permission, just as we did with the JMS destination ACLs. However, it's important to note that the permission applies to the entire JNDI directory. This means that if a user is allowed to list, look up, and/or modify *anything* in JNDI, then they can do it for *everything*. See Chapter 9 for reasons why this might be a security hole.

Deploying message-driven beans

WebLogic fully supports message-driven beans in its application server. Deploying them is simply a matter of creating the proper XML descriptor files and running the *ejbc* compiler as you would with any EJB. If you are not familiar with how to do this, consult the WebLogic documentation and example files to learn how. WebLogic comes with sample message-driven bean compilation scripts you can refer to. Listing 12-3 shows a simple message-driven bean.

Listing 12-3: A basic message-driven bean

```
import javax.ejb.*;
import javax.jms.*;
import javax.naming.*;

public class MDBTest implements MessageDrivenBean, MessageListener
{
    private MessageDrivenContext context;

    public void ejbCreate() {}

    public void ejbRemove() {}

    public void setMessageDrivenContext(MessageDrivenContext c)
    {
        context = c;
    }

    public void onMessage(Message msg)
    {
        TextMessage tmsg = (TextMessage) msg;

        try
        {
            System.err.println("Got message: " + tmsg.getText());
        }
        catch(JMSException e)
        {
            e.printStackTrace();
        }
    }
}
```

To deploy this bean, we need to create two XML deployment descriptor files. The first, ejb-jar.xml, is a standard format for all EJBs. It maps a name to a message-driven bean class, defines the transaction model for the onMessage() method, and says what type of JMS message the bean is supposed to respond to: Topic or Queue.

The second XML file, weblogic-ejb-jar.xml, is WebLogic-specific. It has a variety of options for managing instances of the bean at runtime (consult the WebLogic documentation for a complete description) but its primary responsibility is to map the JNDI name of the Topic or Queue, which the bean will be receiving messages for to the message-driven bean itself.

Listings 12-4 and 12-5 show samples of these two files that presume we want to make our sample bean from Listing 12-3 respond to Queue messages that are sent to the "TestQueue" destination that we defined earlier in this chapter. Refer back to Chapter 7 for a more detailed description of the contents of these files.

Listing 12-4: A sample ejb-jar.xml file

```
<!DOCTYPE ejb-jar PUBLIC "-//Sun Microsystems, Inc.//DTD Enterprise
JavaBeans 2.0//EN" "http://java.sun.com/dtd/ejb-jar_2_0.dtd">

<ejb-jar>
 <enterprise-beans>

    <message-driven>
      <ejb-name>mdbTest</ejb-name>

      <ejb-class>MDTest</ejb-class>

      <transaction-type>Container</transaction-type>

      <message-driven-destination>
        <destination-type>javax.jms.Queue</destination-type>
      </message-driven-destination>

    </message-driven>

 </enterprise-beans>
</ejb-jar>
```

Listing 12-5: A sample weblogic-ejb-jar.xml file

```
<!DOCTYPE weblogic-ejb-jar PUBLIC "-//BEA Systems, Inc.//DTD
WebLogic 6.0.0 EJB//EN"
"http://www.bea.com/servers/wls600/dtd/weblogic-ejb-jar.dtd">
```

Continued

Listing 12-5 *(Continued)*

```
<weblogic-ejb-jar>

  <weblogic-enterprise-bean>

    <ejb-name>mdbTest</ejb-name>

    <message-driven-descriptor>

      <pool>
        <max-beans-in-free-pool>
        200
        </max-beans-in-free-pool>
        <initial-beans-in-free-pool>
        20
        </initial-beans-in-free-pool>
      </pool>

      <destination-jndi-name>TestQueue</destination-jndi-name>

    </message-driven-descriptor>

    <jndi-name>examplesMessageDriven1</jndi-name>

  </weblogic-enterprise-bean>

</weblogic-ejb-jar>
```

Administering iPlanet Message Queue 2.0

In this section, we'll examine the administrative capabilities of a dedicated JMS messaging product, iPlanet Message Queue. After having reviewed WebLogic's admin tools, iPlanet's will provide a useful case study illustrating a different approach to user interface design. Both products support a similar set of features, albeit using somewhat different terminology.

Overview of iPlanet Message Queue 2.0 and JMS

Unlike WebLogic, iPlanet products (the result of the Sun/Netscape/AOL alliance) are more often available as standalone offerings that you can purchase separately and integrate with each other or with third-party products. This is partly by design and partly by happenstance, the result of trying to integrate so many different company's products (Sun, Netscape, NetDynamics, Forte, and more) under the iPlanet rubric.

The iPlanet Message Queue 2.0 (iMQ) — sometimes still referred to as JMQ from its original name, Java Message Queue — is one such standalone product that you can purchase and use without any other J2EE products such as an application server. The iPlanet Application Server (iAS) — the latest version as of this writing is 6.0 — has a nice pluggability capability that allows any standard JMS server (iMQ, MQSeries, and so on) to be integrated into the application server so that iAS EJBs can make use of JMS functionality.

iPlanet is not generally as quick on the draw as WebLogic when it comes to previewing new functionality but it does usually provide full support at or near the time a specification is officially made final. Because iAS 6.0 does not support message-driven beans, we will confine our discussion in this section to administering iMQ only.

Remember, message-driven beans are not part of the JMS specification; they are part of the EJB 2.0 specification. Consequently, it is entirely possible for a standards-compliant JMS product not to support message-driven bean technology.

Administering your JMS server

Administration of an iMQ server involves the following main steps:

- ◆ Running a Broker
- ◆ Running the admin console
- ◆ Defining a broker
- ◆ Creating destinations
- ◆ Defining an object store
- ◆ Adding a connection factory
- ◆ Adding a destination

The walkthrough in this section was developed from an installation on a Windows NT machine. Unix-based installations operate similarly.

RUNNING A BROKER

In iMQ terminology the JMS server daemon is called a *broker*. Before administering anything, you need to run the broker process from the command line (it can also be installed as an NT service). An example command is as follows:

```
jmqbroker -javahome c:\jdk1.3 -name MyBroker
```

The -javahome parameter is optional. The -name parameter is required and is an arbitrary logical name for the broker. No prior configuration is required before running a named broker for the first time. However, you will notice after running a broker for the first time that a directory such as %JMQ_HOME%\var\stores\ MyBroker has been created. This is the home directory for the MyBroker broker where it keeps all configuration information.

Many properties are available to modify the behavior of an iMQ installation. You can specify these properties on the command line when running a broker or in a configuration file. Two of these properties involve the capability to dynamically create topics and queue — that is, they allow or deny the capability for a client to create its own destination names on the fly. The properties `jmq.autocreate.queue` and `jmq.autocreate.topic` have defaults of `true`, which allows clients to create their own unadministered destination names. In contrast, WebLogic prevents a JMS client from creating a destination dynamically under all circumstances (unless you resort to a proprietary API). Autocreating destinations dynamically can be a convenience (especially during development) but can be a security risk as well. See Chapter 8, "Securing JMS," for more information.

RUNNING THE ADMIN CONSOLE

Like most modern systems, you can administer iMQ completely by manually editing the configuration files and by using command-line programs, but for our example here we'll use the administration console because it's easier and clearer. The iMQ administration console is not browser-based like WebLogic's; it is a Java GUI program that, as usual, has the advantage of providing a richer interface but with a loss of flexibility in terms of being able to easily administer the server from a wide variety of locations. To run the admin console, execute the command `jmqadmin.bat` (or a similarly named script on Unix machines).

DEFINING A BROKER

Once the admin console is running, the first step is to define the broker we are interested in administering. Defining a broker is only meant to tell the admin console about the broker; it does not create or run a broker. That is done from the command line as mentioned previously.

To add a broker, select the /Actions/Add Broker menu item from admin console's menu bar. Change the Broker Label to **MyBroker** and enter a password of **admin**. Leave the defaults for the other fields and then click the OK button. Figure 12-12 shows the main iPlanet admin console with the Add Broker pop-up window.

Note that leaving out a password when defining a broker does not mean no password exists, just that, for security reasons, you intend to enter the real password every time you connect to the broker rather than having it cached on disk for you. The default broker password is "admin," which is what we're using here. This can, of course, be changed. Refer to the iMQ documentation to find out how.

After creating the broker you will see the new broker listed on the right side of the admin console, as shown in Figure 12-13.

When a broker is first added, it has a state of "Disconnected." You'll need to connect it to the running broker before proceeding. To do this, highlight the broker line in the right-hand side window and select /Actions/Connect to Broker from the console program's menu bar.

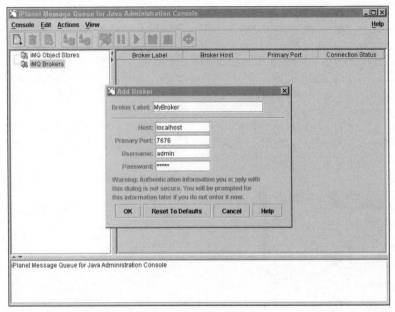

Figure 12-12: The iMQ Add Broker pop-up window

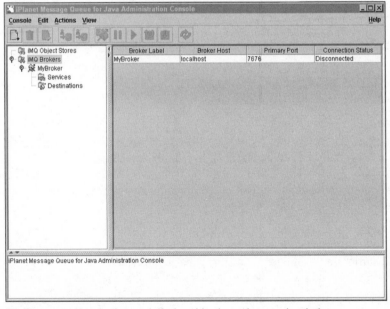

Figure 12-13: New brokers are displayed in the main console window

CREATING DESTINATIONS

The next step we need to take is to create a new JMS destination. This is not just telling the admin console about a destination that already exists; here we are actually creating a new destination. Navigate the pathway /iMQ Brokers/MyBroker in the tree on the left and right-click the Destinations entry. Select "Add Broker Destination" from the pop-up menu. We'll define a queue destination because it involves more options than a topic. Topic destinations are defined similarly to what we'll see here. Enter a destination name of **MyQueue**, select a Destination Type of Queue and select a Queue Delivery Policy of Round Robin. Then click the OK button. Figure 12-14 shows a picture of the Add Broker Destination pop-up.

Figure 12-14: Creating a new JMS queue destination

For queue destinations (but not topics) you have three possible delivery policies: Single, Round Robin, and Fail Over. Here's a description of each:

◆ **Single:** iMQ prevents more than one client from consuming messages for that particular destination at any time.

◆ **Fail Over:** This allows more than one client to register as a consumer for a particular destination. If one disconnects (abnormally or normally), messages start going to the next consumer that registered in the order it had registered. This policy can be good for implementing a simple fail-over strategy, say for the situation where you have a primary machine doing all the work and one or more hot backup machines standing by. However, because the order of connection determines primary and secondary (or tertiary, and so on) status, you will need to be very careful to be sure the consumer on the primary machine connects prior to the one on the hot backup machine and that the hot backup disconnects before the primary does. This requires some sort of out-of-channel synchronization mechanisms and could be tricky to get just right.

◆ **Round Robin:** This is similar to the fail-over policy in that multiple consumers can register to receive messages sent to the same destination. However, each incoming message is delivered to a single consumer in round-robin fashion – the order being determined by the order in which the consumers connected.

This policy can be useful for implementing a simple load-balancing scheme (covered in Chapter 4). The balancing can be done between two or more applications on the same or multiple machines. The only danger to watch out for is that if one of the consumers disconnects, then any messages originally destined for it will be reslotted for delivery to the remaining consumers, possibly resulting in out-of-order delivery. Because we have multiple consumers, however, we're already in a situation where out-of-order processing is okay because there's no guarantee a message delivered to one consumer will be processed entirely before one delivered after it to another consumer, so out-of-order processing shouldn't be a concern.

DEFINING AN OBJECT STORE

Defining an object store is how you tell the admin console about your JNDI data source. Defining an object store does not create a new JNDI directory *per se,* but if you are using a basic file system provider to manage your JNDI information, then it has the same effect as creating an entirely new JNDI directory.

While your main directory can be a remote LDAP installation that you want to use to manage your administered objects, we'll use the local file system as the permanent store for our JNDI directory in order to keep the example simple and straightforward.

To define an admin store, right-click the top level iMQ Object Stores entry in the tree on the left in the admin console. Select Add Object Store from the pop-up menu. Enter an Object Store Label of **MyObjectStore**. A large set of properties can be configured for our object store and they are listed in the middle of the window. Only two are mandatory, however. Select `java.naming.factory.initial` from the option box and enter **com.sun.jndi.fscontext.RefFSContextFactory** in the Value field. Then click the Add button on the right. Next, select `java.naming.provider.url` from the option box. Enter **file:///c:/Program Files/iPlanetMessageQueue2.0/var/stores/MyBroker/filestore** (or the equivalent path on your system) in the Value field and click the Add button again. Figure 12-15 shows what the Add Object Store pop-up window should look like before you click the OK button.

Figure 12-15: Defining a new JNDI object store

Just as with the broker itself, we will need to connect to the new object store before proceeding. To do this, right-click MyObjectStore in the left panel and select "Connect to Object Store" from the pop-up menu.

ADDING A CONNECTION FACTORY

As with all JMS products, connection factories and destinations are administered objects so we must add them to our JNDI directory. To add a connection factory, right-click Connection Factories in the left pane and select "Add Connection Factory Object" from the pop-up menu. In the Lookup Name field, enter **MyQueueConnectionFactory** and select a Factory Type of QueueConnectionFactory from the radio box. You can leave all the other values with their defaults but at some point you should fully explore all the tabbed panes and possible values, descriptions of which can be found in the iPlanet documentation. Some of the key values and behaviors that can be configured for an iMQ connection factory are as follows:

- SSL connectivity for encrypted messaging (as with WebLogic, be sure you're comfortable that all traffic for a given type of messaging is being encrypted appropriately)

- HTTP tunneling options

- A client identifier for durable topic subscribers

- Connection factory lookup authorization; notice that unlike with WebLogic, you can manage access to connection factories on a per-user basis, but unfortunately not a group basis (see the "Administering WebLogic 6.1" section earlier in this chapter for more information)

- JMS message default property values

Figure 12-16 shows the main Add Connection Factory Object pop-up window. After you click OK, the new connection factory will appear in the right-hand pane of the admin window.

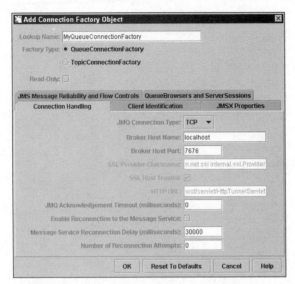

Figure 12-16: Adding a new JMS connection factory
object to JNDI

ADDING A DESTINATION

Before we can start messaging with our new queue, our last step is to add a new destination to the JNDI directory. Find the MyObjectStore folder in the left pane, right-click the Destinations entry, and select "Add Destination Object" from the pop-up menu. Enter a Lookup Name of **TestQueue**, select a Destination Type of Queue and enter a Destination Name of **MyQueue** (the same name we used previously when we created a destination for MyBroker). Now, we are simply mapping a previously created destination to the JNDI name that will be used to look it up, which is TestQueue. Figure 12-17 shows the how the Add Destination Object pop-up window should appear prior to clicking the OK button.

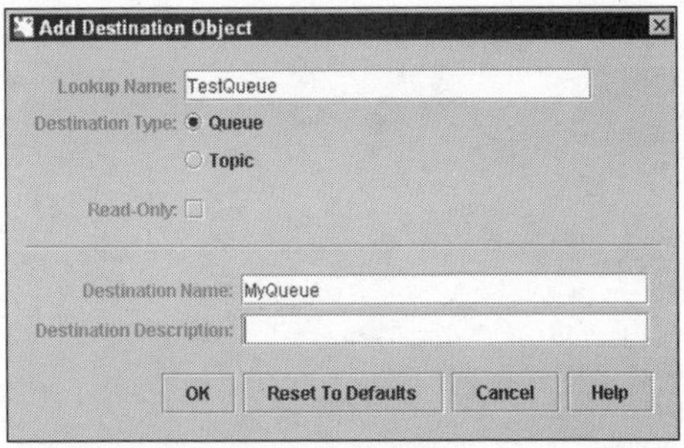

Figure 12-17: Adding a new Queue destination
object to JNDI

WRITING A TEST CLIENT

Listing 12-6 is a test program that you can use to verify if the new iMQ installation is working and if our newly created queue connection factory and destination are operational. As always, the power of a standards-based API such as JMS is that this same basic program will work with any JMS installation – the only difference is in the JNDI lookup code at the beginning. And because the difference is just in simple strings, you can easily keep the variable information outside the compiled program in a configuration file.

Listing 12-6: A sending and receiving test program for the "TestQueue" queue

```
import java.util.*;
import javax.naming.*;
import javax.jms.*;

/* This program will send a simple "Hello World" text message
 * if the parameter passed it is "send". If it is "receive" it
 * will receive what it presumes to be a TextMessage and exit.
 */

public class QueueTest
{
    public static void main(String[] args) throws Exception
    {
        if (args.length != 1 ||
            !("send".equalsIgnoreCase(args[0]) ||
            "receive".equalsIgnoreCase(args[0])))
        {
            System.out.println(
                "Usage: java QueueTest { send | receive }");
            System.exit(1);
        }

        Context ctx = null;
        Hashtable env = new Hashtable();

        env.put(Context.INITIAL_CONTEXT_FACTORY,
            "com.sun.jndi.fscontext.FSContextFactory");
        env.put(Context.PROVIDER_URL,
            "file:///c:/Program
Files/iPlanetMessageQueue2.0/var/stores/MyBroker/filestore");

        ctx = new InitialContext(env);

        QueueConnectionFactory qcf =
            (QueueConnectionFactory)
```

```
        ctx.lookup("MyQueueConnectionFactory");

QueueConnection qc = qcf.createQueueConnection();

QueueSession qs = qc.createQueueSession(false,
    QueueSession.AUTO_ACKNOWLEDGE);

Queue queue = null;
try
{
    queue = (javax.jms.Queue) ctx.lookup("TestQueue");
}
catch (Exception e)
{
    e.printStackTrace();
}

if (args[0].equalsIgnoreCase("receive"))
{
    QueueReceiver qrec = null;

    try
    {
        qrec = qs.createReceiver(queue);
    }
    catch (Exception e)
    {
        e.printStackTrace();
    }

    qc.start();

    System.out.println("Receiving msg");
    TextMessage msg = (TextMessage) qrec.receive();
    System.out.println("Got message: " + msg.getText());

    qrec.close();
}
else
{
    QueueSender qsend = null;

    try
    {
```

Continued

Listing 12-6 *(Continued)*

```
                qsend = qs.createSender(queue);
            }
            catch (Exception e)
            {
                e.printStackTrace();
            }

            TextMessage msg = qs.createTextMessage();
            msg.setText("Hello World");

            System.out.println("Sending msg");
            qsend.send(msg);

            qsend.close();
        }

        qs.close();
        qc.close();
    }
}

<project name="JMSTest" default="compile" basedir=".">

  <property name="JMQ_HOME" value="c:/Program
Files/iPlanetMessageQueue2.0" />
  <property name="jmslib" value="${JMQ_HOME}/lib/jms.jar"/>

  <path id="runclasspath">
    <pathelement location="." />
    <pathelement location="./classes" />
    <pathelement location="${JMQ_HOME}/lib/jms.jar" />
    <pathelement location="${JMQ_HOME}/lib/jmq.jar" />
    <pathelement location="${JMQ_HOME}/lib/fscontext.jar" />
    <pathelement location="${JMQ_HOME}/lib/providerutil.jar" />
  </path>

  <target name="prepare">
    <mkdir dir="./classes"/>
  </target>

  <target name="compile" depends="prepare">

    <javac srcdir="." destdir="./classes" classpath=".;${jmslib}">
    </javac>
```

```
    </target>

    <target name="runsend" depends="compile">
      <java classname="QueueTest" fork="yes">
          <classpath refid="runclasspath"/>
          <arg value="send"/>
      </java>
    </target>

    <target name="runreceive" depends="compile">
      <java classname="QueueTest" fork="yes">
          <classpath refid="runclasspath"/>
          <arg value="receive"/>
      </java>
    </target>

    <target name="clean">
      <delete dir="./classes" />
    </target>

</project>
```

Listing 12-7 shows an ant `build.xml` file that can be used to compile and run the test program. The "runsend" and "runreceive" targets can be used to execute the send and receive sides of the test program, respectively. You may need to tailor the `JMQ_HOME` variable to match your particular installation.

Listing 12-7: An ant build.xml for compiling and running Listing 12-6

```
<project name="JMSTest" default="compile" basedir=".">

    <property name="JMQ_HOME" value="c:/Program
Files/iPlanetMessageQueue2.0" />
    <property name="jmslib" value="${JMQ_HOME}/lib/jms.jar"/>

    <path id="runclasspath">
      <pathelement location="." />
      <pathelement location="./classes" />
      <pathelement location="${JMQ_HOME}/lib/jms.jar" />
      <pathelement location="${JMQ_HOME}/lib/jmq.jar" />
      <pathelement location="${JMQ_HOME}/lib/fscontext.jar" />
      <pathelement location="${JMQ_HOME}/lib/providerutil.jar" />
    </path>

    <target name="prepare">
```

Continued

Listing 12-7 *(Continued)*

```
      <mkdir dir="./classes"/>
  </target>

  <target name="compile" depends="prepare">

    <javac srcdir="." destdir="./classes" classpath=".;${jmslib}">
    </javac>

  </target>

  <target name="runsend" depends="compile">
    <java classname="QueueTest" fork="yes">
        <classpath refid="runclasspath"/>
        <arg value="send"/>
    </java>
  </target>

  <target name="runreceive" depends="compile">
    <java classname="QueueTest" fork="yes">
        <classpath refid="runclasspath"/>
        <arg value="receive"/>
    </java>
  </target>

  <target name="clean">
    <delete dir="./classes" />
  </target>

</project>
```

Evaluating JMS Products

If you'd like to download a free evaluation copy of either the WebLogic or iPlanet JMS product – or if you just want more detailed information about their capabilities – go directly to their home pages on the Web, as follows:

◆ For WebLogic Server: `http://www.bea.com`

◆ For iPlanet Message Queue: `http://www.iplanet.com`

And, of course, remember that just because a product is a market leader does not necessarily make it one of the best. Defining "best" can be difficult in any case when talking about JMS systems. You can evaluate a product in many different ways and many other JMS products are available – some free and/or open source. A few major categories to evaluate a product on are:

- Performance

- Standards compliance

- Supports both JMS topics and JMS queues

- Transaction support and integration

- Ease of administration

- Value-added features

- Security capabilities

- Ease of integration with other products and systems

- Support for Internet-based messaging

- Cost

- Available vendor support

What weight you give to each factor depends on your current environment and your current and future needs.

Summary

Though JMS does an excellent job of defining a standard messaging API, we've seen in this chapter that there is no standard way of approaching the administrative side of a JMS installation. Though you may know JMS very well, it can still be frustrating and time-consuming trying to get a new vendor's product up and running as you try to learn the product's interface, approach, and terminology. Even so, ease of administration is one area the JMS vendors can use to distinguish themselves in the marketplace.

Part III

JMS Architecture

Chapter 13

An Enterprise Real-Time Financial Trading System

IN THIS CHAPTER

- Sample Market Trading System (MTS) overview

- MTS requirements and features

- MTS system architecture using JMS

- Improving throughput with client-side internal queues

IT ALL BEGINS WITH ARCHITECTURE. Architecture is the technical plan that describes how your system will operate – and, by extension, how you will build it. A good, thorough architecture is no guarantee by itself of a successful system – proper requirements, implementation, and testing are all vital ingredients as well – but without a well-thought-out architecture, the chances of ending up with a smooth-running, well-performing system are greatly reduced.

In this book's final chapters we will run through some example architectures for systems that have JMS as a key component. Throughout this book we've tried to focus not just on the nuts and bolts of JMS programming but also on the architectural and design issues you need to be aware of to successfully design systems based on JMS.

For this chapter's exercise, let's assume we're an in-house development team working in a large financial company and that we've been given the task of implementing a proprietary trading system to be used by the company's fixed-income trading desk. The system will be named Market Trading System (MTS).

Users of the MTS system will be traders, analysts, and managers. The total number of users is expected to be fewer than 100 but of course each category of user will have somewhat different needs. In this chapter we'll focus on the system's messaging aspects and put together a system architecture to support it. Among the key messaging features we'll need from our JMS infrastructure are real-time message transmission; safe, transactionalized delivery; and flexible, cross-platform messaging.

The term "real time," as it's used on Wall Street and in many other corporate computing environments, does not mean the same thing it does if you're talking to operating systems engineers. Strictly speaking, in computer jargon, a real-time system is one in which operations can be performed in a predefined amount of time at the exact time an application wants to perform them (that is, with a millisecond or greater resolution). In the general developer population, however, "real time" is generically used to mean "fast" or "as soon as possible after a certain event occurs." This is the meaning of the term as we are using it in this chapter.

System Requirements

As with any system, a development team must design its system to conform with a predetermined set of restrictions and requirements. At a high level, we can break such requirements down into five categories:

- Physical infrastructure
- External and existing systems
- User requirements and required features
- Security requirements
- Performance requirements

For the MTS system, we've been given requirements for each of the categories as described in the following sections.

Physical infrastructure

Most new software has to operate to some extent within an existing physical network and hardware installation. MTS is no exception. We'll assume that our system's users will always be working from a desktop machine of some sort – PC or workstation – and that this desktop machine is connected to the internal LAN. The LAN is an Ethernet (TCP/IP) network and may be physically segmented into one or more subnets (see Figure 13-1). Further, let's assume we've been given the freedom and budget to add whatever server computers we deem necessary to the infrastructure.

External and existing systems

MTS must interact with two main external systems. The first is an existing back-office system that handles clearing and settlement for all the trading systems in the firm, called the Trade Processor (TP). The TP system resides on a mainframe and receives trade records from front-office trading systems via some sort of persistent queue technology. Because TP is currently being used by a variety of systems besides ours we cannot expect it to change the way it operates for us. Nor can we expect it to accommodate any message formats other than the ones it already knows about.

The second system is a market data distribution system (also known as a ticker plant) that receives real-time stock quotes via a connection to a proprietary equity data reseller and redistributes these quotes over our internal network (also in real time). We'll make the assumptions that the ticker plant is co-located on our internal LAN and that we have enough control over it so we can dictate the particular message format of the stock quotes it transmits. However, to complicate matters, we'll say that the ticker plant has been written in C++.

Figure 13-1 illustrates the relationship between the various systems.

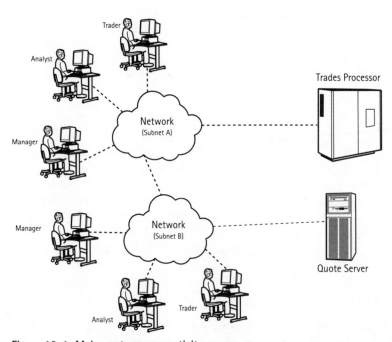

Figure 13-1: Major systems connectivity

User requirements and required features

Previously we identified three classes of MTS users: traders, analysts, and managers. For simplicity's sake, let's assume that the primary activities of each type of user can be cleanly decomposed into one of the following categories. Using these categories, we will be able to determine how to design our messaging infrastructure to support their needs.

◆ **Traders** obviously make trades, buying and selling financial instruments. In our case we'll say they're bond traders. To effect a trade, we need to get a message from the trader's GUI-based program that resides on his or her desktop machine to the trades processing system. We also need to pass back a confirmation message from the trades processing system to the trader indicating either that the trade has been accepted or that it has some sort of error. Traders also need up-to-the-minute quotes from the equity market so they can gauge the effectiveness of their hedging strategies, for which they use equity instruments. Only traders are allowed to make trades.

◆ **Managers** monitor activity. They want to see real-time profit and loss (P&L) numbers so they know how much money the trading desk is making or losing that day. They also need to be alerted about any trade greater than $1 million, as well as any trade that results in a negative account balance (a short sale).

◆ **Analysts** constantly monitor the bond and equity markets so they can suggest new trading strategies to the traders. To accomplish this task, they require as much real-time bond and equity information as possible. Their front-end application uses this information to update a plethora of colorful little moving charts and graphs that nobody but them can make any sense of.

Security requirements

Our trading environment will be physically separated from the rest of the company and our network and machines unreachable because they have been cordoned off by the use of an internal firewall. Even with these precautions, we want to ensure that no unauthorized trades are submitted to the system by people who do have legitimate access to the trading desk's network (for example, developers, system administrators, consultants, and so on) but who are not predesignated traders.

Performance requirements

Performance requirements for this system are high. The equity market generates a huge number of quotes daily and this number comprises the bulk of messages traversing the network. Let's say we've been told to design the system so it can handle a peak rate of 100 quote messages per second sustained over the course of the business day.

By comparison, messages associated with our proprietary trading activity will be low because the number of them can only be directly proportional to the manual entry capabilities of the traders; we can assume no more than 1,000 trade requests per business day. However, the traders are naturally very busy people working in a fast moving market and will require quick confirmations that their trades have been processed so they can move on to the next task. They expect confirmation that each of their trades has been processed and their on-screen position updated within three seconds after entering the trade.

MTS System Architecture

We now have enough information to start fleshing out an architecture for the messaging-related MTS infrastructure. There are many ways to approach an architectural analysis for a system like this. The general approach we'll use here is to first define the basic format of the messages that will be passed between the various applications (client-side, server, legacy, etc.). Second, we'll specify how and when the messages will be delivered. And last, we'll specify some of the key operational behaviors of the applications involved in the messaging.

This approach works well when designing a distributed system because in many ways the messages themselves define the behavioral contract of the various participating components. Just as you'd begin designing a non-messaging component by defining its interface (i.e., its API), you can accomplish the same thing in a loosely coupled system by designing the messages first. After all, it's the messages which define the possible inputs and outputs of a module, just as defining a module's input and output parameters would in a system based on a different communications technology, such as CORBA.

Thus, the first order of business is to decide what types of messages we will be passing around and what they will look like.

Determining message types

From our requirements, it's safe to say we'll need the following distinct messages, which we'll look at in more detail:

- TradeRequest
- TradeReply
- TradeNotification
- EquityQuote

THE TRADEREQUEST MESSAGE

TradeRequest messages are used to submit a buy or sell order to the back-end trades processing system. They should only originate from a trader's application. This message is a request message in two ways. First, it indicates a request for the trades processing system to perform a service – namely, to accept a trade and to perform whatever back-office magic is necessary to ensure the trade is successfully cleared. It is only a request because it's possible for the trades processing system to reject it for a variety of reasons (bad message format, insufficient funds, and so on).

Second, we're calling the message type TradeRequest because it is the request half of a request reply operation. As such, we must somehow ensure that the sender is uniquely identified so that the reply from the trades processing system can be delivered only to the application that initiated the trade initially and no other.

Table 13-1 lists the data elements of a TradeRequest message.

TABLE 13-1 DATA ELEMENTS OF A TRADEREQUEST MESSAGE

Field Name	Java Type	Description
Originator ID	String	A unique ID indicating the message source
Account From	String	The seller's account number
Account To	String	The buyer's account
CUSIP	String	The instrument's identifier
Quantity	Long	The number of bonds to buy/sell (sell quantities are negative)
Price	Double	The sale price in dollars
Trade Date	Date	The date of the trade
Settlement Date	Date	The settlement date of the trade
Message ID	String	A unique identifier for this message

Note that a CUSIP is an industry-standard identifier for some types of fixed-income instruments (for a concise description of what a CUSIP is, and as a starting point for further investigation, see http://www.sec.gov/answers/cusip.htm).

THE TRADEREPLY MESSAGE

TradeReply messages are returned to the originator of a trade request by the trades processing system. A trade reply simply consists of a status code and a human-readable error message. Table 13-2 lists the data elements of a TradeReply message.

TABLE 13-2 DATA ELEMENTS OF A TRADEREPLY MESSAGE

Field Name	Java Type	Description
Status	`int`	0 indicates all OK
Error Message	`String`	An optional message
Message ID	`String`	The identifier for the message that this message is the reply to

THE TRADENOTIFICATION MESSAGE

`TradeNotification` messages are broadcast to all applications that have registered to receive them upon the successful acceptance of a trade request. This broadcast must occur always only after the `TradeReply` message has been delivered and it must always be sent from the same JMS session so that we are guaranteed the messages will arrive at each client in the proper order. The initiator of the trade will receive a trade confirmation followed by a trade notification; all others will receive just a trade notification.

Note that we cannot use JMS to guarantee that a `TradeNotification` message is received by a client immediately following a `TradeReply` because it's possible for a message from another source to end up being delivered to a client in between the two. This will not be a problem for us, however, as long as we ensure that our trader application assumes only the relative ordering of the two messages but not the absolute ordering (and that it receives both messages via the same JMS session).

The data elements of a `TradeNotification` are similar to those of a `TradeRequest` but they have an additional field indicating the profit or loss made on the trade using whatever P&L calculation scheme the firm employs (first-in-first-out, average cost, etc.). The `TradeNotification` message also has a field that indicates the new account position (that is, the new quantity of the bond identified by the CUSIP in the trade in the "Account From" field in the trade). Table 13-3 lists the data elements of a `TradeNotification` message.

TABLE 13-3 DATA ELEMENTS OF A TRADENOTIFICATION MESSAGE

Field Name	Java Type	Description
Account From	`String`	The seller's account number
Account To	`String`	The buyer's account

Continued

TABLE 13-3 DATA ELEMENTS OF A TRADENOTIFICATION MESSAGE *(Continued)*

CUSIP	String	The instrument's identifier
Quantity	long	The number of bonds to buy/sell
Price	double	The sale price in dollars
Trade Date	Date	The date of the trade
Settlement Date	Date	The settlement date of the trade
P&L	double	The money made or lost on the trade
Position	long	The new position after the trade

THE EQUITYQUOTE MESSAGE

EquityQuote messages are very simple. They contain a ticker symbol indicating what stock a quote is for, and the current bid and ask prices for the stock. Table 13-4 lists the data elements of an EquityQuote message.

TABLE 13-4 DATA ELEMENTS OF AN EQUITYQUOTE MESSAGE

Field Name	Java Type	Description
Ticker Symbol	String	The seller's account number
Bid	Double	The buyer's account
Bid Time	Date	The instrument's identifier
Ask	Double	The number of bonds to buy/sell
Ask Time	Date	The sale price in dollars

Creating an initial architecture

Now that we've identified our basic messages, we can start thinking about what components we'll need to build to process the messages, how the messages will flow between the components, and where the instances of the components will reside. This leads us to our initial architecture for the MTS system.

Let's assume we've already made three basic technology decisions:

◆ A Java-based client-side application for users to interact with. The Swing (JFC) toolkit will enable us to get the same look and feel on our desktop machines whatever they are (PC, Unix, Mac).

◆ A J2EE-compliant application server to handle the middleware chores.

◆ A JMS-compliant messaging product to tie all our applications together.

Figure 13-2 shows our initial architecture, incorporating all the main system elements from the requirements and our defined messages.

A review of this diagram highlights a small hole in our design thus far, however. We presumed we would need only one message type to submit a trade (TradeRequest) and one type to get a confirmation (TradeReply), but because we've imposed an application server in the middle of our system, it doesn't seem like this will be possible. We said earlier that the trades processing system already existed and required specific message formats that we could not expect to change. It's highly unlikely our desired formats will match that of the existing processing system, or that we could simply adopt their format, so we will need to define two additional messages that the application server will use to talk to the back office. Let's call them TPTradeRequest and TPTradeReply because they will perform roughly the same function as their front-end counterparts. The application server will be given the job of translating the front-end message into a back-end one and vice versa. Figure 13-3 shows an updated architectural diagram.

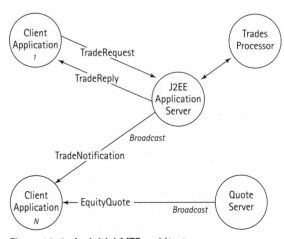

Figure 13-2: An initial MTS architecture

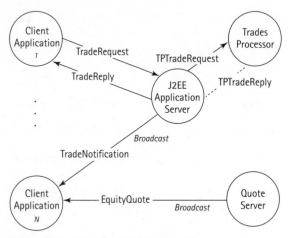

Figure 13-3: An updated MTS architecture

Notice how in our architecture we have not involved the application server in the distribution of equity quotes. This is so for two main reasons. First, application servers only ever operate in response to an initiating action of some sort (a method call on an enterprise bean, the receipt of a message, and so on), and we need our quotes to be proactively delivered to the client applications as soon as they come in so that the information will arrive at the client applications as soon as possible. Sending the quotes to the application server and forcing the clients to request them periodically would not only cause the messages to arrive in a less timely fashion, it would also drive up network traffic as a result of the constant polling by the clients. Certainly, we could have message-driven beans receive the quote messages and then immediately rebroadcast them to the clients but there's not much point in involving the application server in that when the messages are already being broadcast by the ticker plant in the first place.

Second, not involving the application server in quote distribution will enable it to focus solely on trading activity. This leaves it relatively unloaded, improving its scalability and letting it respond faster to user requests.

Determining JMS messaging modes

Now that we have an initial architecture in place, we should decide what type of JMS messaging is most appropriate for each interaction between components. The following are some options.

THE EQUITYQUOTE MESSAGE

Because EquityQuote messages are broadcast in high volumes to many machines, it seems clear they should be delivered using JMS publish/subscribe messaging. We have no need for 100-percent reliable delivery of these messages because by the time a message is recovered, it's likely that a fresher one will have superseded it. Consequently, we will use nonpersistent messaging for these and won't bother to send or receive them in a transaction; not using persistent, transactionalized messaging also helps us achieve higher message throughput where it's needed the most.

We'll also use the lightest weight JMS acknowledgement mode: DUPS_OK_ ACKNOWLEDGE. Provided we design our client applications that receive quote messages such that they are not sensitive to receiving the same quote message twice, DUPS_OK_ACKNOWLEDGE will give us the best performance (see Chapter 10 for an explanation of why this is the case).

Because we'll likely be using different types of acknowledgement and transactional behavior in our clients that receive messages, MTS is an application that will need to create multiple JMS sessions to receive messages. The session that receives quote messages would be created as follows:

```
TopicSession session = topicConn.createTopicSession(false,

TopicSession.DUPS_OK_ACKNOWLEDGE);
```

To make it fast and easy for the clients to manipulate the message and to allow for future expansion, we'll use the JMS MapMessage to deliver the messages. The following code fragment shows an example of how data from an EquityQuote message might be extracted:

```
String symbol = equityQuote.getString("Ticker Symbol");
double bid = equityQuote.getDouble("Bid");
// JMS messages do not support Dates natively so they must
// be sent as longs
Date bidTime = new Date( equityQuote.getLong("Bid Time") );
double ask = equityQuote.getDouble("Ask");
Date askTime = new Date( equityQuote.getLong("Ask Time") );
```

THE TPTRADEREQUEST AND TPTRADEREPLY MESSAGES

We have no choice with these messages; they must be delivered to the back office over the queue product already in place so we must use JMS point-to-point messaging for it. If the JMS product we select automatically converts MapMessages to the required format of the trades processing system, then we can use them. Otherwise, we can fall back on TextMessage or BytesMessage, which lets us finely control the format of the message so that it conforms to the trade processor's requirements.

For example, many mainframe-based systems are written in COBOL and naturally store information in their native format. Because this format differs from the various microcomputer systems (which in turn differ from each other depending on the specific hardware) it is common for mainframe applications providing services to the microcomputer world to communicate entirely with fixed-format text messages. Traditionally, it has just been a more readily available solution to convert ASCII to EBCDIC and, in turn, convert the EBCDIC text to int, floats, and so on, than it is to give the mainframe application enough knowledge to convert back and forth from all the possible native data representations it might see. A sample message format expected by the mainframe Trades Processing system might be as shown in Table 13-5.

TABLE 13-5 A SAMPLE MAINFRAME TRADES PROCESSING QUEUE
            MESSAGE FORMAT

Field	Size	Example
Trade Date	8 chars	"12082002"
Settlement Date	8 chars	"12112002"
Account From	7 chars	"ABC1234"
Account To	7 chars	"XYZ6789"
CUSIP	8 chars	"57391310"
Quantity	7 chars	"0001000"
Price	10 chars	"000109.500"

Some messaging products automatically convert data types, but assuming our trades processing system still expects records in text format, then we'll have to extract the data from the TradeRequest message received from the client and construct an appropriately formatted TextMessage to pass on to the trades processor. And, of course, we must do the reverse for the returned TPTradeReply.

To handle the initial trade request from the trader client, we'll need to employ a message-driven bean in our application server. This bean will be responsible for receiving the trade request message from the trader applications, doing any required processing (e.g. insert the trade into the local database), and then forwarding the trade to the trade processing mainframe.

Listing 13-1 and Listing 13-2 show two sample classes that would be used by the message-driven bean that accepts incoming TradeRequest. The Listing 13-1 class converts incoming MapMessages to a class called TradeRequest. The Listing 13-2 class can be used to produce the fixed-format text message required by the mainframe from a TradeRequest object.

Listing 13-1: A class that converts a TradeRequest MapMessage to an object

```
import javax.jms.*;
import java.util.*;

public class TradeRequest
```

```
{
    String originatorID;
    String accountFrom, accountTo;
    String CUSIP;
    long quantity;
    double price;
    Date tradeDate;
    Date settlementDate;

    public void loadFromMapMessage(MapMessage msg) throws
JMSException
    {
        originatorID = ((Queue) msg.getJMSReplyTo()).getQueueName();
        accountFrom = msg.getString("Account From");
        accountTo = msg.getString("Account To");
        CUSIP = msg.getString("CUSIP");
        quantity = msg.getLong("Quantity");
        price = msg.getDouble("Price");
        tradeDate = new Date(msg.getLong("Trade Date"));
        settlementDate = new Date(msg.getLong("Settlement Date"));
    }
}
```

Listing 13-2: A class that converts a TradeRequest object to a TextMessage

```
import javax.jms.*;
import java.util.*;
import java.text.*;

public class TPTradeRequest
{
    String originatorID;
    String accountFrom, accountTo;
    String CUSIP;
    long quantity;
    double price;
    Date tradeDate;
    Date settlementDate;

    public TPTradeRequest(TradeRequest trade)
    {
        originatorID = trade.originatorID;
```

Continued

Listing 13-2 *(Continued)*

```
        accountFrom = trade.accountFrom;
        accountTo = trade.accountTo;
        CUSIP = trade.CUSIP;
        quantity = trade.quantity;
        price = trade.price;
        tradeDate = trade.tradeDate;
        settlementDate = trade.settlementDate;
    }


    static SimpleDateFormat dateFormat = new
SimpleDateFormat("MMddyyyy");
    static DecimalFormat priceFormat = new DecimalFormat("#.000");

    public TextMessage toTextMessage(Session session) throws
JMSException
    {
        StringBuffer s = new StringBuffer();

        s.append( toPad(accountFrom, 7) );
        s.append( toPad(accountTo, 7) );
        s.append( toPad(CUSIP, 8) );
        s.append( toZeroPad("" + quantity, 7) );
        s.append( toZeroPad( priceFormat.format(price), 10) );
        s.append( toPad( dateFormat.format(tradeDate), 8) );
        s.append( toPad( dateFormat.format(settlementDate), 8) );

        TextMessage tm = session.createTextMessage(s.toString());
        tm.setJMSCorrelationID(originatorID);

        return tm;
    }

    static String toZeroPad(String s, int len)
    {
        if (s == null) s = "";

        if (s.length() > len) return s.substring(0, len);
        else if (s.length() < len)
        {
            StringBuffer ret = new StringBuffer(s);
            for (int i=0; i < len-s.length(); ++i) ret.insert(0,
'0');
```

```
            return ret.toString();
        }
        return s;
    }

    static String toPad(String s, int len)
    {
        if (s == null) s = "";

        if (s.length() > len) return s.substring(0, len);
        else if (s.length() < len)
        {
            StringBuffer ret = new StringBuffer(s);
            for (int i=0; i < len-s.length(); ++i) ret.insert(0, '
');
            return ret.toString();
        }
        return s;
    }
}
```

Handling the TPTradeReply message that is returned from the mainframe application presents us with a bit of a problem. The simplest solution would be to have the same message-driven bean that accepts the TradeRequest message block and wait for the TPTradeReply after sending the TPTradeRequest message to the mainframe. This is a basic request/reply situation for which we could use the QueueRequestor class in our message-driven bean. There are two problems with this approach, however.

The first problem relates to the fact that it's generally not a very good idea to perform any blocking operations inside an EJB, especially if the blocking will occur for relatively long periods of time, such as we might experience while waiting for a response from the mainframe. Blocking inside an EJB keeps that particular instance of the EJB occupied and unavailable to handle new requests. This will negatively impact the scalability of a system. It's a much better idea in such cases to process the reply message in such situations asynchronously by using a second message-driven bean.

The second problem we have — and this is a general issue related to performing request/reply messaging — is that it is not possible to initiate a request/reply operation from inside a transacted session. The reason for this is that messages that are sent from inside a transacted session are held until the transaction is committed. Since your application will block inside the transaction waiting for the reply message, a deadlock situation will have been created: the request message cannot be sent until the reply message is received.

There is no reason why a message-driven bean cannot receive a request message and send out a reply message within a single transaction. It is, in fact, a common function of message-driven beans to service request/reply operations on behalf of clients. It's only when you have a message-driven bean with container managed transactions acting as the *client* of a request/reply that you will get into trouble.

For these two reasons we will need to write one message-driven bean to receive the TradeRequest message and send the TPTradeRequest to the mainframe – all inside of a single transaction. And we will need to write another message-driven bean to receive the TPTradeReply from the mainframe and deliver it back to the trader client – also all within a single transaction.

Because we cannot block waiting for a reply from the mainframe, we'll need some way to identify the reply message when it comes back. That is, we'll need to figure out which client application initiated the corresponding TradeRequest so that we can respond to it. This type of message matching is exactly what the **JMSCorrelationID** property is meant for; we'll just need to be sure our trade processing application fills it in properly on the TPTradeReply messages it sends out (with the incoming TPTradeRequest message's correlation ID).

THE TRADENOTIFICATION MESSAGE

The decision on how to send TradeNotification messages is also straightforward: (1) a single trade notification must be sent to an unknown number of client applications, and (2) if a client application is not running at the time it is sent, then the application does not need to receive it. Clearly, nonpersistent pub/sub messaging is the way to go.

We should make clear at this point that our architecture assumes that the applications that need to know about every trade will not need to actually receive every trade notification message that is broadcast. Though it might seem obvious to use durable topic subscribers, this is not the best approach. For one reason, a lot of trade notifications will be going out and if a client application is not available for a while – say, because its user is on vacation for a couple weeks – the queue of waiting messages could grow quite large.

In addition, you probably don't want applications that report on trading – perhaps an application that displays the number of trades during the day having quantities greater than some user-configurable amount – to be keeping all the information they need to generate the report in local memory. It's much better to design such reporting applications to retrieve the required data from the central relational database that can do most of the slicing and dicing for them as well as giving them up-to-the-minute information.

Some data storage mechanism outside of JMS is required in any case, because if a client application crashes in the middle of the day, there must be some way for it to get the historical information it needs so it can represent the current state of the world to the user when it comes back up. Naturally, clients will not access the central database directly in two-tier fashion, but will instead get any needed data from the J2EE application server that will expose services that mediate access to the database.

SYNCHRONIZING AT START-UP   Given the architecture we've outlined, it is vital that a proper start-up and synchronization procedure be employed. A client application that crashes and restarts in the middle of the day needs to retrieve the necessary historical and summary information from the database. But it will be doing so at the same time that messages likely to have an effect on the content of that data are being hurled at it.

Unfortunately, there's no simple answer to this problem; JMS explicitly does not define any particular delivery behavior for applications that start receiving messages from an already active bus. If you delay subscribing to JMS messages (and hence delay their receipt) until *after* reading any initialization data from the database, then it's possible you'll miss some messages that were delivered during the small window between reading and subscribing. If, on the other hand you subscribe *first* and *then* read your initialization data, you may end up processing messages pertaining to data that was already reflected in the database.

In most cases, the latter technique is better. For instance, if the data in question is of the "only the most recent value matters" variety, such as an account position, then the appropriate sequence of events would be as follows:

1. Subscribe to the messages but don't read any that arrive. Your JMS provider will begin delivering messages to your application but they will be held in a provider queue until your application is ready to process them.

2. Load any initialization data and update the internal state of your application with it.

3. Process any held messages and any subsequent incoming messages as normal, updating the internal state of your application.

These steps will ensure that your application's internal state reflects the accurate current values. One problem that would arise is if your initialization process takes so long to complete that any buffers being used to hold incoming JMS messages overflow, resulting in dropped messages. But this is unlikely.

Keep in mind that in order for this procedure to work correctly, your messages must contain absolute, current values, not changes in value (deltas). In the case of an account position, for example, if an account balance started at 200 and three trades occurred with quantities of 100, 500, and 1000 (in that order), then your `TradeNotification` messages should report current balances of 300, 800, and 1800.

In circumstances such as this, designers often mistakenly opt to send out `TradeNotification` messages that contain just the changes to the position (which in this case is simply the trade quantity) and rely on the client applications to add the received quantity to the current position. Due to the difficulties associated with startup synchronization, this is not the best approach. After all, short of employing some very convoluted algorithms, there's no way to tell whether a position delta received in a message was already applied to the position amount an application retrieved from the database or not. In a system where message order was not guaranteed, then you would have to use the delta approach, but since JMS guarantees that messages will be delivered in the order they were sent, you're much better off using the absolute value method.

Furthermore, a system that makes use only of absolute value messaging is self-healing, whereas a delta value one is not. Consider, if a message containing a delta value is lost in transit, a client's position value will never be correct afterwards, whereas, a client receiving absolute value messages will have the correct values as soon as the next message is received.

As we said earlier, it's probably not a good idea to keep a list of historical data in local memory, but if you do need to do this for some reason, then you could properly synchronize your application's internal state with the database by following the preceding numbered sequence of events except for Step 3. In place of this, you would need to throw out any pending messages that contained data already in your application's internal list. To do this correctly, you will need a way to uniquely identify records or to timestamp them with a high degree of accuracy so that messages that duplicate those already loaded can be discarded.

THE TRADEREQUEST AND TRADEREPLY MESSAGES

The `TradeRequest` and `TradeReply` messages are the most problematic to figure out what to do with from a messaging mode perspective. Certainly, we'll need to use message-driven beans in the application server to receive the `TradeRequest` message because our application server will be sitting in between the client applications and the trades processing system — that much is a given. But how best to get the message there?

Trade messages get delivered to only one central location, so a point-to-point message or a durable topic message is in order. Because durable topics provide no advantages over point-to-point messages when there is only a single reader, we can eliminate their use.

The question, then, is do we want persistent point-to-point messaging or non-persistent? Trade requests are too important to lose, so persistent messaging seems to be the obvious answer. However, the implication of using this mode is that, if the application server were to crash for some reason, the trades will be queued while waiting for it to come back up. Is this really what we want? Probably not. In reality, if the application server is down, then the entire trading system is effectively down because there is nothing to route trades to the back office. While it can certainly do so when it comes back up, it is unlikely the traders would want to continue trading when there is no way for them to know what the current state of their accounts are (such as current positions) as a result of the trades.

Assuming we've thoroughly analyzed the situation and decided that trading should not continue if the application server or anything it depends on (e.g. the database) were to fail, there's really no need to take the performance hit of using persistent point-to-point messaging. Instead, we'll go with nonpersistent point-to-point messaging. As it turns out, we can even use nonpersistent pub/sub messaging and get the same results. It's six of one, a half dozen of the other.

Since we're using nonpersistent messaging, though, it's possible a trade request may get lost. In order to compensate for this unlikely event, the best thing to do is to implement a timeout mechanism in the client application. If, for instance, we decide to use the QueueRequestor class to send out a TradeRequest and wait for a TradeReply, we need to start a timer at the moment the TradeRequest message is delivered. If the timer expires prior to the receipt of a TradeReply, then the user should be alerted so that a human can determine if the trade needs to be reentered or not. (Note that some providers allow you to administratively configure a timeout when defining a connection factory.)

Note also that by using the QueueRequestor class, we will not need to explicitly populate a Message ID field from the message format in Tables 13-1 and 13-2; the **JMSReplyTo** message property can serve this purpose. On the sender side, the QueueRequestor will automatically fill in the **JMSReplyTo** property with a unique ID. On the server side, we will need to use **JMSReplyTo** as the destination to send the reply message (see Chapter 6 for more information on using the QueueRequestor class). Following the procedure outlined earlier in the chapter, we'll use the **JMSReplyTo** property as the correlation ID to tie together all the messages related to a single trade request.

Additionally, even though we are actually performing four asynchronous messaging operations passing through two systems (our application server and the mainframe), from the trader application point of view all this activity is hidden behind a single synchronous call by the use of the QueueRequestor class.

In reality, even if we were using persistent messaging, a timeout mechanism would be necessary because it would be possible for the request message to be accepted but still not processed due to the unavailability of the application server, back-office trades processor, or other critical system.

The necessity of using timeout mechanisms illustrates how request/reply messaging can eliminate some of the basic advantages of JMS's asynchronous behavior. As we've discussed on many occasions so far in this book, asynchronous messaging is great in as much as it allows applications to operate independently and at their own pace. By employing a request/reply paradigm on top of an asynchronous infrastructure, we've essentially switched to a synchronous messaging model. Unfortunately, while asynchronous messaging is preferable, sometimes synchronous messaging cannot be avoided.

Finally, to ensure the integrity of our application database, we must be sure to enclose the receipt of the TradeRequest message, the sending of the TPTradeRequest message, and any local database activity related to the two messages in a distributed transaction. We should also do likewise with the receipt of the

`TPTradeReply` message by the application server and any local database operations it performs.

MESSAGE VERSUS METHOD CALL

One question you may be asking your self is, why bother with all the rigmarole of request/reply messaging between the client and application server when you could simply have the client application make a remote method call on an enterprise bean running in the application server? In many real-world systems this is, in fact, exactly what you would do.

The problem with doing it in our fictional MTS system is that a call to an EJB method is synchronous but the interaction between the EJB and the trades processor system is asynchronous. This means that after the EJB is invoked by the client, it would need somehow to block and be alerted when the reply came back. In an application server, this is a bad idea from a scalability point of view because too many EJB instances may be blocked for relatively long periods of time. Blocked EJB instances would not be available to service new requests. And, of course, they too would need to implement timeout mechanisms to handle the case where the back office never returned a reply message.

Figure 13-4 shows our final MTS messaging architecture.

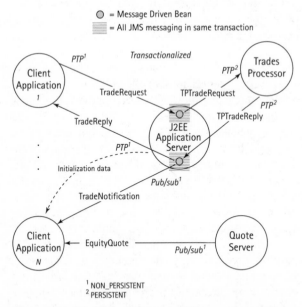

Figure 13-4: The MTS architecture with messaging modes

Selecting products

After coming up with a requirements document and putting together a solid initial architecture, now is the time to begin thinking about what third-party products might suit our needs. From an application server point of view the primary requirement is a product supporting EJB 2.0, particularly message-driven beans .

From a JMS provider point of view, an ideal JMS product would have these features:

◆ Supports both publish/subscribe and point-to-point messaging.

◆ Handles pub/sub messaging between Java and C++ clients (i.e. will automatically convert `MapMessage`s from Java applications to C++ ones and *vice versa*).

◆ Handles point-to-point messaging between JMS clients and whatever queue product is used by the trades processing system to accept and return messages.

◆ Can broadcast an adequate number of pub/sub messages per second (measured by peak as well as average volume).

◆ Is designed in a way such that it can be configured to work seamlessly over our LAN topology (that is, including multiple subnets). Or, if there's a way we can reconfigure our network slightly, will work over the reconfigured network.

◆ Interoperates with our application server.

◆ Supports distributed transactions encompassing our message-driven beans and local database

Finding a JMS provider that supports all these bullet points might be a tall order, especially when cost issues are factored in. Unfortunately, if we can't find the perfect product or if, as often happens, we are stuck with a previously purchased software suite, then our architecture might have to change somewhat. Most JMS products, however, are rapidly evolving to include all these features if they don't already. The feature to pay the most attention to for a system like MTS is performance because you can't rely upon a marketing brochure to determine if a product's performance will meet your needs.

Improving client-side throughput

One of the key, but under-appreciated, elements in any messaging architecture involving GUI clients is the way in which messages are handled once they leave the bus and are inside the client application. The reason this piece of the puzzle is so important is that the inefficient handling of messages inside an application can cause the queue of undelivered messages to back up, resulting in lower-than-ideal throughput. Remember that the queue we're talking about here is the client-side queue the provider caches the messages in until your application is ready to process them; it exists regardless of the actual JMS messaging mode used to deliver the messages. Only if an application can process the messages it receives as fast or faster than they are delivered to it will you get maximum throughput out of your messaging infrastructure.

This problem can beset any type of application but it manifests itself most often in GUI-based applications because the process of updating and redrawing GUI components typically takes a lot longer to complete than the time it takes to receive a single message. Applications that contain numerous individual GUI components that need to be updated in response to incoming traffic are the most likely to have problems because often many of these components need to be updated each time a new message arrives. This is certainly the case with the analyst application in our fictional MTS system, which suffers from having a large number of graphical components and a high rate of incoming messages.

If there existed, for instance, ten individual graph and table components in the analyst application – each of which had to be updated whenever a new equity quote arrived – we would need to perform 1000 internal updates per second whenever the peak load of 100 quote messages per second was reached; this may be beyond the capabilities of an application running on a relatively underpowered desktop.

The problem with most internal application message delivery mechanisms is that they are serial. Information based on an incoming message is delivered to each component one at a time. One problem with serial processing is that it causes the performance to degrade linearly as each new component is added to the system. Another problem is that the entire system is held hostage to the performance of a single slow component because the next incoming message cannot be consumed until each and every component is finished processing the current message.

Figure 13-5 illustrates a typical internal architecture.

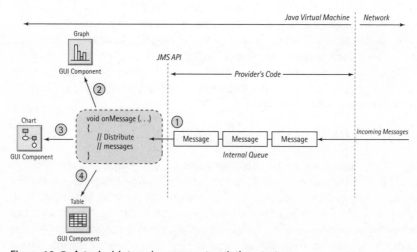

Figure 13-5: A typical internal component updating strategy

Step 1 is the receipt of the message from the bus. Steps 2, 3, and 4 happen in sequence. The problem is that Step 1 cannot be executed again (that is, a new message cannot be received) until Step 4 has been completed.

IMPROVING PERFORMANCE WITH AN INTERNAL QUEUE ARCHITECTURE

Clearly, overall throughput can be increased if each component processes messages in parallel. Just as a JMS system that broadcasts messages to many applications at once operates faster than one that delivers messages to each application sequentially, so too inside an application. A good way to achieve this is to interpose an in-memory queue in between the JMS `onMessage()` method and the application's GUI components. Using this strategy, the `onMessage()` method can accept a message, deliver it to one internal location – the queue – and then return to accept a new message. The GUI components would be designed to read messages off the queue as needed, which lets each one operate at its own pace while not holding up the other components.

Figure 13-6 illustrates an internal queue architecture.

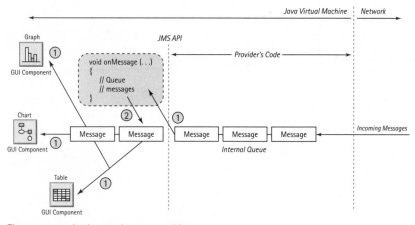

Figure 13-6: An internal queue architecture

Let's examine the operation of the internal queue in more detail. In Java applications, GUI components do not run independently – they all run within a single GUI event thread. Thus, to achieve any sort of parallelism we need to employ a helper thread for each GUI component that receives messages. It is the responsibility of the helper thread to read messages from the queue and to update the component's display, which, to be correct, should be done using the `SwingUtilities.invokeLater()` method (refer to the `javax.swing.SwingUtilities` class documentation to see what this method does if you are not familiar with it).

Because we're using a single queue to hold messages for many components, helper threads cannot "read" messages in the sense that they remove them from the queue. They can only "peek" at them – that is, read them without removing them. To be as efficient as possible, each peek operation should retrieve all available unseen messages, not just the single one at the head of the queue.

There must be some mechanism by which messages get removed, of course, otherwise the queue would grow indefinitely. This can be done by employing a thread that runs periodically and removes any messages that have already been seen by all components. Alternatively, the system could be designed so that when the last component reads a message from the queue, that message (or messages) is also removed from the queue.

In either case, the API that controls access to the queue needs to be written such that it internally keeps track of which components are reading messages and which messages have been delivered to whom. In this way it can discard messages that are no longer required and keep the size of the queue manageable. All access to the queue should be through this API so it can perform the necessary housekeeping.

Finally, so that the helper threads can avoid polling for new messages, they should synchronize on a common object so that they can all be woken up at the same time with an `Object.notifyAll()` call whenever a new message is placed on the end of the queue.

Figure 13-7 shows a blow-up of the internal queue architecture and how it operates.

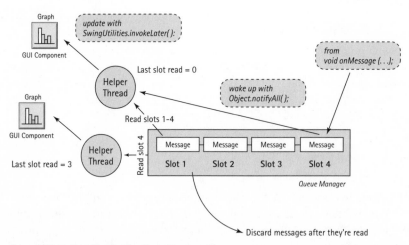

Figure 13-7: Detailed internal queue operation

As with all buffering infrastructures, the system will still break down if the incoming messages arrive faster than they can be processed because the buffer eventually overflows. Using this architecture, however, increases this threshold in your application because instead of the time to process a single message being as follows (where T_i is a single component's processing time):

$$T_1 + T_2 + T_3 + \ldots T_N$$

it will be instead:

$$\max(T_1, T_2, T_3, \ldots T_N)$$

discounting the small additional performance hit you get from employing the required helper threads.

Finally, remember that employing an internal queue or similar architecture is not necessary for all applications. Many applications receive messages at a slow enough rate that trying to process the messages asynchronously as described in this section would be more trouble than it's worth, especially because it can be tricky to get just right. Applications that have very high performance requirements, on the other hand, can benefit greatly by implementing such a solution. Furthermore, it's a solution that can be written generically and used across many different applications.

Securing the system

We pointed out in Chapters 9 and 10 that security and performance considerations are often left out of the initial design of a new system. The preceding requirements for our fictional MTS system do include specific security and performance data so we're off to the right start.

To satisfy the performance requirements, we've designed the system so that it will support high enough message rates and response times. The only way to know for sure, however, is to prototype the key infrastructure elements and run some benchmarks.

Security requirements, on the other hand, have not been incorporated into the MTS architecture yet. As we said previously, we know our system will be running on a network segregated from the rest of the world by a firewall so we don't need to worry about the systems and network being probed by the general public (or, for that matter, the rest of the company). This does not mean we don't want a still higher level of security. Many non-traders will have access to the network and we want to prohibit them from submitting false trades to the back end. We can do this in two ways (see Chapter 9 for a detailed discussion of each):

1. Prohibiting access to the messaging infrastructure through whatever authentication and authorization mechanisms (such as logon) our JMS provider and application server provide.

2. Tagging each trade message with a message authentication code that the server can use to verify the origin of each trade request message.

The simplest solution is the one in which the messaging software can be configured to prevent unauthorized usage. However, we may need to go with the second option if the security features of our provider are inadequate and it's possible that messages could be spoofed.

For many systems, we would also want to explore the possibility of encrypting the trade traffic to prevent unauthorized users and systems from examining the contents of a trade request message. For a system such as MTS we can achieve this in one of three ways:

1. Employ a virtual private network (VPN) that encrypts all traffic sent between machines on the LAN.

2. Use our JMS providers' built-in message encryption capabilities, if any.

3. Encrypt/decrypt the contents of trade request messages within our application code.

Option 1 is a simple enough solution but has a major drawback: Encrypting/decrypting a message is an expensive operation and we intend to flood our LAN with a large number of stock quote messages. Not only would encrypting them all result in a big performance hit, it's not even necessary because it's doubtful we'd be required to encrypt public information such as stock quotes.

Many JMS providers have the capability of using SSL to secure messaging traffic. If the one we use does, then the second option is a good solution because we'll be able to encrypt just the traffic we care to – the trade message traffic – and let the quote traffic continue to be sent in the clear. Be careful, however, because use of SSL implies a connection-oriented (socket-based) message-delivery mechanism and this hub-and-spoke topology may not be sufficient to deliver messages in a high enough volume. A provider based on a broadcast technology such as UDP or IP Multicast will probably give us a high enough message throughput to meet our requirements, but rules out the use of SSL because SSL is a connection-oriented protocol.

Lastly, we could, with some difficulty, encrypt the trade messages in application code. Whether this makes sense – or even whether it matters that we encrypt the trade messages at all – is a close call. `TradeNotification` messages in the MTS system are intended to be broadcast to all users indiscriminately – not just to traders – so it may not be worthwhile to bother encrypting `TradeRequest` or `TradeReply` messages (because notifications contain the same information as requests). On the other hand, if it's important enough to ensure the confidentiality of the firm's proprietary trading activity to the greatest degree possible, it may be worth the extra effort after all.

Summary

We've seen in this chapter that the process of developing a solid architecture is an exercise in choosing between a variety of alternatives. All third-party software presents a designer with choices regarding how and how best to use it; JMS software probably offers more design choices than most. In addition to the built-in options – pub/sub versus point-to-point messaging, persistent versus non-persistent, and so on – there can be many proprietary features that you'll need to consider as well. To the extent a proprietary feature deals with an area outside the domain of the JMS API (e.g., performance tuning) you simply need to consider the merits of using the feature or not. Vendor's proprietary APIs, on the other hand, are probably best avoided entirely to ensure the portability of your application.

In this chapter we saw how to analyze an infrastructure, derive requirements, and create a new messaging architecture from scratch. You must also anticipate from the beginning that an architecture will evolve over time. Certainly, in the initial design stage it will change rapidly as it gets reviewed and refined. Changing requirements during development can also cause an architecture to change as well, though hopefully you won't have too many of those.

Once you have a stable initial architecture, the most important step to take is to prototype the system's key elements. This is the only way to be sure you haven't overlooked something in your design. But it is also critical when incorporating a software suite like you'd get from a JMS provider because you'll want to verify the provider's claims regarding performance and functionality before fully committing to the product.

Ultimately, though, there is no one right answer for most architectural decisions. That's why it is so important to verify and re-verify your assumptions as often as is practical.

Chapter 14

An Integrated Workflow System

IN THIS CHAPTER

- ◆ Using JMS to unify legacy systems
- ◆ Requirements for a simulated workflow system
- ◆ Advantages of durable pub/sub messaging
- ◆ Bridging multiple JMS providers

CORPORATIONS HAVE MUCH MORE OF A TENDENCY to grow organically than by design. Naturally, the same is true of the computer systems that keep a company running. Even when they're originally built according to carefully thought-out requirements and employ a bulletproof design – which is rare – systems are constantly updated and tweaked to conform to ever-changing business needs and opportunities.

The tipping point when management decides it's finally time to replace an aging infrastructure usually arrives when it becomes cost-efficient to rewrite the existing system or systems from scratch. But in the interim period, generally measured in years, various techniques are typically used to increase the useful life of systems that are already in place.

One strategy for supporting new business needs is to link together various enterprise systems that are already operational so that they can share information and work as a team to satisfy required business processes. Given the large number of advertisements by companies offering to help "integrate" your business, you could say this must be a pretty common desire.

One possible way to integrate systems is to give several systems access to the same primary data sources – in essence, giving them access to the same database. This is typically a very troublesome undertaking, however, because it's pretty much guaranteed each system will have at least a slightly different view of any shared data.

For example, say that System A maintains a "customer" table with a 30-character `last_name` column. System B has the same table but calls the column `lname` and expects it to be no more than 25 characters long. You could standardize on System A's schema but would still need to hunt down and change every reference to `lname` and any dependency on the 25-character limit in System B. For this simple example alone, the effort to update System B would be time-consuming and require much regression testing. Magnify this problem by hundreds of similar little issues and you suddenly have a big conversion project on your hands.

Additionally, many other issues can plague any effort to merge two or more databases together, such as:

- **Table dependencies.** e.g. One database might put all customer information into one table row. Another might break it up into several tables.

- **Data types.** e.g. One database might store a quantity as a string, another as an integer.

- **Concurrent access.** e.g. When is it safe for an application to manipulate some data and how can we ensure it's not stepping on some other application's toes?

- **Transactional control.** How do you ensure an operation that begins in one application and ends in another takes place within a single transaction to maintain database integrity?

For these reasons and others, giving two legacy applications access to the same database is not usually the easiest way to leverage the functionality of both systems. Considering the amount of code rewriting and re-testing that must be undertaken, you're generally better off developing a brand new system that encompasses the functionality of all the legacy systems in question.

When an organization is not ready to undertake a major rewrite, a good interim solution utilizing interapplication messaging, such as that provided by JMS, can be employed to tie existing applications together. The advantage of this approach is that each application can continue to operate largely how it currently does without your having to do major surgery to get them to share data and functionality.

Rather than having System A create a record in a database so it's available for System B's use, it is often better, for example, to let System A keep its own version of a customer record and let System B keep its own version. Systems A and B can share customer information by agreeing on a common JMS message format that is used to pass information back and forth between them.

In addition, by using the JMS XA distributed transaction capabilities (discussed in Chapter 8), we can execute business logic within the context of a database update operation in conjunction with associated JMS operations. In this way, you can use JMS to ensure data integrity between applications. Proper use of JMS transactions and persistent messaging will ensure that when a customer record is stored in its local database by System A, for instance, that it will also be stored in System B's database as well (eventually, in any case).

This chapter illustrates the way JMS can be used to link existing systems together with JMS by using the example of a cellular service provider that wants to include several internal systems in one business process: the enabling of new cell-phone service for a customer.

System Requirements

As we did in the previous chapter, I'll first describe the systems and business processes we'll be working with and then break down the requirements for the areas that are addressed in this excercise along the lines of a few categories. Then we'll move on to architecting a solution.

System background

In what is currently a very labor-intensive process, a cell phone company, CellExpress, must complete the following four internal processes before a new customer's cell phone service is turned on:

1. The order must be taken

2. The customer's background must be checked by the credit department

3. The equipment department must ship out any hardware the customer requires (cell phone, accessories, and so on) .

4. The customer's service must be enabled with the physical phone network.

These processes must occur in sequence.

As things stand today, each step of the process is supported by its own legacy computer system. All systems are networked together for e-mail and whatnot, but the systems are not connected in any way that supports the phone service enablement business process. Hard-copy reports are delivered by interoffice messenger several times a day from each department to the next one in line. CellExpress would like to greatly speed up the overall customer-enablement process but doesn't have the time or staff to undertake a significant development project that would produce a single new system that had the functionality of all the old systems.

Figure 14-1 shows the general relationship of the systems involved in the service enablement process. The numbers correspond to the numbered list of business process steps from earlier in this section.

Except for the mainframe-based system that talks to the cell phone network, all the systems in question are fortunately pretty new and based on J2EE technology. CellExpress architects (eager to play with the latest technology) realize it would be relatively quick and easy to link the systems together using JMS and message-driven beans.

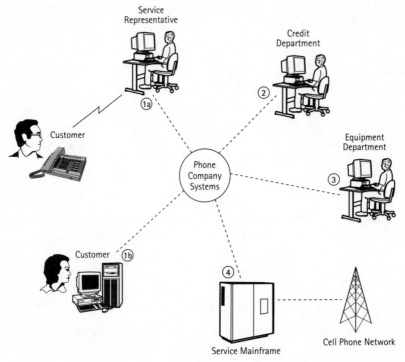

Figure 14-1: The CellExpress internal phone service enablement procedure

We'll begin analyzing the system as we did in the previous chapter, with the following categories:

◆ Physical infrastructure

◆ External and existing systems

◆ User requirements and required features

◆ Security requirements

◆ Performance requirements

Physical infrastructure

All the departmental systems in question are islands in that they run on their own server machines and associated client machines. The applications are designed well, but each one uses a somewhat different combination of products from various vendors, such as databases, application servers, physical hardware, and operating systems. Fortunately, all systems can readily talk to each over the same internal LAN. This LAN is also adequately protected from the Internet by the corporate firewall.

External and existing systems

We previously identified the four primary existing systems at CellExpress as follows:

1. The customer service representative system

2. The credit department system

3. The equipment department system

4. The network control system

Each of the four primary systems is described in the following sections.

THE CUSTOMER SERVICE REPRESENTATIVE SYSTEM

The job of the customer service representative is, among other things, to take orders for new cell phone service. The customer service reps work at the call center and probably use a Java telephony (JTAPI) enabled CRM (customer relationship management) system to handle incoming service calls from their desktop PCs. At the center of the system is a J2EE application server that their desktop applications access over the local LAN.

In addition, customers can order phone service for themselves over the Internet using a browser-based interface. The front-end servlets that manage this interaction also talk to the same application server as the customer service rep's desktop programs.

THE CREDIT DEPARTMENT SYSTEM

The credit department has a simple application architecture consisting of a single application server running on a central workgroup hardware server. The desktop systems used by the credit department consist of a variety of hardware architectures running Swing-based Java applications. These applications talk directly to the application server over the LAN.

After an order is taken, personnel in this department run a credit check on the customer. If the customer passes the credit check, the order is passed on to the equipment department. If the customer fails the credit check, then an e-mail message is sent to the customer denying the service request.

THE EQUIPMENT DEPARTMENT SYSTEM

The equipment department is set up exactly the same way as the credit department. They have a central application server that the desktop applications access in a client/server manner. The main difference is that the equipment department's application server vendor is not the same as the credit department's.

The equipment department's responsibility is to fulfill the hardware order that accompanied the original service request. They deliver the new phone and any accessories to the customer's address, and also pass along the phone's new phone number to the network control system so the service can be enabled.

THE NETWORK CONTROL SYSTEM

The network control system is an older mainframe-based system that communicates directly with the cell phone network so that it can enable new phone numbers. It is accessible via TCP/IP connectivity over the corporate LAN and is capable of running the JMS client software of our choice.

With all these systems, we will make the assumption that we have a free hand to implement whatever application changes we need to incorporate JMS messaging into them. Figure 14-2 expands on Figure 14-1 to show how all these systems are related architecturally.

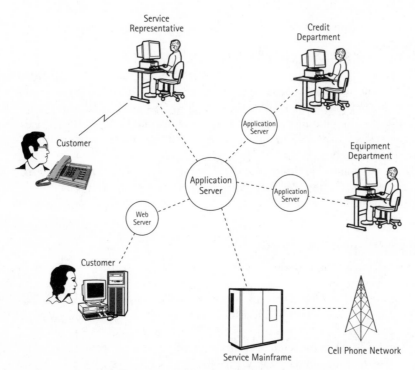

Figure 14-2: Relationships of the CellExpress systems and processes

User requirements and required features

We don't really have new business requirements for this system *per se* because we're happy with the business functionality as it currently exists in the various systems. Our main goal and requirement is to streamline the service creation process by electronically passing the required data between the various in-house systems as a replacement for the current manual process. This will reduce the time needed to turn on new phone service as well as eliminate any data entry errors that previously occurred as a result of all of the manual re-entering of information that took place when tasks were passed from system to system.

Security requirements

Because the data we're passing between the systems is not expected to be particularly sensitive and because we're only shuttling it back and forth on the internal corporate network, we've decided not to bother encrypting it. On the other hand, to ensure that no one inside the company attempts to submit an unauthorized message – or tries to submit a message to a system that has not visited each required system before being delivered to the next in line – we need to implement some sort of authorization scheme.

Performance requirements

As this is a completely internal system that requires human input to generate traffic, we do not need to be overly concerned about designing with specific performance criteria in mind. During later testing phases, however, it will be a good idea to quantify what the maximum processing capacity of each individual system is – both in terms of computational capacity and human processing capacity – because it is the service enablement rate of the slowest link in the chain that determines the maximum rate at which the integrated system will be able to handle requests for new service.

System Architecture

As in the previous chapter, we'll take a message-centric approach to the architectural analysis for the new system. The main difference in this case is that the functionality of the various endpoint programs participating in the overall application is expected to change very little. In many ways, the business logic that determines when a message is delivered, where it is delivered to, and what it contains is really the entire application we're creating.

Determining message types

To keep things simple and straightforward, we'll define just a single message type. More specifically, we'll define an expandable message type that can be used in a variety of situations. By using a non-fixed format message, we'll be able to add elements to the message at each stop as it passes through each point in the workflow business process. The message will contain all the information needed to set up a customer's new phone service and we'll pass the same message (same message format and content, not necessarily the same message object) between the various systems.

In the case where a system needs to add information to the message so it can be passed on to another system down the line, we will assume that the particular field or fields that hold such information will be null or nonexistent until the system that first uses the fields populates them. The `javax.jms.MapMessage` class will easily do the trick because it does not require a fixed-format message structure and we can easily add fields to the message as we pass it from system to system.

Alternatively, a `javax.jms.TextMessage` containing an XML message would work as well. Since we don't expect performance to be a big factor, XML might be a good choice, especially if we think that at some point we might want to include systems in the workflow that, for whatever reason, will not be able to participate in the JMS messaging bus and, hence, would not be able to send and receive `MapMessages`.

Let's call this new message the `CellularService` message. Its data elements will be as listed in Table 14-1.

TABLE 14-1 THE CELLULARSERVICE MESSAGE'S DATA ELEMENTS

Field Name	Java Type	Description
First Name	String	The customer's first name
Last Name	String	The customer's last name
Address 1	String	Billing address line #1
Address 2	String	Billing address line #2
City	String	Billing address city
State	String	Billing address state
Zip Code	String	Billing address Zip code
E-mail	String	Customer's e-mail address
Account Number	String	The customer's new account number (assigned by the customer service system)
Billing Plan	String	Some plan identifier (assigned by the customer service system)
Credit OK	boolean	Credit approved flag (assigned by the credit system)
Phone Number	String	The customer's new phone number (assigned by the equipment system)
Customer Service Signature	byte[]	Message authentication code (assigned by the customer service system)
Credit Dept Signature	byte[]	Message authentication code (assigned by the credit system)
Equipment Dept Signature	byte[]	Message authentication code (assigned by the equipment system)

Listing 14-1 shows a code fragment illustrating how to create a `MapMessage` representing the `CellularService` message.

Listing 14-1: Creating a CellularService MapMessage

```
MapMessage cellularService = jmsSession.createMapMessage();

cellularService.setString("First Name", "Matthew");
cellularService.setString("Last Name", "Damon");
cellularService.setString("Address 1", "123 23rd St.");
cellularService.setString("Address 2", "Apt 1000");
cellularService.setString("City", "New York");
cellularService.setString("State", "NY");
cellularService.setString("Zip Code", "10011");
cellularService.setString("E-mail", "mdamon@maildomain.com");
cellularService.setString("Account Number", "123-456-789");
cellularService.setString("Billing Plan", "Extended");
cellularService.setBoolean("Credit OK", true);
cellularService.setString("Phone Number", "212-555-1212");

// These fields can be left out until needed or placeholders can
// can be used as is done here.
cellularService.setBytes("Customer Service Signature", new byte[0]);
cellularService.setBytes("Credit Dept Signature", new byte[0]);
cellularService.setBytes("Equipment Dept Signature", new byte[0]);
```

Creating an initial architecture

As we pointed out in the last section, almost the entire system we're developing is the manifestation of the service enablement process. Mostly we're just building new glue to tie together the old applications. The first order of architectural business will be to decide precisely how the "glue" should be designed. Then we'll figure out what kind of JMS support we'll need. And finally, we can decide how to architect the security requirements of the system.

USING A WORKFLOW ENGINE

It seems clear from the business requirements that a workflow engine of some sort can help us achieve our goals. We can write our own or use a third-party product. In either case, we expect the workflow engine to be responsible for sending the `CellularService` message we described previously to each appropriate subsystem at the appropriate time – the appropriate time being after the message is success-fully processed by the previous system in the chain.

The workflow engine will not itself be directly responsible for any messaging, however. Generally, such systems operate by invoking specific enterprise bean methods on an application server with some specific parameters; the individual beans that get called are responsible for performing any required underlying messaging.

The particular beans that get called are determined by consulting a rule base that a developer or operator has created. The way this is done is proprietary to the workflow engine and often can be created using a graphical interface of some sort.

In our system, we'll say the workflow engine will operate on enterprise beans in the customer service system's application server. We will need four stateless session beans to get the job done, as follows:

1. The bean that starts and controls the workflow process (i.e. the workflow engine) – called by the customer service desktop client initially

2. A bean to send the message to the credit department system – called by the workflow engine

3. A bean to forward the message to the equipment department's system – called by the workflow engine

4. A bean to send the message to the network control system

Because sending a message to the credit and equipment beans does not alone imply that the operation has been completed – remember, we need human interaction at each of these systems before proceeding – we'll need two additional beans:

1. A message-driven bean that handles the returned message from the credit system

2. A message-driven bean that handles the returned message from the equipment system

For the first bean, the workflow engine's rule base will need to be configured so that it looks at the "Credit OK" field before sending the message to the equipment system. If the field is false, then the process should be aborted and an e-mail sent to the user as the system requirements state. Figure 14-3 shows the workflow engine operation.

After either message-driven bean receives the message back from a departmental system, it will have to then pass the message to the workflow engine bean, which will determine the next course of action. Because the workflow bean is stateless, some means of identifying the current workflow instance will need to be implemented. This can be done easily by assigning a unique identifier to the message that will identify the flow instance to the workflow engine so it can figure out where in the overall business process the message is when it is received. We can simply add a "WorkflowID" field to the `CellularService` message to accomplish this goal. Note that the **JMSMessageID** message property would not adequately serve as a workflow identifier because the provider assigned message ID will change every time we transmit the message between systems.

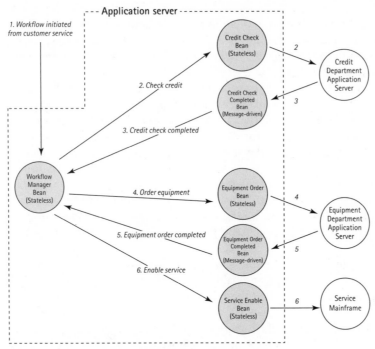

Figure 14-3: Messaging controlled by a workflow engine

SELECTING MESSAGING TYPES

Now that we have a good idea of the messaging flow, we need to figure out what type of JMS messaging we want to use. Certainly, we don't want to lose any messages anywhere along the way because losing a message at any point in the process means that someone's service request will not be fulfilled. This would be bad for business and bad for customer relations.

Fortunately, our message volumes will not be that high, so we're in a good position to use JMS's transacted sessions for all messaging without being overly concerned about the resulting performance hit. Likewise, any database operations a system does as a result of sending or receiving a message must be included in a distributed XA transaction, so we'll need to be sure our JMS provider(s) support them.

Because we cannot lose messages, the use of nonpersistent messaging is ruled out as well. Even if we could use nonpersistent messaging, we probably wouldn't want to in an environment such as this. The main reason is that we're integrating a variety of departmental-level systems. Typically, such systems are not engineered for 24/7 operation, meaning that they could be down or unavailable for fairly long stretches of time. This being the case, we need persistent messaging to ensure that all delivered messages ultimately make it to their destination regardless of whether the target system is currently running or not.

All messages are only being routed between two systems at a time, so this would indicate that point-to-point messaging is the preferred option, which would work just fine. However, to anticipate future requirements, we're probably better off using durable pub/sub messaging instead, at least for the messages that are delivered to the departmental systems.

Why use pub/sub? Suppose somewhere down the road it is decided that the billing department's system needs to receive a copy of every message sent to the network control system. In this situation, durable pub/sub messaging enables us to accomplish this goal much more easily than point-to-point messaging. With a single point-to-point queue between the workflow engine and the network control system, we'd need to write a new bean to send messages to the billing department and also add a step to the workflow rule base to invoke this new bean whenever a message is sent to the network control system. By using durable pub/sub messaging, all we need to do is be sure the billing system subscribes to the same message destination as the network control system; no other changes need to be made to any other system.

Certainly, we could also use durable subscription messaging for the messages returned to the workflow engine. It's probably okay just to stick with regular point-to-point messaging, though, for the messaging from the departmental systems to the workflow engine and from the workflow engine to the service mainframe. The reason for this is that it's highly likely there will only ever be one application that needs to receive these messages. On the other hand, we keep the most flexibility by using durable subscription messaging for everything. The choice is up to you.

Keep in mind, though, that durable pub/sub is not a good option (for performance reasons) when many clients receive the same message. But when just a handful of recipients are involved, the durable subscriber amalgam of pub/sub messaging and persistent queue messaging can be quite useful indeed.

Figure 14-4 shows the basic architecture with messaging types.

TIP

Remember from Chapter 5 that messages sent over durable topic subscription queues are subject to slightly different rules than those sent via regular point-to-point queues. A message in a point-to-point queue will stay in the queue until a client application removes it, whenever that may be. A message in a durable subscription queue will wait for a client to read it only if the client has previously registered as a consumer through a call to `TopicSession.createDurableSubscriber()`.

For the CellExpress application, once a departmental system has registered as a durable subscriber, messages will be held for it during any period the departmental system is not running. Prior to this first registration, however, any messages sent to the departmental system will be silently discarded.

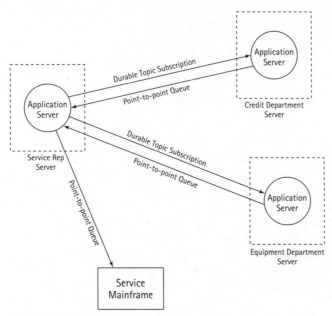

Figure 14-4: The architecture with messaging types

BRIDGING JMS PROVIDERS

We noted earlier in our description of the current implementation of the existing systems that the customer service system and the credit system, though both J2EE-based, are running on different vendor's software products. This might present a problem when it comes to JMS messaging because, currently, there's no JMS requirement that application servers be able to work with all vendors' JMS products. Though the industry is definitely moving in the direction of providing pluggable JMS support (that is, allowing any vendor's JMS product to be used with any vendor's application server product), at present some do and some don't.

If we can find a JMS product that operates with all the various application servers employed by the customer service, credit, and equipment systems, then we're home free. If not, we'll need to be sure that our application server vendor — though it may not let us replace the default JMS provider that comes with it — at least lets us use a secondary JMS provider for sending messages. We'll be able to accomplish our architectural goals that way.

Barring either of these solutions, the only way to route a message from one application server to another is to have a non-application server–based daemon process running between the two application servers. The sole job of this daemon process is to route messages received on one provider to the other provider. Because this process is not running in an application server, it will have no restrictions on how many JMS products it can access at the same time. Figure 14-5 shows how to bridge providers in this manner:

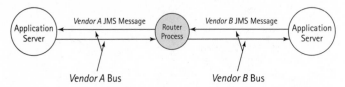

Figure 14-5: Routing JMS messages from one provider to another

Also, remember from Chapter 3 that JMS does not require provider interoperability. This means that you cannot necessarily take a `MapMessage` object received from one provider, for instance, and simply turn around and send it using another provider. Depending on how your providers are implemented, it's possible you may be able to send a message object received via one provider over another provider without modification. If not, a new `MapMessage` object would have to be created using the second provider and the fields must be copied one by one from the first `MapMessage` to the second before sending the second one. Note that to avoid hard-coding field names, this task requires the router process to iterate over all the fields in the message using `javax.jms.MapMessage.getMapNames`.

Listing 14-2 shows a simple program that is a client for two distinct JMS providers. It receives messages from an iPlanet Message Queue queue and routes them to a WebLogic queue. With these two particular providers it is possible to use the same message object received from the former to send directly to the latter (and *vice versa*), so there's no need to create and populate a new `MapMessage` object before forwarding it to the second provider.

Listing 14-2: JMS message forwarding between two different provider's queues

```
import javax.jms.*;
import javax.naming.*;
import java.util.*;

/* This program routes Messages sent over a queue from iMQ to
WebLogic.
 */

public class Router
{
    public static void main(String[] args) throws Exception
    {
        // Setup iMQ ****************************

        Hashtable envIMQ = new Hashtable();

        envIMQ.put(Context.INITIAL_CONTEXT_FACTORY,
            "com.sun.jndi.fscontext.RefFSContextFactory");
        envIMQ.put(Context.PROVIDER_URL,
```

```
        "file:///c:/Program Files/iPlanetMessageQueue2.0/var/
stores/MyBroker/filestore");

    Context contextIMQ = new InitialContext(envIMQ);

    QueueConnectionFactory qcfIMQ =
        (QueueConnectionFactory)
        contextIMQ.lookup("MyQueueConnectionFactory");

    QueueConnection qcIMQ = qcfIMQ.createQueueConnection();

    QueueSession qsIMQ = qcIMQ.createQueueSession(false,
        QueueSession.AUTO_ACKNOWLEDGE);

    Queue queueIMQ = (javax.jms.Queue)
contextIMQ.lookup("TestQueue");

    QueueReceiver qrecIMQ = qsIMQ.createReceiver(queueIMQ);

    // Setup WebLogic *****************************

    Hashtable envWL = new Hashtable();

    envWL.put(Context.INITIAL_CONTEXT_FACTORY,
                "weblogic.jndi.WLInitialContextFactory");
    envWL.put(Context.PROVIDER_URL, "t3://localhost:7001");

    Context contextWL = new InitialContext(envWL);

    QueueConnectionFactory qcfWL =
        (QueueConnectionFactory) contextWL.lookup("QUEUEFACTORY");

    QueueConnection qcWL = qcfWL.createQueueConnection();

    QueueSession qsWL = qcWL.createQueueSession(false,
        QueueSession.AUTO_ACKNOWLEDGE);

    Queue queueWL = (javax.jms.Queue)
contextWL.lookup("QUEUENAME");

    QueueSender qsendWL = qsWL.createSender(queueWL);


    // Do the routing ***********************************
```

Continued

Listing 14-2 *(Continued)*

```
        qcIMQ.start();

        while (true)
        {
            // Read from iMQ and send to WebLogic

            System.out.println("Waiting for message ...");
            Message msg = qrecIMQ.receive();

            System.out.println("Routing message: " + msg);
            qsendWL.send(msg);
        }
    }
}
```

SIGNING THE MESSAGES

Finally, to ensure that each message not only comes from where it says it comes from but also that it has not skipped any steps along the way, we will have each system digitally sign each message by generating a message authentication code using the utility program from Chapter 9. For this to work, each message end point must be assigned a unique digital key. This key must remain known only to the application it is assigned to and to the central workflow application, which must hold copies of all the keys for all the other systems.

When a message is sent, the sending system generates a message authentication code (MAC) and places it in the message with the appropriate field name (for example, "Credit Dept Signature"). The receiving system (which is always the workflow engine) must then use what it believes to be the sending system's key and check that the message is valid before continuing with any business operations.

Figure 14-6 shows the key assignment strategy.

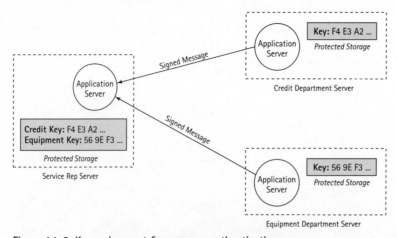

Figure 14-6: Key assignment for message authentication

Digital signatures will not only ensure that the message actually comes from the system it says it does but that the message contents have not been changed en route. This is particularly valuable in an architecture such as ours where a message might reside in permanent storage for a relatively long time before being read. An attacker that gained access to the disk could, after all, change the contents of the message.

Listing 14-3 shows how each departmental system would use the `MACUtil` utility from Chapter 9 to sign the `CellularService` message before they returned it to the workflow engine.

Listing 14-3: Code fragment showing how to use MACUtil to sign CellularService messages

```
// This operation is performed by the customer service system
SecretKey custServiceKey = (get customer service's key from somewhere);
MACUtil.tagMessage(cellularService, custServiceKey, "Customer
Service Signature");

// This operation is performed by the credit department system
SecretKey creditDeptKey = (get credit dept.'s key from somewhere);
MACUtil.tagMessage(cellularService, creditDeptKey, "Credit Dept
Signature");

// This operation performed by the equipment department system
SecretKey equipDeptKey = (get equipment dept.'s key from somewhere);
MACUtil.tagMessage(cellularService, equipDeptKey, "Equipment Dept
Signature");
```

Summary

Linking legacy applications together with messaging is a great way to get extended mileage out of old systems. Of course, no one would ever claim this is an ideal solution to the problem of getting different applications with different databases to work together. Duplicate and dispersed data is not, for instance, very conducive to efficient system-wide rollup and reporting. On the other hand, integrating them with JMS is an expedient and simple solution. And when time is money, expediency and simplicity are often the overriding factors.

Chapter 15

A High-Volume Extranet System

IN THIS CHAPTER

- ◆ Analyzing push-and-pull delivery models
- ◆ Branch office system requirements
- ◆ Sample BOSS system architecture
- ◆ Alternatives to JMS over the Internet

ARCHITECTS ALL HAVE THE SAME PROBLEM with the Internet: getting large amounts of data out to a broad user community in a quick and efficient manner. The Internet was not designed for broadcast messaging. IP Multicast and the Multicast Backbone are relatively new technologies that can be used to perform broadcast messaging over the Internet. And while they are good initial steps, they are still not in widespread use, partly because they require large amounts of bandwidth and partly because delivery of messages is not guaranteed.

The "push" technology craze of a few years back is a good object lesson of the difficulties one encounters when trying to build large-scale, Internet-based data distribution systems. Push systems were touted as being capable of actively delivering real-time messages such as stock quotes, weather, and news to a large community of clients, but under the covers the majority of these systems were built using what you might call "intelligent pull" infrastructures.

A true push infrastructure involves clients passively waiting for data to be delivered to them — but the clients don't necessarily know when or how frequently the data will arrive. A data distribution model such as this could easily be implemented on top of a true broadcast technology. We've seen examples of this already in this book where pub/sub providers use UDP messaging to get exactly this kind of behavior. It's an efficient and low-cost data-delivery model for LAN-based environments but unfortunately doesn't work well over the Internet because there are too many potential clients and data must typically pass through too many routers to get from point A to point B.

Another way to implement true push technology over the Internet is by using connected sockets. In such a model, each client maintains an open socket connection between itself and the server, as shown in Figure 15-1. This is typically how true push infrastructures are built when implemented over the Internet as well as, oftentimes, over a LAN.

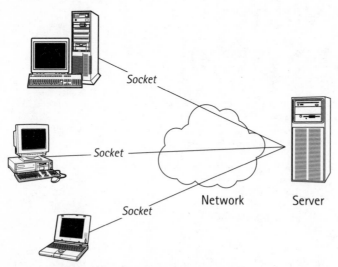

Figure 15-1: A connection-oriented push model

From an efficiency point of view, a connection-oriented model works well because client applications can receive a steady stream of information without having to initiate a new connection to the server in order to receive each new batch of data. Unfortunately, because clients maintain open connections for long periods of time, this approach presents severe scalability problems. What works well for a handful of clients does not work well for thousands of clients. In this case, it's not the Internet that is to blame but the inability of server-based software to efficiently deal with so many simultaneous connections.

Figure 15-2 illustrates the reasons for this limitation. A server-based application that sends a message to all connected clients must do so serially – a message must be written sequentially to each open socket via a call to the socket's write() method. For many thousands of clients this means that many thousands of write() calls would have to be made per message. Clearly this does not scale very well.

Complicating the matter further are clients that are nonresponsive or slow to respond. A single slow or malfunctioning client might, for instance, cause the write() call to block or take a long time to complete, which would hold up message delivery to all clients.

You could try to avoid this problem by dedicating a single writer thread to each client. However, not only would this require many more threads than is generally practical to use in an application, but it still leaves you with the job of maintaining individual outbound message queues for each client and the unpleasant task of writing a lot of housekeeping code to keep track of and maintain state for all active clients.

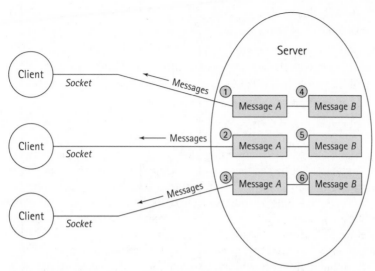

Figure 15-2: Sequence of writes to connection-oriented sockets for messages A and B

Because of the problems associated with connected socket solutions, Internet-based applications that need to deliver information to large numbers of clients almost always use a disconnected pull approach. In this on-demand delivery model, clients request data from the server by opening up a socket to the server, retrieving the required data (based on some small amount of request information sent to the server), and closing the socket. This approach has the advantage of greater scalability because only a small percentage of the current client population is actually connected to the server at any given time. Servers also do not need to be concerned with malfunctioning clients. A client that is suffering from environmental or network problems won't even bother the server.

The downside to on-demand message retrieval is, among others, a higher message latency and the inability of the server to force the client to take some immediate action as a result of receiving a message.

The disconnected pull model is exactly that of the HTTP-based Web we all know so well, and it is the reason a Web server running on a smallish machine can successfully service (albeit sometimes slowly) a large number of clients (i.e., Web browsers).

Many enterprises require a solution that falls somewhere between pure push and pure pull. They want to be able to push information to a large number of clients but they need the scalability achieved by employing a pull infrastructure.

Unfortunately, there are no easy answers. If there were, there'd be a standard for Internet-based message broadcasting instead of the hodge-podge of third-party and proprietary solutions in use today. This chapter talks about some of the possible ways to deliver messages to a large number of client applications communicating with a central corporate server over an extranet.

Extranet is one of those computer lingo terms without a specific definition. Here, we use it to refer to an environment where the client base is well known (for example, the employees of a firm's partner companies but not the public at large) and is linked to a main server either over the public Internet or over a private WAN (wide-area network).

A lot of companies want more functionality than they can get using basic Web technologies and a standard browser. They want their extranet users to have the custom, rich functionality you get from, say, a standalone Swing application or applet, but want those applications to communicate with their server using reliable, scalable Web technologies. This chapter describes a sample architecture that you can use to provide messaging services in such a situation.

As an illustration, let's say we are building a system called the Branch Office Status System (BOSS) that employees will use in a bank's branch offices to monitor financial transactions flowing through the bank's central computers.

System Requirements

Continuing the pattern of the previous two chapters, we'll first analyze the BOSS system requirements along the lines of the following five categories:

◆ Physical infrastructure

◆ External and existing systems

◆ User requirements and required features

◆ Security requirements

◆ Performance requirements

Physical infrastructure

For our computing platform let's assume we've been budgeted to purchase one or more large Unix-based servers. These machines will run our application, Web server, database, and JMS software. Front-ending this computing environment will be a secured demilitarized zone (DMZ) employing appropriately configured firewalls that allow only HTTP(S) and/or SSL (Secure Sockets Layer) traffic through from the Internet to our main server.

The client applications running in the branch offices will be provided by us and will run on a variety of desktop computing platforms. They will all have secure socket access to the public Internet, which they will use to connect to our application's server. Client desktop machines will reside in a large number of branch offices nationwide. The total number of employees accessing the system will be in the thousands.

External and existing systems

For the BOSS system let's presume we're in the enviable position of being able to write the entire system from scratch. We won't need to talk to any external or existing systems. Except for any third-party packages we employ, both the server application and client application will be written by our development team.

User requirements and required features

Many classes of users might exist in a bank branch office. For our purposes, we'll focus on three functions: loan processing, targeted sales, and branch monitoring. A *sales representative* is responsible for the first two functions and the *branch manager* the last. Branch employees will need to perform many other business functions via their desktop applications, but we're going to assume that the communication mechanism will be a synchronous call from the application to the server using some standard Web-based technology, such as SOAP (Simple Object Access Protocol). JMS is not appropriate to use in this case.

On the other hand, the three types of activity we'll look at here will require applications to receive messages asynchronously, so JMS is relevant.

SALES REPRESENTATIVE

Sales representatives are responsible for generating new business. To do this they analyze customer accounts so they can recommend new products, services, or investments to customers. For our purposes we'll just focus on one feature the sales representatives would like the BOSS system to provide them: to be alerted whenever a customer who belongs to their home branch makes a deposit over a certain amount into an account. Each sales representative may choose a different amount that he or she wants to be alerted for.

In addition, sales representatives take loan applications from customers in the branch office and submit each application to the central server. The loan is not approved immediately, however. Even if a loan can be approved automatically, it generally takes too much server-side processing time to make it feasible to use a single synchronous call to submit the loan and return the approval status to the user. Sometimes, as well, loans must be manually reviewed and approved or rejected by an employee from the central office.

Sales representatives can check the current status of any outstanding loan applications by periodically running a report. But, rather than waste their time, we'd like to be able to proactively alert sales representatives when an application they previously submitted has been approved or rejected. For this task we'll need to send a message to their application asynchronously, which will cause an alert to pop up on their screen.

BRANCH MANAGER

Branch managers need to be able to see all the activity related to their particular branch office. The application they use will be entirely passive; it will display a running total of all accounts opened at that branch as well as other similar activities.

The amounts shown on the screen are updated without interaction by the user and increase over time for the run-time life of the application or until reset to zero by the branch manager.

Security requirements

Because we are sending sensitive financial information across the public Internet, we must encrypt all traffic. Users will need to be properly authenticated as well, of course, to prevent the wrong people from accessing the system.

Inside the branch office, we won't try to limit access to any of the messages to particular users because we won't be sending any so sensitive that they should be hidden from any bank employee. Business functions, remember, will not take place over a JMS pipe; they will be transmitted over another channel and we'll use other means of permissioning to limit access to business functions to specific users.

While we don't need to secure any JMS traffic from internal spying, we do want to be sure that loan-status messages are delivered only to the sales representative who initiated the loan application.

Performance requirements

We do not anticipate message traffic to any particular desktop application to be extremely high. The main challenge, though, will be to ensure that we do not flood each client application with large numbers of messages that it is not interested in because the overall number of messages generated by the system will be quite large. If we assume we have a large number of branch offices and that all the activity going on at the office and associated ATMs results in JMS messages that someone, somewhere is interested in – say, on the order of one million messages per day – then clearly it is not practical to send all messages to all desktop machines so they can be filtered by the client.

System Architecture

As we did in the last chapter, we'll begin our architectural analysis from the inside out by specifying the formats of our essential messages and then designing a mechanism for their transmission.

Determining message types

We can easily identify the few simple messages we'll need:

- `LoanStatus`
- `AccountOpen`
- `AccountDeposit`

Obviously, a system such as BOSS would have many, many more message types, but for our purposes we can limit our discussion to these three; they will serve to highlight the main use of JMS in the system.

THE LOANSTATUS MESSAGE

The `LoanStatus` message is issued by some server-based component when the disposition of a loan application has been determined, either through automated or manual means. This message will not be generated unless a loan application has been submitted previously, but remember that the application is delivered to the server via a non-JMS mechanism so there's no "upstream" message we need to specify. Table 15-1 lists the data elements of a `LoanStatus` message:

TABLE 15-1 LOANSTATUS DATA ELEMENTS

Field Name	Java Type	Description
Officer ID	String	The unique ID of the loan officer
Branch ID	String	The loan officer's branch office
Account Number	String	The applicant's account number
Loan Number	String	A unique loan identifier
Status	String	"APPROVED" or "REJECTED"

THE ACCOUNTOPEN MESSAGE

`AccountOpen` messages are broadcast to all interested parties at the branch where the account was opened. Table 15-2 lists the few fields in this message:

TABLE 15-2 ACCOUNTOPEN DATA ELEMENTS

Field Name	Java Type	Description
Branch ID	String	The home branch office of the account
Account Number	String	The new account number
Customer	String	The customer's full name
Initial Amount	double	The initial amount deposited in the account

THE ACCOUNTDEPOSIT MESSAGE

AccountDeposit messages are broadcast to all interested parties at the branch that owns the account. AccountDeposit messages will be generated by the server whenever a deposit is recorded in the server's database. The mechanism for reporting and recording these deposits is beyond the scope of our analysis. Table 15-3 lists the fields in an AccountDeposit message.

TABLE 15-3 ACCOUNTDEPOSIT DATA ELEMENTS

Field Name	Java Type	Description
Branch ID	String	The home branch office of the account
Account Number	String	The account number
Customer	String	The customer's full name
Deposit Amount	double	The amount deposited in the account

Creating an initial architecture

Designing a messaging architecture for a system such as BOSS presents many problems. The Internet is a relatively slow medium, and subject to frequent temporary interruptions and slowdowns. This makes it difficult if not impossible to reliably send messages at a high rate from a server to even one client. The situation is further complicated when all messages must be delivered over an encrypted channel such as HTTPS, which imposes an additional performance penalty on communications. To help mitigate the performance impact, we will probably need to use a hardware-based encryption solution on the server.

In addition, it's not likely that desktop machines in a bank's branch office will have enough horsepower to cope with a high message rate even if the Internet was conducive to delivering them all there.

Before creating a software architecture, let's first review the physical infrastructure and technical decisions we've made so far (see Figure 15-3).

We have elected to use synchronous SOAP remote procedure calls over HTTPS from the client applications to the server for any case where we need to invoke some business logic. The server-side code invoked by the SOAP call will in most cases merely turn around and invoke an Enterprise JavaBean running in an application server to perform the actual business logic.

We've identified three types of business logic calls that generate JMS messages. A call that submits a loan application results in a LoanStatus message being generated. A call to open a new account results in the generation of an AccountOpen message. Finally, a call to make a deposit into an account results in an AccountDeposit message being generated. Figure 15-4 illustrates this relationship between the server-side components.

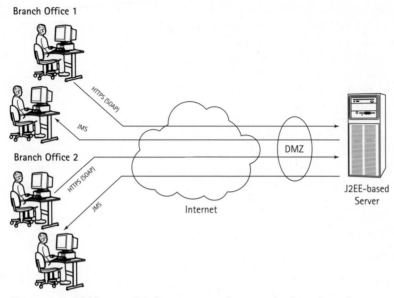

Figure 15-3: BOSS network infrastructure and communications channels

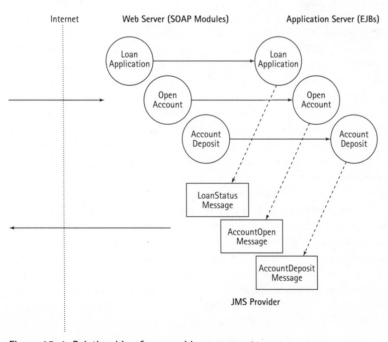

Figure 15-4: Relationship of server-side components

The main issue before us now is how to get the JMS messages out to the client applications in the branch offices. The simple answer, of course, is to find a JMS provider that supports messaging over HTTPS tunneling or direct SSL and have our client applications subscribe to the messages they are interested in. Unfortunately, this solution may not work as well as it might first seem. This is a situation where the way in which a provider implements its messaging has a big impact on the feasibility of using its product.

For instance, consider the `AccountDeposit` message. The applications used by sales representatives need to register for the receipt of these messages through a combination of destination name and message selector. As we mentioned previously in this chapter when describing the system requirements, the key pieces of information the application uses to determine if it's interested in a message are as follows:

◆ Message type

◆ Branch ID of account

◆ Deposit amount

The broadcast nature of the messaging mandates JMS pub/sub messaging, but we have several ways to route the messages, some more efficient than others. If, for instance, we were to simply send all account deposit messages with an address of "ACCOUNT_DEPOSIT," a sales representative's application would be swamped with all bank-wide deposit notices – clearly many more messages than the application needs or than could be delivered efficiently over the Internet.

So what if we decide to make our addressing scheme more specific and include the branch office ID, such as "ACCOUNT_DEPOSIT.BRANCH123," in the destination? Now we can have our clients subscribe to deposit messages using the new addressing scheme that causes only the account deposit messages for a particular branch to be sent over the Internet to that branch. This should reduce the account deposit traffic to a manageable level but, unfortunately, we've also decreased the flexibility of our architecture.

Because we encoded variable information into the message's address, it is now much harder for any other applications that may want to receive all account deposit messages to get them. Some JMS providers support wildcard addressing, which makes it possible to subscribe to all account deposit messages by subscribing to the following address: "ACCOUNT_DEPOSIT.*". This capability is not mandated by the JMS specification, however, so we have no guarantee of being able to do this and, even if we could, it would not be portable.

Furthermore, this type of addressing scheme has its limitations. For example, in the case of an account deposit message, we want the sales representatives to also receive messages based on the deposit amount. Because the amount that triggers a message will vary from sales rep to sales rep within the same branch office, it's impossible to encode it into the address.

JMS message selectors were designed to provide a much more flexible way of receiving only the messages you are interested in. Instead of trying to stuff all the important information into a message's address, you just need to be sure it's part of the message's properties (see Chapter 2 for more information on message properties). This way we can keep the address simple and maintain maximum flexibility regarding which applications are able to receive the message. With selectors we can then simply make our clients subscribe to the destination "ACCOUNT_DEPOSIT" with a message selector, "BranchID = 'BRANCH123' AND DepositAmount >= 10000" (where 10000 is replaced with whatever amount the sales rep prefers).

Problem solved? Not quite. This is a situation where you need to know the underlying implementation of your JMS provider. As we saw in Chapter 10, it is possible for a provider to use message selectors to do client-side or server-side filtering. Most providers do client-side filtering because that's easiest to implement, but it means that a message must travel over the network to its destination before it gets dropped if it doesn't match the current selector. If the main reason we're using message selectors is to minimize the number of messages sent over the network, then a client-side filtering implementation will not help us accomplish our goal.

In fact, using a typical JMS product over the Internet is usually fraught with problems. In addition to the client-side filtering issue, JMS pub/sub messaging in general can be problematic. If non-persistent pub/sub messaging is chosen, many messages will likely be lost. If persistent or durable pub/sub messaging is used, the server-side resources required can be quite high; after all, the provider will need to manage many thousands of logical server-side queues if it has many thousands of users.

Does all this mean that you should absolutely not consider JMS products for Internet-based messaging? Not at all. Messaging software is improving all the time and you may find a program that meets your needs. Just be sure to do your homework and test the product in a *realistic* environment before making a decision. Most JMS providers that are designed explicitly for optimized, secure Internet delivery make a point of explicitly advertising themselves as such.

Alternative solutions

So we can't find a JMS product that works well over the Internet; or we don't have the budget for it; or we're stuck with an unacceptable previously purchased product. What then? A good architect can always come up with different ways to solve a problem; if we can't get our JMS solution to work the way we need it to, we can always eliminate it — at least, that is, the Internet portion of it that's giving us trouble.

PROXYING JMS CLIENTS
One way to get around a JMS product with a poor Internet delivery story is by proxying the client side of the JMS messaging bus on the server. To do this, we need to write a small module that serves as the actual entity that receives messages from the JMS bus and then forwards them to the client. The actual format of the forwarded message needs to be agreed upon by the proxy and the client but there is no reason we couldn't write our own very minimal JMS provider to fool the client application into thinking it is talking directly to a real JMS provider.

The advantage of proxying clients on the server side is that we eliminate any potential inefficiencies that might arise with JMS providers that do client-side message selector filtering as described previously. Figure 15-5 illustrates this solution.

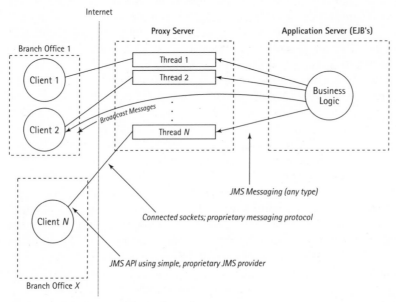

Figure 15-5: Proxying JMS clients on the server

Notice, in Figure 15-5, how we've made the assumption that a server-side proxy is an active instance of a thread that maintains an open connection to both the JMS provider and the client application. Many thousands of clients, however, mean many thousands of threads and many thousands of simultaneously open sockets. This may be more than the server can handle (see Chapter 10 for tuning and performance recommendations).

One way to reduce the server-side resource requirements is to institute a polling scheme. Instead of maintaining an open connection, a client application polls every few seconds – that is, it opens a new connection to the server, receives any new messages, and closes the connection. This eliminates the need for our server to support so many open sockets – at the cost of slightly higher message latency. So we don't lose any messages that arrive when a client is disconnected, we need to use durable topic subscriptions that hold the messages until the client reactivates the connection.

To eliminate the use of so many proxy threads on the server, all we need to do is have the client supply its unique durable subscription ID (see Chapter 5 for details on client IDs and durable subscription messaging) every time it polls (as shown in Figure 15-6).

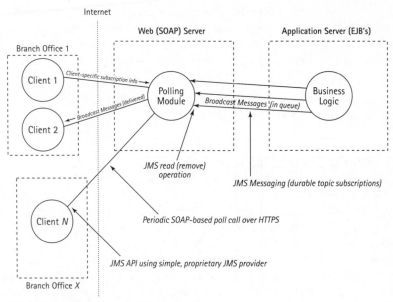

Figure 15-6: Proxying clients using polling

The polling and reinitiating of durable subscription connections all the time will, of course, slow down the messaging somewhat but if that is acceptable, then we are able to greatly reduce the server-side resource requirements.

EMPLOYING POLICY-BASED POLLING   Polling is traditionally a dirty word in architecture circles and, indeed, you shouldn't employ polling if you don't have to – sometimes there's no choice, though. The dumb polling most often used in applications generally involves a simplistic policy of having a client poll the server every x seconds.

Policy-based polling, whereby a client application changes its polling rate based on some set of rules, can reduce the overall amount of poll requests seen by the server. Some sample policies are as follows:

◆ Slide the polling rate up or down depending on the current average message rate. Higher message rates would cause a client to poll more frequently; lesser rates, less frequently. By doing this, clients that receive a lot of messages will get better service and those that receive fewer messages will not bother the server as much.

◆ Dramatically reduce (or suspend) polling outside of normal business hours. If your client applications generally aren't going to be receiving messages most of the day, there's no reason for them to be polling 24 hours a day. This reduction can help reduce the load on your server quite a bit if you have client applications running in many different time zones all accessing the same server. Keep in mind that your application may require some sophistication to use this scheme; for instance, consider an employee on a business trip who requires access to the system.

◆ Develop quality-of-service levels and associated polling policies. Systems should be configurable to allow more important applications and users to poll more frequently than less important ones.

REDUCING DURABLE SUBSCRIPTION OVERHEAD

With the durable subscription architecture, we've done a good job of reducing the need for so much per client active state (this is, client-specific information cached in memory) on the server. Unfortunately, the need for one durable subscription queue per client still may cause our provider to use an inordinate amount of disk space in its database.

If, for example, a JMS provider is implemented so that it adds a row to its database for every durable subscriber who should receive a given message, then we'll certainly have problems with this architecture if we ever want to send the same message to thousands of clients. Thousands of rows would need to be added to the database just to send one message. This is clearly not conducive to a high-performance, highly scalable system.

The way to solve this is to use a single queue for all clients. First, let's drop the idea of using multiple durable subscriptions and instead put all our outbound messages in a single point-to-point queue. Second, to get the right messages out to the right clients, we'll have our server-side JMS proxy *browse* the queue on behalf of the clients instead of reading the messages on the queue. Thus, all clients can access a single queue, dramatically reducing the amount of disk space required and increasing scalability.

For this scheme to work, each client needs to supply (or the server has to maintain) a list of destinations it is interested in and any message selectors that may go along with them. The client also needs to remember and supply to the server on each poll request a "pointer" to the last message it received from the queue. When a client polls for messages, the server-side JMS proxy activates a QueueBrowser for the requested destination and message selector and it uses it to retrieve all the pending messages for the client (if any) that come after the pointer in the queue.

The "pointer" used could be a variety of things. If the provider's JMSMessageID property is guaranteed to be unique and numerically or lexically increasing, then that would be ideal. Then the proxy could augment the client's supplied message selector with the fragment "AND JMSMessageID > X", where X is the last message ID (that is, pointer) supplied by the client.

Alternatively, you could have your application set an application-specific header on each message inserted into the queue with a sequence number that could be used as the pointer. You need to ensure, however, that the sequence numbers are unique and increasing (but not necessarily absolutely sequential).

You may be tempted to use the message's timestamp as the pointer, but that's probably not a good idea because you might miss messages if more than one message is inserted into the queue within the same millisecond.

The pseudo-code for a sender using sequence numbers would look something like this:

```
QueueSender sender = queueSession.createSender(queue);

MapMessage msg = queueSession.createMapMessage();

msg.setIntProperty("SequenceNumber", seqNum);

// Populate the rest of the message here

sender.send(msg);
```

The pseudo-code for a receiver (i.e., the proxy) would look something like this:

```
int lastSeqNum = -1;  // The appropriate sequence number would be
supplied
                    // by the requesting client.

QueueBrowser browser = queueSession.createBrowser(queue,
                            "SequenceNumber > " + lastSeqNum);

for (Enumeration en=browser.getEnumeration(); en.hasMoreElements();)
{
    Message msg = (Message) en.nextElement();
    lastSeqNum = msg.getIntProperty("SequenceNumber");

    // Forward the message to the client over the Internet
connection here.
    // The client will keep track of the highest sequence number for
all
    // messages received by it and pass it back to the proxy the
next time
    // it polls for messages.
}
```

The main strengths of the single-queue strategy are as follows:

◆ No information (beyond any basic session information) about currently logged-in users or information about who's interested in what messages needs to be maintained on the server.

◆ The number of writes to the database for each message is minimal.

◆ The number of writes is the same regardless of the number of users currently accessing the system. Because the writes are independent of the number of clients, the scalability of the messaging infrastructure will be excellent.

◆ Most access to the queue will be read access. This allows for a better-performing, more scalable system because it enables the database to do what it does best (by caching frequently accessed data in memory).

◆ Any required state information (primarily queue indexes and topics) can be maintained on the client side. This reduces the load on the server and again allows for better scalability because there are no messaging-related state-maintenance requirements on the server that depend on the number of users currently accessing the system.

One key factor you'll have to watch out for when implementing a single-queue solution is the efficiency of the browse operation. You'll likely need to use whatever proprietary data store configuration features your provider and/or database vendor has to ensure the browse operation on the queue does not take an excessively long time and does not start to perform more slowly as the queue grows.

Figure 15-7 shows the single-queue architecture diagrammatically.

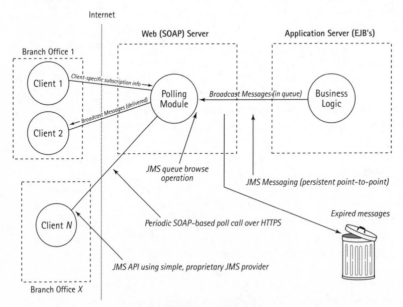

Figure 15-7: A single-queue distribution architecture

GETTING RID OF UNUSED MESSAGES   Because the JMS provider does not know which or how many users are interested in the messages in it, the JMS provider cannot know precisely when to remove unneeded messages from the permanent queue. All we're doing, after all, is browsing the queue, not reading (and hence removing) any messages from it. The queue obviously cannot be allowed to grow infinitely, so a strategy must be in place for deleting unneeded messages.

The obvious method, of course, is to set the time-to-live (see Chapter 2, for a description of the **JMSExpiration** property) on each message that goes into the queue to some appropriate value and let the JMS provider get rid of the messages as it would normally. (If your provider does not support message expiration you could always write a process that periodically runs and purges the queue of expired messages.)

You would set the time to live when placing outbound messages on the queue as follows:

```
QueueSender sender = queueSession.createSender(queue);

sender.setTimeToLive(24 * 60 * 60 * 1000);  // Expire messages after
1 day
```

The main issue, however, is determining what constitutes a safe amount of time to allow a message to be removed. The preferred scenario is simply to keep the messages in the database for a long time. This would mean that messages are deleted only if they are so old that there is no chance a user's session could have been active for that long. But how to determine, of course, what a reasonable period for this is? A day? A week? A month? You will need to decide based on your system requirements and physical resources available to you.

Also, whatever the safe period is, you must also determine whether the database will have the capacity (in terms of disk space and performance) to hold all the records that will be generated during that period. This decision clearly depends on the message-generation rate and the size and configuration of the database environment.

Securing the system

Security's pretty straightforward with the BOSS system as it is. All traffic is fully encrypted automatically with HTTPS/SSL, so there's no chance of interception or sending of false messages by nonbank personnel. Login access to the system can also be easily controlled through the use of client-side certificates and/or a plain old password.

One task we do need to watch out for is the use of client-generated message selectors to retrieve messages. If, for instance, we want to be sure no employees at one branch office can receive any messages directed to another branch office, then we need to have the server examine every message selector it receives to ensure that a properly logged-on user from one branch is not attempting to retrieve messages for a different branch. A properly working client application would always have the right branch ID in its selector, naturally, but who's to say a knowledgeable hacker wouldn't change a configuration file or database somewhere to cause the program to think it's in a different branch? The only sure way to prevent this is to confirm every client's branch affiliation every time he or she accesses the system. You may also want to have the client digitally sign each message to ensure that it has not been tampered with. This signature should contain the proper branch ID (or other distinguishing information) so that the server can compare it to a pre-computed value.

Summary

In this chapter we saw that there are often no simple answers when designing a system that requires Internet-based messaging. In a world of infinite bandwidth and unlimited processing power, our systems would support a correspondingly unlimited number of users at however many locations we desired without much thought on the architect's part. Because we're nowhere near that world, we're going to have to change our software architectures to accommodate the realities of limited performance in our system and network infrastructure. Primarily, you need to be aware of performance limitations and know your requirements. This will help you figure out what parts of your architecture require special treatment.

When it comes to integrating third-party products into your architecture, it's always important not to swallow the marketing literature's claims hook, line, and sinker. Find out for yourself whether a product performs as advertised by testing it in the way you intend to use it before committing to it.

As with the example in this chapter, the challenge of finding out late in the development process that a JMS product is not up to snuff may not necessarily be solved simply by swapping in another vendor's JMS package; it may instead require some drastic redesigning.

Chapter 16

An Internet Order-Taking System

IN THIS CHAPTER

◆ Business integration with JMS

◆ Techniques for integrating varied architectures

◆ Migrating functionality by redirecting messages

IN MANY CASES, you can use JMS messaging software to link together a few legacy systems to help make them appear to operate as one. There are a few important reasons for this. First, messaging infrastructures are not terribly invasive; they operate mainly outside other applications, providing an access path to an application's existing functionality without having to dig deep into the application itself.

Second, messaging lets you tie together independently running programs without having to try to componentize all of the applications so that they can run in a single executable image. Furthermore, messaging enables legacy applications to communicate while continuing to operate in their original environment, be it Solaris, Linux, Microsoft, or whatever. In other words, messaging systems enable you to exercise good object-oriented design strategies such as encapsulation and decoupling.

Finally, as we've said many times in this book already, JMS operates asynchronously. This allows all the involved applications to talk to each other while continuing to operate at their own pace and in their own way. There's no need to try to modify them to get them to work in lock-step fashion. Using JMS, application A can invoke application B without having to care about how long application B is going to take to handle its request or about many of the possible failures that might occur.

Of course, having emphasized what an architect's friend asynchronicity is, many circumstances still require synchronous behavior – when you need the answer *now*. It's like the stateless versus stateful design debate. There's no question stateless modules are easier to design and operate; they also scale and perform better than stateful ones. That doesn't mean, of course, that you can avoid using stateful design patterns in all circumstances.

This chapter attempts to illustrate all these concepts and shows how you can use JMS effectively by exploring a situation where we're the architecture team for an Internet-based bookseller called PrintedMatter.com. PrintedMatter.com sells a lot of books but profits are somewhat lagging. To placate our restless investors,

PrintedMatter.com has decided to acquire two other companies that sell merchandise over the Internet and add their wares to its shop. OneFishTwoFish.com sells exotic, live fish and AntiquesGalore.com sells, naturally, antiques.

We have been charged with integrating these three businesses as quickly as possible. Time to market is of the essence. We know there's nowhere near enough time to start rewriting applications, so our main focus is on linking them together as best we can. However, being the good architects we are, we want to do this in a way that's amenable to the applications we are porting, slowly and piece by piece, to our preferred, unified J2EE environment. This will enable us to better maintain and enhance the newly integrated system in the future as well as improve its performance.

System Requirements

As usual, we'll begin our architectural exercise by breaking down what we know about the various systems along the following lines:

- ◆ Physical infrastructure

- ◆ External and existing systems

- ◆ User requirements and required features

- ◆ Security requirements

- ◆ Performance requirements

For this system, however, we need to keep in mind that there are actually four systems we need to be concerned with: the three we are integrating plus the new system, which results from unifying the original three.

Physical infrastructure

Let's say each of our three systems is running in a physical and OS environment as follows:

- ◆ **PrintedMatter.com:** PrintedMatter.com's operations are housed on a large Unix-based system with plenty of spare horsepower. It is an Internet-based application so the environment is secured from intrusion by the judicious use of firewalls. All of its operations, except fulfillment, take place on this primary system. The application and supporting software is all J2EE-compliant. An Oracle database is used for local permanent storage of customer activity. Currently, when a customer orders a book through the site a message is sent over an extranet to a third party's distribution system for order fulfillment. This third-party extranet connection is secured with a virtual private network (VPN).

♦ **OneFishTwoFish.com:** OneFishTwoFish.com is basically a home-based, budget-conscious operation, so its applications run on low-cost Intel architecture hardware running the Linux operating system, an Apache Web server, and a MySQL database. All fulfillment, customer service, and other business functions take place on OneFishTwoFish.com's local systems; it has no communications with other company's systems.

♦ **AntiquesGalore.com:** AntiqueGalore.com's systems run on Intel-based hardware and the Windows OS and use an SQLServer database. Like PrintedMatter.com, AntiquesGalore.com has a VPN link to a larger distributor where the company sends its orders for delivery.

Figure 16-1 shows the configuration of our three existing systems. At present they are not integrated, and the different hardware and software environments each runs in will pose some interesting architectural challenges when trying to link them together.

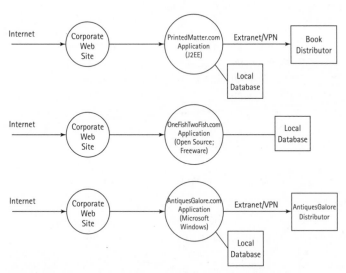

Figure 16-1: The current unintegrated systems configuration

External and existing systems

In a situation such as this where we're integrating several applications, in some ways all the systems are external systems. Assuming we're pretty happy with the design and function of our main system (PrintedMatter.com's), then it makes the most sense to maintain as much of that infrastructure as possible, leveraging it as the core of the new system. This leaves us with the job of figuring out how best to integrate the two remaining "external" systems (OneFishTwoFish.com and AntiquesGalore.com) into the original system. Figure 16-2 shows the desired future configuration.

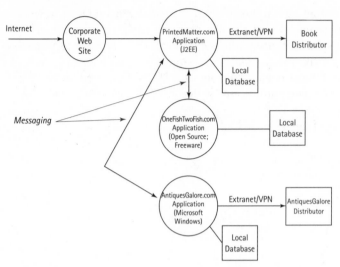

Figure 16-2: The desired short-term integrated systems configuration

Of course, this is just a short-term configuration so we can get the system up and running as quickly as possible. When designing a solution to support this configuration, we need to keep in mind that a major goal is to be able to slowly migrate functionality from the "external" legacy systems into the main system. Because we don't want to do this in a big-bang manner, however, it will be critical to structure our messaging solution so that specific messages and types of messages can be easily rerouted to different applications over the system's life.

User requirements and required features

Naturally, as with any sort of online retail site, we have a plethora of requirements regarding presentation, functionality, and user experience. Because none of this impacts the behind-the-scenes messaging infrastructure, we can ignore it here. As a general principle, however, we need to keep in mind that what we're really trying to accomplish by integrating the three systems is to provide for the user-management layer of the application as much of a common view of each system's data and business functionality as possible. By creating a good service abstraction layer, we can gradually port underlying functionality from its native environment to a single J2EE-based one where it can be better managed and enhanced.

Unfortunately, we must overcome many challenges when doing something like this. Chief among them is the issue of how to best invoke another application's business logic from within our primary EJBs. Partly this is a function of how cleanly an application exposes its services to begin with. AntiquesGalore.com's application has a nice, simple EJB-based application programming interface (API) that another application can call to, say, determine an order's status. It should be a relatively simple matter for one of PrintedMatter.com's EJBs – the original one on which we are basing our new system's functionality – to call AntiquesGalore.com's bean whenever we need to retrieve the status of an order placed on AntiquesGalore.com's system.

The situation becomes a lot more complicated, however, if we want to have one of our enterprise beans make a call outside its container to a non-J2EE application. There's no simple way to call outside an EJB to a DCOM (Microsoft's distributed object technology)-based component, for example, and though you *can* write native code that will call the DCOM module from your Java module, this is not recommended practice for enterprise beans and is also not likely to leave you with a very scalable, maintainable application.

Another hurdle to overcome in some cases is the situation where an application does not even have a straightforward, method-centric means of invoking its business functions. This is often the case with less professionally developed applications that tend to be two-tiered — for example, the business-related code is intertwined tightly with the presentation/user management code — instead of *n*-tiered where the business functions are cleanly demarcated, focused, and easily callable by another module. Figure 16-3 contrasts the two styles.

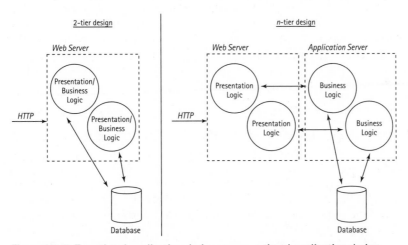

Figure 16-3: Two-tiered application design versus *n*-tiered application design

One of the advantages of n-tier design, of course, is that it's possible to get directly at an application's business logic without having to go through any unrelated presentation code first. This enables you to use the same supporting business logic for a variety of applications that all look or operate somewhat differently. Or, in our case, it lets us incorporate the existing business logic from the acquired companies into our existing site's look and feel.

Because OneFishTwoFish.com and AntiquesGalore.com have designs that are not conducive to direct invocation by a J2EE application, our main challenge architecturally is to figure out how to link these systems to our PrintedMatter.com infrastructure.

Security requirements

Though we can't dramatically change any of OneFishTwoFish.com's or AntiquesGalore.com's software and hardware environments, it's safe to assume that we'll be able to physically relocate the systems so that all three are co-located in a secure server room somewhere and linked together over the same LAN. Presuming the LAN is secure, then we're covered as far as network security is concerned because we've already said our Internet connection is properly secured with firewalls and that the external links from the applications to the distributors are secured with a VPN.

Though our systems can be deemed safe from attack, we're still left with the challenge of navigating the different security technologies supported by each system. This is the "single sign-on" problem so often encountered when various legacy applications need to talk to each other. In a mass-market order-taking system such as ours, the problem is somewhat simpler than in many other cases because the core functionality is typically all executed under a single user ID that has a fixed set of permissions. This is because all system users – at least all customers, that is – tend to be treated equally and, thus, there's no need to define separate security roles for each. However, we still have the problem of System A having to login to System B prior to being able to access B's functionality. The three options for doing this are as follows:

1. A logs in to B every time it needs to invoke B.

2. A logs into B once and holds the connection open, reusing it as desired.

3. A maintains a pool of open, validated connections to B for use by A's components as needed.

Options 1 and 2 are not terribly attractive because they will not give us optimal performance and scalability. Option 3 is best but still requires us to write custom code to manage the login and pool for each application/technology combination we need to communicate with.

Connection pooling techniques are used quite frequently in application servers to help them achieve greater scalability. Application servers typically have so many enterprise beans that need to talk to external resources (databases, JMS, and so on) that it makes no sense for each module to maintain its own open connection to the resource. In these situations, the application server maintains a pool of connections to the resource and doles them out to the EJBs on an "as needed" basis.

JMS defines support for this type of behavior through the `javax.jms.ServerSessionPool` interface, which is used by application servers that support JMS session pooling. As an EJB JMS developer, session pooling will be transparent to you, however, so you don't need to be too concerned about it.

Connection pooling is a valuable technology — even more so when somebody else has implemented it for you already.

Interposing a JMS messaging channel between the applications enables us to side-step the login issue entirely because, in order to send a message to an application, we only need to log in to the JMS provider, not to the application that is the message's final destination. This is a valuable feature because this way we can keep any application-specific knowledge regarding how to log in to secondary applications – OneFishTwoFish.com and AntiquesGalore.com in our example – out of the main application. Not only will this reduce the time it takes to integrate all the systems but it will help us move around functionality in the future because we've reduced inter-system dependencies.

Performance requirements

Certainly, any large retail order-taking system is going to have demanding performance requirements, particularly when it comes to response time. This is one of those cases, though, where it's unlikely messaging will be the gating factor. It's more likely a function of how well the system is coded and how well-designed the database schema is. This is because our messaging will be taking place between only a handfull of server-side components and will thus be able to completely run over our local high-speed LAN or even the super-charged system bus you often find in high-end servers these days. These are optimum conditions for high-volume messaging, so we won't focus on it as a performance factor from an architectural point of view. This is not to say, however, that it should not be a point of focus when it comes time to code the system's messaging-related aspects (see Chapter 10 for a discussion of the importance of lower-level code optimizations in a JMS-based system).

System Architecture

In this chapter we'll take a slightly different approach to architectural analysis than in previous chapters. We'll dispense with defining particular messages because the contents are not as important as the flow. As such, we'll just identify a few basic message types so we can plot their lifecycles and map them to an architecture. This will also serve to highlight some of the higher-level issues surrounding integrating systems with JMS, as opposed to the lower-level API and design issues.

Determining message types

The basics of any retail order-taking system are, of course, inventory and orders. All three of our existing systems must have the capability to determine what products are available in the site (inventory) and a method of purchasing them (orders).

Most order-taking sites force consumers to add their prospective purchases to a virtual shopping cart before submitting the order. Other order-taking sites, such as online brokerages, follow a more direct-purchase model where each order (such as a stock purchase) is effected immediately. For our purposes, we're just going to concern ourselves with what can be considered the main business function (the order entry) and not worry about how the orders are collected in the first place because that is a function of the application's user-management layer.

The inventory-listing capabilities of order-taking systems all follows pretty much the same pattern: some sort of selection criteria is pieced together (color, price, product type, and so on) and supplied to the inventory-lookup module, which responds with a list of items that match the supplied search criteria. While order traffic basically flows in one direction — from front to back — inventory traffic flows both ways because it is essentially a request/reply mechanism.

Creating an initial architecture

Given what we know about our requirements, we can now begin to construct an architecture. So far, we've identified the following three main logical application layers or tiers:

◆ **The Presentation/User Management Layer:** This layer is responsible for the look and feel. It manages the consumer's view of the site through, for example, the use of standard technologies such as Java Server Pages (`http://java.sun.com/products/jsp/index.html`), servlets, and XML. This layer also manages the site operation through the use of open-source toolkits such as Apache Struts (`http://jakarta.apache.org/struts/index.html`) and other technologies that control the user's page flow. Presentation layer frameworks like Struts also help the developer map HTTP-based input to Java objects. Naturally, a large amount of proprietary code is also required to implement business logic such as field-level value checking. The code and toolkits supporting this layer will reside in the site's Web server.

◆ **The Application Layer:** The application layer is where the site's primary business function resides. As we said earlier, these functions can typically be considered as independent of any particular look and feel. We'll see a module for accepting a product order, for instance, but nothing related to how an order form is displayed to the user. Clearly, the presentation layer and the application layer need to be in constant communication. Orders will be accepted and preliminarily validated by the presentation layer before being passed to the application layer for final processing. Also, the presentation layer formulates inventory search requests that it gives to the application layer, which returns a list of matching items to be displayed to the user. We'll want to implement these services as enterprise beans running in an application server so that they are scalable and the presentation layer can easily invoke them.

◆ **The Legacy Layer:** This is the layer that, for the time being, is doing all the heavy lifting. This layer basically consists of the three existing systems we're trying to integrate. Our goal, though, is to eliminate this layer over time. It should only exist for as long as it takes to chip away at the functionality inside it and migrate it to the main application layer.

Figure 16-4 shows the relationship between the three application layers.

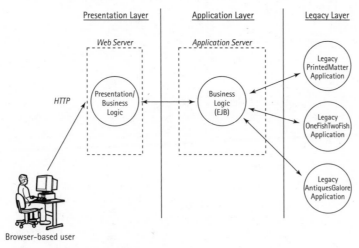

Figure 16-4: Application layers

HIDING THE LEGACY SYSTEMS

As a J2EE shop we've already said we want to stick with the current application layer model we're using for PrintedMatter.com's Web site, which exposes all application-layer services as EJBs. So at first blush it would seem that this part of the job — making PrintedMatter.com's functionality available to the new system — is already done for us. To some extent this is true because, even though we have described PrintedMatter.com's site as being part of the legacy layer, there's still no reason it can't reside inside the new application layer (that is, it can run in the main application server).

However, if our main goal is to provide a uniform way of accessing back-end services to our presentation layer, then simply giving it access to the current PrintedMatter.com EJB API will not quite get the job done for us. Unless we are sure that PrintedMatter.com's API supports all the features and data elements we'll need to have for the other two legacy sites as well, then we'll have to rewrite

PrintedMatter.com's EJB interface to some extent. This, of course, requires rewriting code that has been working perfectly, and any time we start doing that we've immediately increased our time to delivery.

It would be much safer and quicker to place a thin wrapper layer on top of the existing functionality. This wrapper would take the form of an EJB with an external interface that supports all the required functionality that the user-management layer needs to interact with all three legacy systems. Internally, the wrapper bean will have to examine each incoming data packet, determine which system it should go to, and reformat it into the form required by the particular legacy system where it is destined. And, of course, it must do the reverse for any returned values.

By mediating access to the legacy applications this way we are free to change the underlying implementations of each at any time without impacting the presentation layer. Figure 16-5 shows how access to legacy functions can be mediated by an EJB (or EJBs).

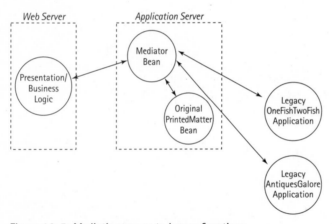

Figure 16-5: Mediating access to legacy functions

TALKING TO THE LEGACY SYSTEMS

Now that we've figured out what we want the external interface of the application layer to look like, we need to figure out what the internal interface should be. That is, how should the application layer talk to the legacy applications?

In the case of a legacy PrintedMatter.com module, the choice is obviously RMI (Remote Method Invocation) because this is the typical way beans in a container talk to each other – there are exceptions to this rule but they're not important for our purposes here – and both our mediator bean and legacy bean will be running in the same application server.

On the other hand, we want our mediator bean to be able to communicate with the other two legacy systems that are not only running on different technologies but are running on different machines. Here is where JMS comes to the rescue because its cross-platform, intermachine messaging capabilities enables us to easily send messages back and forth between the two environments.

Our only problem is that, assuming we can find an acceptable JMS provider that runs on all our various computing platforms, the OneFishTwoFish.com and AntiquesGalore.com applications were not originally designed to work with JMS. To get around this problem, we can simply (or perhaps not so simply, depending on how well the original applications were designed) write an adapter module to run in each application's native environment. The adapter is responsible for sending and receiving our JMS messages, interpreting them, and invoking the required internal functionality. This requires writing some new code for both the OneFishTwoFish.com and AntiquesGalore.com systems but, like the use of the mediator pattern referred to previously, it is the least intrusive way to integrate all the legacy systems.

Figure 16-6 shows the latest architecture with the communications paths identified.

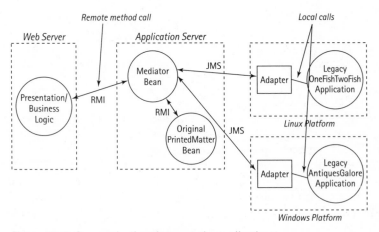

Figure 16-6: Communications between the applications

SIMPLIFYING THE ARCHITECTURE

There's nothing wrong with the architecture as we've defined it; it will work just fine. But having arrived at a workable solution is not always the best time to stop analyzing the problem. After all, there's almost always a simpler solution than the one you first come up with.

In our case, it seems apparent after review that there's really no need for all traffic to go through the mediator bean. One of the great features of JMS is that is takes on the responsibility of routing messages to interested parties without us having to specifically encode that logic into our application. As the mediator bean stands now, it has to be designed in such a way that it examines all the incoming "messages" (that is, data received from the remote method call) and effectively decides where to forward the request. By relying solely on JMS to do this for us we can simplify our design.

In fact, if we refocus the mediator bean to solely be a proxy for the legacy PrintedMatter.com bean and turn it into a message-driven bean, then the entire architecture will be one that is uniformly driven by messages emitted from the presentation layer, as shown in Figure 16-7.

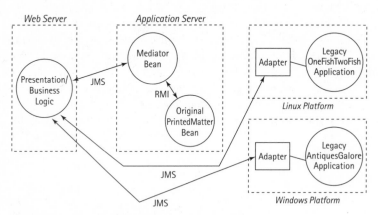

Figure 16-7: A fully message-driven architecture

MIGRATING FUNCTIONALITY

While the use of JMS messaging between the presentation layer and the application layer may not seem like the best long-term solution at first, what we've accomplished is an increase in flexibility in terms of what system components handle what messages. This is important because, when the time comes to move functionality out of the legacy systems into the J2EE infrastructure, we can do so simply by enabling the new J2EE-based module (the message-driven bean) and configuring it (through its deployment descriptor) to receive the traffic that was originally intended for the legacy system.

To illustrate how to reroute behavior through the use of JMS naming, let's say, for instance, that we've named our JMS destinations, as shown in Figure 16-8. The actual type of JMS delivery mechanism can be either point-to-point or pub/sub and either persistent or non-persistent, depending on our specific application requirements. Note, however, that one advantage of pub/sub delivery is that more than one component can receive the same message. This can be handy in the case, for example, where we send an order to a legacy system but also want to have a J2EE component record the same order in its database, perhaps for tracking or customer-support purposes.

At some point we're going to write a brand new order bean that can handle book, fish, and antique orders. Instead of trying to implement all this new functionality at once we could, for instance, just implement the book order functionality. Configuring this bean to accept all "ORDER.BOOK" messages and unconfiguring the original order mediator bean from receiving the same messages has the effect of redirecting all book orders to the new bean. This configuration takes place in the bean deployment descriptor (see Chapter 7 for more on deployment descriptors) so we can do it without changing any of the original bean's code. This is valuable because if we discover a problem with the new bean, we can readily redirect messages back to the old bean.

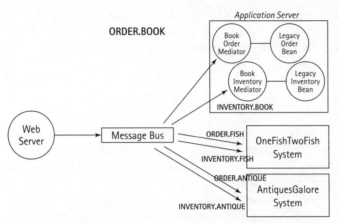

Figure 16-8: Distributing functionality with JMS destination names

Likewise with the other functionality we plan on migrating. When we're ready, for instance, to have our new order bean start handling fish orders, too (this way we can throw in a free fish to everybody who buys $50 worth of books!), then we can route the "ORDER.FISH" messages to the new bean as well.

On top of this, we could use the JMS message selection capabilities to route just some of the fish order traffic to the new bean. By configuring the bean to receive only orders for goldfish, we can split the fish order traffic between the legacy OneFishTwoFish.com system and our new infrastructure, as shown in Figure 16-9.

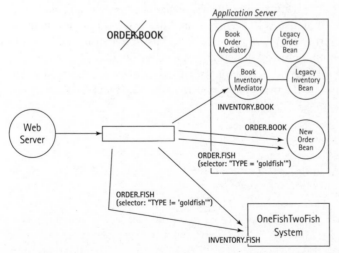

Figure 16-9: Redirecting functionality into the application server

Over time, we can follow this same process until all legacy functions are running satisfactorily in our new J2EE environment. At this point we can finally get rid of the old systems – or keep them in place as an emergency backup.

Summary

This chapter's main aim has been to show how you can leverage JMS to distribute functionality across a broad range of systems, beans, applications – any type of component, actually. The big advantage of employing messaging in this way is that we are able to roll out new, targeted pieces of functionality with minimal impact on the system at large. By manipulating the valves that control the flow of messages through the pipes, we can redirect traffic to new components either bit by bit or all at once.

When supporting a 24/7 production system, this functional redirection capability can be quite a useful tool. Unlike the typical model of application upgrade where you replace an older code module with a newer one, a message-based invocation model lets both the old and new modules exist side-by-side for a while. If designed properly, we can gradually shift traffic over from the old module to the new one, which gives us a chance to detect any problems with the new code while their impact is still limited. Furthermore, if a problem is detected, we are in a position to rapidly redirect traffic back to the old module while we diagnose and correct the problems in the new one.

Naturally, the architectures described in the last four chapters of this book are all somewhat idealized and simplified. In the real world there's always some bizarre condition or requirement that invariably throws a monkey wrench into your nice clean architecture. The challenge is to keep your architecture as close to pristine as possible while still ensuring that it supports all the business requirements. High-level models are one thing, but the devil, as they say, is in the details.

There's no formula for designing a complex yet efficient and functional architecture. It's still largely based on skill and experience – and that's why architects make the big bucks.

Appendix A

API Listing

This appendix provides a JMS API listing for version 1.02b of the JMS specification. The APIs have been grouped by general function according to the following categories, so that classes related to each other can be easily located:

- JMS Message Classes

- JMS Exception Classes

- JMS Common and Support Classes

- JMS Publish/Subscribe (Topic) Classes

- JMS Point-to-Point (Queue) Classes

Within each category the classes are listed alphabetically. You should consult the official Javadoc located at `http://java.sun.com/products/jms` for a complete description of each class and method. While it's not explicitly written herein, please remember that all constructors and methods in this chapter can potentially throw a `javax.jms.JMSException` exception, excluding the following:

- `MessageListener` (all methods)

- `JMSException` and all its subclasses

- `ExceptionListener` (all methods)

- `Session.run()`

- `XASession.getXAResource()`

- `Topic.toString()`

- Queue.toString()

JMS Message Classes
Interface javax.jms.BytesMessage

Implements `javax.jms.Message`

METHODS
```
boolean readBoolean()
byte readByte()
int readUnsignedByte()
short readShort()
int readUnsignedShort()
char readChar()
int readInt()
long readLong()
float readFloat()
double readDouble()
String readUTF()
int readBytes(byte[] value)
int readBytes(byte[] value, int length)
void writeBoolean(boolean value)
void writeByte(byte value)
void writeShort(short value)
void writeChar(char value)
void writeInt(int value)
void writeLong(long value)
void writeFloat(float value)
void writeDouble(double value)
void writeUTF(String value)
void writeBytes(byte[] value)
void writeBytes(byte[] value, int offset, int length)
void writeObject(Object value)
void reset()
```

Interface javax.jms.MapMessage

Implements `javax.jms.Message`

METHODS
```
boolean getBoolean(String name)
byte getByte(String name)
short getShort(String name)
char getChar(String name)
int getInt(String name)
long getLong(String name)
float getFloat(String name)
double getDouble(String name)
String getString(String name)
byte[] getBytes(String name)
Object getObject(String name)
java.util.Enumeration getMapNames()
void setBoolean(String name, boolean value)
```

```
void setByte(String name, byte value)
void setShort(String name, short value)
void setChar(String name, char value)
void setInt(String name, int value)
void setLong(String name, long value)
void setFloat(String name, float value)
void setDouble(String name, double value)
void setString(String name, String value)
void setBytes(String name, byte[] value)
void setBytes(String name, byte[] value, int offset, int length)
void setObject(String name, Object value)
boolean itemExists(String name)
```

Interface javax.jms.Message

METHODS

```
String getJMSMessageID()
void setJMSMessageID(String id)
long getJMSTimestamp()
void setJMSTimestamp(long timestamp)
byte[] getJMSCorrelationIDAsBytes()
void setJMSCorrelationIDAsBytes(byte[] correlationID)
void setJMSCorrelationID(String correlationID)
String getJMSCorrelationID()
javax.jms.Destination getJMSReplyTo()
void setJMSReplyTo(Destination replyTo)
javax.jms.Destination getJMSDestination()
void setJMSDestination(Destination destination)
int getJMSDeliveryMode()
void setJMSDeliveryMode(int deliveryMode)
boolean getJMSRedelivered()
void setJMSRedelivered(boolean redelivered)
String getJMSType()
void setJMSType(String type)
long getJMSExpiration()
void setJMSExpiration(long expiration)
int getJMSPriority()
void setJMSPriority(int priority)
void clearProperties()
boolean propertyExists(String name)
boolean getBooleanProperty(String name)
byte getByteProperty(String name)
short getShortProperty(String name)
int getIntProperty(String name)
long getLongProperty(String name)
float getFloatProperty(String name)
```

```
double getDoubleProperty(String name)
String getStringProperty(String name)
Object getObjectProperty(String name)
java.util.Enumeration getPropertyNames()
void setBooleanProperty(String name, boolean value)
void setByteProperty(String name, byte value)
void setShortProperty(String name, short value)
void setIntProperty(String name, int value)
void setLongProperty(String name, long value)
void setFloatProperty(String name, float value)
void setDoubleProperty(String name, double value)
void setStringProperty(String name, String value)
void setObjectProperty(String name, Object value)
void acknowledge()
void clearBody()
```

FIELDS
```
static final DEFAULT_DELIVERY_MODE
static final DEFAULT_PRIORITY
static final DEFAULT_TIME_TO_LIVE
```

Interface javax.jms.ObjectMessage

Implements `javax.jms.Message`

METHODS
```
void setObject(Serializable object)
java.io.Serializable getObject()
```

Interface javax.jms.StreamMessage

Implements `javax.jms.Message`

METHODS
```
boolean readBoolean()
byte readByte()
short readShort()
char readChar()
int readInt()
long readLong()
float readFloat()
double readDouble()
String readString()
int readBytes(byte[] value)
Object readObject()
void writeBoolean(boolean value)
```

```
void writeByte(byte value)
void writeShort(short value)
void writeChar(char value)
void writeInt(int value)
void writeLong(long value)
void writeFloat(float value)
void writeDouble(double value)
void writeString(String value)
void writeBytes(byte[] value)
void writeBytes(byte[] value, int offset, int length)
void writeObject(Object value)
void reset()
```

Interface javax.jms.TextMessage

Implements `javax.jms.Message`

METHODS
```
void setText(String string)
String getText()
```

JMS Exception Classes

Interface javax.jms.ExceptionListener
METHODS
```
void onException(JMSException exception)
```

Class javax.jms.IllegalStateException

Extends `javax.jms.JMSException`

CONSTRUCTORS
```
IllegalStateException(String reason, String errorCode)
IllegalStateException(String reason)
```

Class javax.jms.InvalidClientIDException

Extends `javax.jms.JMSException`

CONSTRUCTORS
```
InvalidClientIDException(String reason, String errorCode)
InvalidClientIDException(String reason)
```

Class javax.jms.InvalidDestinationException

Extends `javax.jms.JMSException`

CONSTRUCTORS
```
InvalidDestinationException(String reason, String errorCode)
InvalidDestinationException(String reason)
```

Class javax.jms.InvalidSelectorException

Extends `javax.jms.JMSException`

CONSTRUCTORS
```
InvalidSelectorException(String reason, String errorCode)
InvalidSelectorException(String reason)
```

Class javax.jms.JMSException

Extends `Exception`

CONSTRUCTORS
```
JMSException(String reason, String errorCode)
JMSException(String reason)
```

METHODS
```
String getErrorCode()
Exception getLinkedException()
synchronized void setLinkedException(Exception ex)
```

Class javax.jms.JMSSecurityException

Extends `javax.jms.JMSException`

CONSTRUCTORS
```
JMSSecurityException(String reason, String errorCode)
JMSSecurityException(String reason)
```

Class javax.jms.MessageEOFException

Extends `javax.jms.JMSException`

CONSTRUCTORS
```
MessageEOFException(String reason, String errorCode)
MessageEOFException(String reason)
```

Class javax.jms.MessageFormatException

Extends `javax.jms.JMSException`

CONSTRUCTORS
```
MessageFormatException(String reason, String errorCode)
MessageFormatException(String reason)
```

Class javax.jms.MessageNotReadableException

Extends `javax.jms.JMSException`

CONSTRUCTORS
```
MessageNotReadableException(String reason, String errorCode)
MessageNotReadableException(String reason)
```

Class javax.jms.MessageNotWriteableException

Extends `javax.jms.JMSException`

CONSTRUCTORS
```
MessageNotWriteableException(String reason, String errorCode)
MessageNotWriteableException(String reason)
```

Class javax.jms.ResourceAllocationException

Extends `javax.jms.JMSException`

CONSTRUCTORS
```
ResourceAllocationException(String reason, String errorCode)
ResourceAllocationException(String reason)
```

Class javax.jms.TransactionInProgressException

Extends `javax.jms.JMSException`

CONSTRUCTORS
```
TransactionInProgressException(String reason, String errorCode)
TransactionInProgressException(String reason)
```

Class javax.jms.TransactionRolledBackException

Extends `javax.jms.JMSException`

CONSTRUCTORS
```
TransactionRolledBackException(String reason, String errorCode)
TransactionRolledBackException(String reason)
```

JMS Common and Support Classes

Interface javax.jms.Connection

METHODS

```
String getClientID()
void setClientID(String clientID)
javax.jms.ConnectionMetaData getMetaData()
javax.jms.ExceptionListener getExceptionListener()
void setExceptionListener(ExceptionListener listener)
void start()
void stop()
void close()
```

Interface javax.jms.ConnectionConsumer

METHODS

```
javax.jms.ServerSessionPool getServerSessionPool()
void close()
```

Interface javax.jms.ConnectionFactory

Empty interface

Interface javax.jms.ConnectionMetaData

METHODS

```
String getJMSVersion()
int getJMSMajorVersion()
int getJMSMinorVersion()
String getJMSProviderName()
String getProviderVersion()
int getProviderMajorVersion()
int getProviderMinorVersion()
java.util.Enumeration getJMSXPropertyNames()
```

Interface javax.jms.DeliveryMode

FIELDS

```
static final NON_PERSISTENT
static final PERSISTENT
```

Interface javax.jms.Destination

Empty interface

Interface javax.jms.MessageConsumer

METHODS

```
String getMessageSelector()
javax.jms.MessageListener getMessageListener()
void setMessageListener(MessageListener listener)
javax.jms.Message receive()
javax.jms.Message receive(long timeout)
javax.jms.Message receiveNoWait()
void close()
```

Interface javax.jms.MessageListener

METHODS

```
void onMessage(Message message)
```

Interface javax.jms.MessageProducer

METHODS

```
void setDisableMessageID(boolean value)
boolean getDisableMessageID()
void setDisableMessageTimestamp(boolean value)
boolean getDisableMessageTimestamp()
void setDeliveryMode(int deliveryMode)
int getDeliveryMode()
void setPriority(int defaultPriority)
int getPriority()
void setTimeToLive(long timeToLive)
long getTimeToLive()
void close()
```

Interface javax.jms.ServerSession

METHODS

```
javax.jms.Session getSession()
void start()
```

Interface javax.jms.ServerSessionPool

METHODS

```
javax.jms.ServerSession getServerSession()
```

Interface javax.jms.Session

Implements Runnable

METHODS
```
javax.jms.BytesMessage createBytesMessage()
javax.jms.MapMessage createMapMessage()
javax.jms.Message createMessage()
javax.jms.ObjectMessage createObjectMessage()
javax.jms.ObjectMessage createObjectMessage(Serializable object)
javax.jms.StreamMessage createStreamMessage()
javax.jms.TextMessage createTextMessage()
javax.jms.TextMessage createTextMessage(String text)
boolean getTransacted()
void commit()
void rollback()
void close()
void recover()
javax.jms.MessageListener getMessageListener()
void setMessageListener(MessageListener listener)
void run()
```

FIELDS
```
static final AUTO_ACKNOWLEDGE
static final CLIENT_ACKNOWLEDGE
static final DUPS_OK_ACKNOWLEDGE
```

Interface javax.jms.XAConnection

Empty interface

Interface javax.jms.XAConnectionFactory

Empty interface

Interface javax.jms.XASession

Implements `javax.jms.Session`

METHODS
```
javax.transaction.xa.XAResource getXAResource()
boolean getTransacted()
void commit()
void rollback()
```

JMS Publish/Subscribe (Topic) Classes

Interface javax.jms.Topic

Implements `javax.jms.Destination`

METHODS
```
String getTopicName()
String toString()
```

Interface javax.jms.TopicConnection

Implements `javax.jms.Connection`

METHODS
```
javax.jms.TopicSession createTopicSession(boolean transacted, int
acknowledgeMode)

javax.jms.ConnectionConsumer createConnectionConsumer(Topic topic,
String messageSelector, ServerSessionPool sessionPool, int
maxMessages)

javax.jms.ConnectionConsumer createDurableConnectionConsumer(Topic
topic, String subscriptionName, String messageSelector,
ServerSessionPool sessionPool, int maxMessages)
```

Interface javax.jms.TopicConnectionFactory

Implements `javax.jms.ConnectionFactory`

METHODS
```
javax.jms.TopicConnection createTopicConnection()
javax.jms.TopicConnection createTopicConnection(String userName,
String password)
```

Interface javax.jms.TopicPublisher

Implements `javax.jms.MessageProducer`

METHODS
```
javax.jms.Topic getTopic()
void publish(Message message)
void publish(Message message, int deliveryMode, int priority, long
timeToLive)
void publish(Topic topic, Message message)
```

```
void publish(Topic topic, Message message, int deliveryMode, int
priority, long timeToLive)
```

Class javax.jms.TopicRequestor

CONSTRUCTORS
```
TopicRequestor(TopicSession session, Topic topic)
```

METHODS
```
javax.jms.Message request(Message message)
void close()
```

Interface javax.jms.TopicSession

Implements `javax.jms.Session`

METHODS
```
javax.jms.Topic createTopic(String topicName)
javax.jms.TopicSubscriber createSubscriber(Topic topic)
javax.jms.TopicSubscriber createSubscriber(Topic topic, String
messageSelector, boolean noLocal)
javax.jms.TopicSubscriber createDurableSubscriber(Topic topic,
String name)
javax.jms.TopicSubscriber createDurableSubscriber(Topic topic,
String name, String messageSelector, boolean noLocal)
javax.jms.TopicPublisher createPublisher(Topic topic)
javax.jms.TemporaryTopic createTemporaryTopic()
void unsubscribe(String name)
```

Interface javax.jms.TopicSubscriber

Implements `javax.jms.MessageConsumer`

METHODS
```
javax.jms.Topic getTopic()
boolean getNoLocal()
```

Interface javax.jms.TemporaryTopic

Implements `javax.jms.Topic`

METHODS
```
void delete()
```

Interface javax.jms.XATopicConnection

Implements `javax.jms.XAConnection, javax.jms.TopicConnection`

METHODS
```
javax.jms.XATopicSession createXATopicSession()
javax.jms.TopicSession createTopicSession(boolean transacted, int
acknowledgeMode)
```

Interface javax.jms.XATopicConnectionFactory

Implements   `javax.jms.XAConnectionFactory`,   `javax.jms.TopicConnection Factory`

METHODS
```
javax.jms.XATopicConnection createXATopicConnection()
javax.jms.XATopicConnection createXATopicConnection(String userName,
String password)
```

Interface javax.jms.XATopicSession

Implements `javax.jms.XASession`

METHODS
```
javax.jms.TopicSession getTopicSession()
```

JMS Point-to-Point (Queue) Classes

Interface javax.jms.Queue

Implements `javax.jms.Destination`

METHODS
```
String getQueueName()
String toString()
```

Interface javax.jms.QueueBrowser

METHODS
```
javax.jms.Queue getQueue()
String getMessageSelector()
java.util.Enumeration getEnumeration()
void close()
```

Interface javax.jms.QueueConnection

Implements `javax.jms.Connection`

METHODS
```
javax.jms.QueueSession createQueueSession(boolean transacted, int
acknowledgeMode)
javax.jms.ConnectionConsumer createConnectionConsumer(Queue queue,
String messageSelector, ServerSessionPool sessionPool, int
maxMessages)
```

Interface javax.jms.QueueConnectionFactory

Implements `javax.jms.ConnectionFactory`

METHODS
```
javax.jms.QueueConnection createQueueConnection()
javax.jms.QueueConnection createQueueConnection(String userName,
String password)
```

Interface javax.jms.QueueReceiver

Implements `javax.jms.MessageConsumer`

METHODS
```
javax.jms.Queue getQueue()
```

Class javax.jms.QueueRequestor

CONSTRUCTORS
```
QueueRequestor(QueueSession session, Queue queue)
```

METHODS
```
javax.jms.Message request(Message message)
void close()
```

Interface javax.jms.QueueSender

Implements `javax.jms.MessageProducer`

METHODS
```
javax.jms.Queue getQueue()
void send(Message message)
void send(Message message, int deliveryMode, int priority, long
timeToLive)
void send(Queue queue, Message message)
void send(Queue queue, Message message, int deliveryMode, int
priority, long timeToLive)
```

Interface javax.jms.QueueSession

Implements `javax.jms.Session`

METHODS

```
javax.jms.Queue createQueue(String queueName)
javax.jms.QueueReceiver createReceiver(Queue queue)
javax.jms.QueueReceiver createReceiver(Queue queue, String
messageSelector)
javax.jms.QueueSender createSender(Queue queue)
javax.jms.QueueBrowser createBrowser(Queue queue)
javax.jms.QueueBrowser createBrowser(Queue queue, String
messageSelector)
javax.jms.TemporaryQueue createTemporaryQueue()
```

Interface javax.jms.TemporaryQueue

Implements `javax.jms.Queue`

METHODS

```
void delete()
```

Interface javax.jms.XAQueueConnection

Implements `javax.jms.XAConnection, javax.jms.QueueConnection`

METHODS

```
javax.jms.XAQueueSession createXAQueueSession()
javax.jms.QueueSession createQueueSession(boolean transacted, int
acknowledgeMode)
```

Interface javax.jms.XAQueueConnectionFactory

Implements `javax.jms.XAConnectionFactory, javax.jms.QueueConnection
Factory`

METHODS

```
javax.jms.XAQueueConnection createXAQueueConnection()
javax.jms.XAQueueConnection createXAQueueConnection(String userName,
String password)
```

Interface javax.jms.XAQueueSession

Implements `javax.jms.XASession`

METHODS

`javax.jms.QueueSession getQueueSession()`

Appendix B

JMS-Compliant Products

JMS developers are fortunate to have numerous products available that support the JMS specification — including free, commercial, and open-source software. Table B-1 presents a selected list of products and vendors that JMS system developers should know about. You can learn more about each product by visiting the vendor's Web site.

TABLE B-1 PARTIAL LIST OF VENDORS WITH PRODUCTS SUPPORTING SOME VERSION OF THE JMS SPECIFICATION

Product Name	Vendor	Web Site	Status
Advanced Queuing	Oracle	www.oracle.com	Commercial
Borland AppServer	Borland	www.borland.com	Commercial
Dynamo	ATG	www.atg.com	Commercial
EAServer	Sybase	www.sybase.com	Commercial
FioranoMQ	Fiorano	www.fiorano.com	Commercial
iBus	Softwired	www.softwired-inc.com	Commercial
iMQ	iPlanet (Sun Microsystems)	www.iplanet.com	Commercial
JBossMQ	JBoss	www.jboss.org	Open source
jBrokerMQ	SilverStream	www.silverstream.com	Commercial
Joram	Scalagent	www.objectweb.org	Open source
JRun	Allaire	www.allaire.com	Commercial
MQSeries	IBM	www.ibm.com	Commercial
OpenJMS	ExoLab Group	www.openjms.org	Open source
Orion	Orion	www.orionserver.com	Commercial

Continued

TABLE B-1 PARTIAL LIST OF VENDORS WITH PRODUCTS SUPPORTING SOME VERSION OF THE JMS SPECIFICATION *(Continued)*

Product Name	Vendor	Web Site	Status
SonicMQ	Sonic Software	www.sonicsoftware.com	Commercial
SwiftMQ	IIT Software	www.swiftmq.com	Free, source for sale
TIB/Enterprise for JMS	Tibco	www.tibco.com	Commercial
WebLogic	BEA Systems	www.bea.com	Commercial
Workbench for JMS	Talarian	www.talarian.com	Commercial

Index

A

continued

367

continued

continued

continued

Q

288. JMS guarantees msgs are delivered in order they are sent.